The Swiftie Story

This book is dedicated to Taylor Alison Swift.

Thank you for being there for all of us when we needed you the most. You've taught us so much and continue to do so each day. You've changed all of our lives, even if you don't know it. It's my sincerest hope that somehow this book finds its way to you, and you're able to hear how you've helped each and every one of us, and that you recognize just how much you and your music mean. We wouldn't be here if it weren't for you, and we're eternally grateful. Thank you for trusting us with your words, and allowing us to give them a life of their own.

long live the walls we crashed through,
how the kingdom lights shined just for me and you.

I was screaming, "long live all the magic we made"
and bring on all the pretenders, I'm not afraid.

long live all the mountains we moved,
I had the time of my life fighting dragons with you.

"LONG LIVE (TAYLOR'S VERSION)"

Dear Reader,

T he book you now hold in your hands is a
collection of the blood, sweat, and tears of
hundreds of swifties from all over the world.
These stories have been thoughtfully shared, and carefully
selected, in an effort to create a collection of tales from
people with one underlying similarity: their love for Taylor
Swift. Even though the stories in this volume differ in
length and detail, they all share a passion and undying
appreciation for the artist who has been there for them
through it all. It's truly amazing how one person can
manage to tie so many together, yet Taylor has managed
to do this and more. She has created a community fueled
by love and respect, and her songwriting has united people
across the globe. Her music spans generations, and it's
astonishing to see how one song can be applicable to so
many people for so many different reasons. This project
started as a random shower thought: what if I tried to
create a collection of people's stories of how they became a
swiftie? I turned to my trusty subscribers (I run a YouTube
channel called "All Too Swift" where I upload all sorts of
Taylor-related videos) and told them about my idea, and
how I thought it would be cool if we could create it as a
surprise for Taylor's birthday. My original goal was to try
and collect around a hundred submissions in a month...
the swifties clearly had other plans, because this was
achieved in just three days. The swifties took my idea and
ran with it, sharing it all over the internet. Before I knew

it, I had three hundred submissions, then five hundred, then a thousand, and then over two thousand. My account (talesfortaylor@gmail.com) was filled with emails, day in and day out. I'd go in and read a bunch, and then by the time I refreshed the page, there'd be more waiting for me. These beautiful stories were all being given to me, to treasure and to take care of.

Every effort has been made to preserve the original stories, although in some cases edits were made in an effort to condense certain portions, in order to allow for as many submissions as possible. I can't begin to express my gratitude to all of you, for trusting me to share your words, and for using your presence to further this project. I was truly humbled by the sheer amount of participation and am so thankful to everyone who contributed. All of the stories chosen for this collection stuck out to me in one way or another, but that isn't to say that I didn't love reading each and every one of the stories that didn't make it in. You are all incredible people, and I feel so lucky to have been chosen to hear your tales. Thank you for your contributions, and for your presence in this fandom that means so much to all of us. None of this would be possible if it weren't for Taylor, and all of you.

It seems only fitting for me to begin with my own swiftie story, so without any further ado, here it is!

"I was born in 2006, so growing up, I'd pretty much always been surrounded by Taylor's music in public, even though my family didn't listen to much of it. My dad always preferred rock over country and pop, and as a result, I'd been raised on Metallica instead!

Eventually, the 1989 era came along, and the world was enamored by Taylor's music. One of my earliest memories when it comes to Taylor is when my best friend (at the time) and I choreographed a dance to Shake It Off, which we used to audition for our school's talent show in second grade. We didn't make it in, but the experience was so fun and gave us a cool song to listen to. A few years later, one of my brothers was born (I have five younger brothers and two younger sisters, for reference), and we soon discovered that one of the only things that would help him fall asleep was a Taylor Swift song called Bad Blood.

Next came the reputation era! I can still recall exactly how it felt sitting in the multipurpose room before school in sixth grade, crouching around one of my friends' phones to watch the new Taylor Swift video that everyone was talking about. I thought the song (LWYMMD) was really cool and loved the video, but when I heard people talking about getting tickets for her reputation tour, I unfortunately wasn't interested.

A few months passed, and I finally got my own phone for my twelfth birthday. I made a playlist for myself of songs that I'd listen to while doing homework, and a few Taylor songs made their way onto it, including Delicate and …Ready For It?, which I'd heard on the radio recently and enjoyed. I didn't particularly care about anything relating to Taylor at that point, and I really only liked the few songs that I'd heard.

My swiftie story really started to pick up speed about a year later, in April of 2019. I'd recently turned thirteen in March (fitting, isn't it?) and had begun spending more time online, including on YouTube. One day, I was scrolling through my feed when I noticed a community post from Taylor Swift, with the caption "4.26". I wish I could remember which picture accompanied it, but unfortunately, I can't. I was confused and intrigued because the aesthetic seemed to directly contrast what I'd seen from reputation. The next day, I checked back, and there was another post with the same caption. This cycle continued for a few days, until finally, one day, Taylor announced that she'd be releasing a new music video the next day, on 4/26.

This music video, of course, was ME!, the lead single for her seventh album, Lover. I waited all day long for the music video, and eventually, the time came. I sat in my bed and watched the premiere on my old, glitchy iPad.

I was stunned. I loved it, so much. The moment the snake burst into butterflies, I was hooked. Taylor Swift was a genius, I just didn't know it yet.

The following day, people were talking about it at school, and all day long, I kept watching the view count climb and climb. One girl asked me if I was a swiftie (in a mean way, she wasn't a fan of Taylor) and I defensively proclaimed "No! I'm just seeing if she breaks a record for the amount of views!".

I lived in denial for a while, even though I continued to listen to the song every chance I got. Eventually, YNTCD dropped, and I loved that song as well, thinking it was so fun, and loving the fact that Taylor was urging people to sign a petition for the Equality Act. Eventually, I learned that her seventh album, Lover, would be released on August 23rd, 2019, and although I tried to pretend like I didn't care, I couldn't quite hide my excitement.

I had told myself that I wouldn't stay up to listen to the album as soon as it dropped, but that night, I couldn't sleep, so I decided to try it. I was obsessed, and while I didn't become a fully-fledged swiftie at that moment, that was the point that marked my descent down the rabbit hole into swiftie-dom.

For the next few weeks, I listened to Lover on repeat and eventually began to take a deep dive into Taylor's discography. I started watching interview clips and learned more and more about her, and loved absolutely everything I saw. I also asked for a guitar for Christmas that year, because of Taylor, and then taught myself how to play her songs.

Miss Americana came out in January 2020, and it was exactly what I needed. I loved it so much and watched it so many times in those first few weeks. Eventually, as we all know, the world shut down, and because I was bored, I decided to start a YouTube channel dedicated to Taylor Swift, which I called All Too Swift. That same channel has over thirteen thousand subscribers now!

In May, my baby sister was born, which was super significant because I had always wanted a little sister, and all I had were brothers. I played Taylor's music for her as a baby, and as she got older, she began to love it as well. Eventually, Taylor became our thing, which I'll touch on in a little bit.

When Ruthie was born, she was a very fussy baby, and as a result, taking care of her took a lot. I became very close with my youngest brother, Reid (who was almost 3 at the time), because he needed someone to cuddle him every night in order to fall asleep, and I was the one he chose, since my mom wasn't avaliable.

Every night, he'd request a song be sung to him, and while it varied at first, eventually Hey Stephen became the song he asked me to sing every time. That became our song, and even though he no longer needs it, it'll always be special to me for that reason.

Folklore came out in July, and that marked the first time I'd baked a dessert for one of Taylor's album releases, a tradition I still continue to this day. I also listened to it as soon as it dropped, because ever since Lover, that's been what I do for all of Taylor's new releases. When evermore came out, I was in absolute shock because I had never in my wildest dreams guessed that she'd drop not one, but TWO surprise albums in the same year. I loved evermore even more than I had loved folklore, and the lead single, willow became super important to me.

When I was younger, I had been a Harry Potter kid through and through, and my Taylor Swift obsession kind of took the place of my witchcraft one. But willow was a combination of the two. I watched the premiere of the music video with my mom, and when Taylor came onscreen dressed as a witch, my mom looked at me and said, "Taylor made this for you!", which was absolutely how it felt in that moment. Ever since then, willow has been my favorite song in the entire world, and probably always will be.

Eventually the re-recordings rolled around, and not to brag, but I find it pretty cool that the album that made me a swiftie was actually the first one Taylor ever owned, so I've gotten to experience watching her own all of her albums! Nothing else super significant happened until my sister, Ruthie, got a little older, and started to show more of an interest in Taylor's music. After Midnights dropped, I noticed that she'd begun to sing along to Bejeweled and Anti-Hero, and even more so, one of Taylor's older songs. For whatever reason, Delicate stuck out to her, and even now, over a year later, it's her favorite song in the entire world! She even forced me to memorize the music video choreography with her, and to this day, she'll ask me to "do Delicate!" with her, and we'll play the music video on the TV and dance along with Taylor.

Eventually, Taylor announced the Eras Tour, and I was so desperate for tickets, because at this point, the thing I wanted most in the world was to see Taylor perform live. I'd recently converted one of my friends (who I'd later come to consider my best friend) to a swiftie, and we decided that the two of us would go together. By some miracle, my parents were able to get three tickets, so that I could go with my friend and my mom.

Months later, on April 28th, 2023, I experienced the best day of my entire life. I got to see Taylor perform live at Mercedes Benz Stadium, and it was my first concert ever. It was incredible, and I sobbed so hard during willow, and I got to scream "I'm only seventeen, I don't know anything" at age seventeen, in a stadium full of swifties just like me. I traded so many bracelets, and the atmosphere was truly astonishing- I'd never felt that safe or loved in such a large setting before, but somehow, even though I hardly knew anyone there, it felt like I was where I belonged.

My sister wasn't able to come with us, but luckily I was able to recreate the experience for her a few months later, at the movie theater. She wore a Delicate dress, and I wore my outfit from the Eras Tour, a recreation of the dress Taylor wears in the ME! music video, a callback to the song that started my swiftie journey in the first place.

And yeah, that's basically it! It might be long, but it's important to me, and as Taylor once said, you should never make people "feel bad, dumb, or stupid for being excited about something". I really hope you enjoy reading the rest of the entries, and I hope you respect and appreciate the love and passion that went into each and every one of them.

Taylor, if you're reading this, thank you for absolutely changing my life in the best way possible. You're my biggest role model for so many reasons, but mostly because of your writing. Words are my passion, and you wield them so beautifully. It's my biggest dream to have something I've written read by you, and I'm sure so many others can say the same.

I love you endlessly, and it feels like you're the older sister I never had. Thank you for teaching me so much and for making me feel less alone. I feel so lucky to have gotten the opportunity to fall in love with your music as I've grown up, and I know there are millions who feel the same way. Becoming a swiftie is the best decision I've ever made, and having a place in this fandom is truly the best thing that's ever been mine." -Ellie

***

And now, please enjoy the rest of the swiftie stories!

"I have been listening to Taylor for as long as I can remember. My first ever favorite song was I Knew You Were Trouble, and I was in love with a lot of her older stuff. With that being said, I became a full on swiftie a little after Evermore came out. I had seen some things online about people talking about Folklore, and how incredible it was, so I decided to give it a listen. I fell in love with it, and after that I started listening to her whole discography. Then I fell in love with not only her music, but her personality. I could talk for hours about why I love Taylor, but I'll try to summarize.

To start, she has the biggest heart. She cares for her fans more than anyone in the world, and although I don't know her personally, you can clearly see how much she cares. She is unapologetically herself, and she has bounced back from so many hardships in her life. The way she cares for people is something that everyone should aspire to do. She makes everyone she meets feel like the most special person in the world. She never stops working for what she wants, even when people around her try to tear her down. She is the most down to earth, kind hearted celebrity (and human being) in the world. Her songwriting is on top of the world. Everything about her is amazing. That is why I love Taylor.

Taylor's music means so much to me, more than I'll ever be able to explain. When I feel alone, ashamed of myself, regretful of something I've done, or just absolutely drowning in self-loathing, I can always count on Taylor's music to be there for me. I can come home from having a horrible day at school, put my headphones on, and let the sound of Folklore drown out all the sadness and negativity.

As you can probably tell, I'm a big Folklore girly, so lots of my favorite songs are from Folklore. Asking me my number one Taylor song is a very hard question, but the song that I have always considered to be my favorite song is Cornelia Street. The first time I heard this song I was absolutely in love with it. Her vocals, the lyrics, the vulnerability, the soft yet desperate melodies, everything about it is perfect. I know a lot of people have deep and meaningful stories about why their favorite song is their favorite song, but I don't think it always has to be that way. Cornelia Street has always connected with me, not because I relate to it, but just because of the way the song was written.

Being a swiftie is amazing. The best part of being a swiftie to me is the community. The excitement we share when Taylor releases something. The friendship bracelets we trade with people we've never met, but can relate to. The fact that we don't care if you just discovered Taylor's discography yesterday, or you've been a swiftie since her country days, our community will accept you no matter what.

If I got the chance to tell Taylor something (I would probably be speechless at first) here's what I would say: Taylor, I want you to know that you'll always be loved by us. I know you hear thousands of swifties telling you that they love you everyday, but you probably don't understand the amount that we really do love you. Think about how it feels hearing "I love you" from a significant other for the first time. It's an amazing feeling. But hearing it from thousands of fans, you probably forget the meaning that those words really hold. But just know that when you hear that, we really do love you. There will never be a time when we don't love you. So next time you feel sad and miserable, remember the millions of swifties that truly love you." - Evelyn R.

***

"The first Taylor Swift song I've ever heard was Welcome To New York. As soon as I heard it, I completely fell in love. My favorite Taylor song is "Miss Americana and the Heartbreak Prince". It's such a great song with a great meaning. If I could tell Taylor something, I would tell her thank you. Through the highs and the lows she's been there for me. I love you Taylor!" -Alice

***

"Nothing convinced me to become a Swiftie. I just became one when I first listened to her songs, the first of which was Blank Space. I love Taylor because she's a role model to so many people and she's taught me to never give up. To me, Taylor's music means to always be happy and don't let people get under your skin. Taylor's music has helped me through some really hard times. When I lost my family members I lost myself and Taylor's music helped me find myself again and I'm so grateful that I had her music to help me. My favorite song is "All Too Well" because it's like she's reliving memories and when I listen to it, I start to relive memories and it just takes me back to a happy time. The best part about being a Swiftie is being among other Swifties who love Taylor as much as I do. If I could tell Taylor something it would be thank you for everything you've done" -Emily

***

"I became a swiftie when I was five years old. I've always loved Taylor's music. The first song I ever heard of hers was I Knew You Were Trouble! When I was

3

about 12 or 13, I rediscovered her music and fell in love with it all over again! I love Taylor Swift because she is beautiful and she is a very powerful yet gentle person. Finally, if I could say one thing to Taylor Swift, I would say I appreciate her so much for her glowing personality and her beautiful music!" -anonymous

***

"Dear Taylor, I just wanted you to know that ilysm and I love everything you do for the fans, community and music industry! The first song I ever heard from you was Welcome to New York. As a five year old girl with her little iPod playing Taylor Swift, I used to dance my heart out to this song for multiple years! When 1989 (Taylor's Version) came out I was in awe, listening to the songs that had been my childhood and seeing them finally owned by mother.... WOW (and I might have shedded a tear or two).The music you make is so inspirational to me because I love to write, and your depth throughout your lyrics give me ideas to write stories and even songs!

I can't wait for more albums and songs to be made! The best part about being a swiftie is all the easter eggs throughout music videos, Eras Tour outfits and even Instagram posts, that we get to dive into and figure out the meaning behind. Taylor, keep up the good work, I love you sosososooooosososooooooo much!"-Claire

***

"'Dad, can you play some music?'
'Sure honey.'
This is where it started. ME! Started playing. 'Woah, who sings this? She sounds so good!' I said, smiling at my dad.

'Taylor Swift.'

'I love her voice!'

Taylor has been a huge inspiration for me. She's taught me how to get through hard things, be confident, have a good time, and be a good person. She's changed me. Taylor's music inspired me to sing more, and even to join chorus! Her music means so much to me. I listen to her almost everyday, I listen to her journaling, making food, showering, etc. She's helped me through tough times, fighting with friends, my mom's sickness, so much more. Taylor is such a creative person, she's created many things: music, perfume, clothing. Taylor is probably one of the kindest people in the world. She donates money to people who need it, invites people to her house for a listening party, and she is always up for pictures and videos.

Taylor's songwriting skills are out of this world, she words things so beautifully. She's inspired me to write my own songs. Taylor's songs are most times out of her perspective, but she writes them in a way where everybody else can be reminded about something in their life. I love singing, yelling her songs out. They are so beautiful and relatable. Being a swiftie is also a beautiful thing. We have a whole community, it's so inviting.

Taylor, you are an amazing person and you help so many people." -Irelynn

***

"Taylor Swift is one of my favorite people in the world. She is helping me through everything just like a friend would, even though I don't know her in real life. I know that I might just be "another basic teenage girl", but if that means I get to obsess over Taylor Swift, I am

5

completely okay with that!

Taylor will forever & always be my comfort person. I think the thing that convinced me to be a swiftie was myself. I heard cardigan for the first time again-after I used to listen to it a lot-in like mid 2022 and told myself "I want to memorize this whole song." Then, after I did that, I said "I really like this song, let me add some more of her songs to my playlist." That was when my journey as a swiftie really started, and even though I listened to her a lot as a kid, I was more of a fan and not a real swiftie. As my path began, I watched Miss Americana for the first time. That really helped me get to know her and her music. When I started listening to her more, I watched my life begin again. She opened a whole new door of music for me. As I started becoming a swiftie, I was so eager to learn more about her because hearing her music and seeing her happy changed my life.

The first song by her I ever heard was either Blank Space or I Knew You Were Trouble. When they came on the radio in the car, I screamed them. Before my teenage years, my friend and I made up a dance to Look What You Made Me Do when reputation came out. I grew up with her music. I think that's why the re-recording of 1989 was so important to me. Taylor is my inspiration. I love her because no matter what I am going through, whether it be sad or happy, she is always there with me. I guess you could say there is an invisible string tying her to me. I love her because she has a positive attitude through everything. She doesn't let other people's opinions break her! Every day, she reminds me why I should have a smile on my face. Her music makes me feel heard.

Before I became a real swiftie, I didn't know how to express myself through music, then, I found Taylor again. I realized that she is the artist that has a song for every single situation you could be going through at the moment. Her music and her lyrics make me feel completely the opposite of alone, and I realized that I am not the only one going through the situation I am currently in. She puts into words what I can't put into words, and somehow her words are almost always the exact thing that I am trying to say. Her music means the world to me, and it sickens me when someone makes fun of it. When people tear her down, they tear me down too. Taylor has helped me in so many ways, more than I can even count. If I had a bad day or just wasn't feeling myself, my solution is literally listening to reputation (because, you know, reputation), just listening to my Taylor playlist, or I'll watch Miss Americana. She helps me calm down and realize that everything is going to be okay. She gives me something to live for.

One of my all time favorite songs of hers is Long Live. I physically cannot put into words how much that song means to me. Every time I listen to it I cry. It reminds me of how far she's come, from singing the national anthem and writing songs in school to performing to sold out stadiums. It makes me feel emotions I didn't even know were possible. When SNTV came out, I was in utter shock and was completely breaking down listening to her owning this song because I was so incredibly proud of her. "long live the walls we crashed through, I had the time of my life with you." is one of my favorite lines from the song. It reminds me of everything she's been through and how she's had us by her side and to encourage her to keep going the whole time. The best part of being a swiftie is having so much to look forward to, regarding her album releases, concerts, and more. One more thing (out of the many) of my favorite things about being a swiftie is always having her to look up to. She has had such a positive impact on my life and I love her so much. I love getting excited when I hear her music in public. I love getting merch and vinyls. I love talking about her to my friends that aren't swifties. I love seeing her vinyls and CDs in public.

Being a part of the swiftie community is almost like being part of a family. At the The Eras Tour movie I became friends with people I'd never met before. Seeing swifties in public wearing Taylor's merch is so magical because I love complimenting them on whatever they are wearing. Swifties are some of the kindest people on earth and I love connecting with them over our love for Taylor. It is truly beautiful how she brings people together.

If I could tell Taylor anything, I'd tell her how proud I am of her. I'd also tell her how she makes me feel heard and seen, and how she's such an incredible, gorgeous, and talented human being. I'd make sure she knows the impact she had on my life. I will forever hold onto the memories I have made with her, because they will always hold on to me. I'd tell her that no matter if I have children some day or grow up and move to a cold big city, I will always love her. She will always hold a special place in my heart. Seeing how much she's grown makes me so so proud, and I hate it when she gets choked up sometimes because she deserves the world. Becoming a swiftie was honestly the best decision I have ever made. Although it is hard to put into words how much she means to me, this is the best I can do. Long story short, Taylor made my life 113% better and I cannot wait to continue my life with her by my side. She is, truly, the best thing that's ever been mine." -Julia

***

"I've always liked Taylor but didn't really start knowing everything about her until about 3 years ago. When I was younger I really knew her popular songs with some less popular ones. Taylor has inspired me so much and I love her so much. She is the kindest person ever and I hope she knows that. I don't have a favorite album or song because all of them are equally good."- Grace

***

"What convinced me to become a swiftie was honestly the 1989 album, I have so many good memories with the amazing songs on the album. The first ever song I listened to was Shake It Off (an amazing classic). I personally love Taylor because she's such an incredible songwriter, singer, and person. Taylor's music just means so much to me because it's gotten me through the worst of times, but also has helped me have some of the best memories of my entire life. It feels like Taylor just gets me even though she doesn't have a clue who I am.

To me the best parts of being a swiftie is the loving and incredible community, and that we don't have to wait 3 years to get something exciting from Taylor (mother always spoils us). If I could tell Taylor something it would definitely be, you have gotten me through so much, it feels like you are always there for me when I need you most, I can not explain how grateful I am to have you to look up to: an incredible, amazing, talented, wonderful woman. I love you so much, you have saved my life." -Peighton

***

"I first was a swiftie when my mom bought her first 4 albums on cd and my family listened to it all the time. My favorite song was IKYWT and I would always call Taylor "trouble" when I was little. I then got really hooked when she released folklore, I then backed up and got to know her other albums.

I love Taylor so much and she has such a kind hearted soul, and I love how she is truly unique with her emotional songwriting abilities, and she has gotten to be so important in my life. I truly think that Taylor Swift is one of the best songwriters in the world right now and it's wonderful to see her grow. What I would like to say to Taylor is, to tell her how much she has helped me in life. I get so excited whenever there is a new album or mv released and it gives me so much joy in my life. I love how she keeps us swifties on our toes all the time with the easter eggs and the surprises. I love her with all my heart and I could only wish the best for her." -Bella

***

"I've been a swiftie for as long as I can remember; my parents are both huge swifties so of course I grew up the biggest swiftie ever. People at school would always ask me about my fav songs or artists and I could scream Taylor Swift with no hesitation. I remember screaming the red album with my dad whenever we were in the car. I am 14 years old so I was around 3-4 years old at this time, I remember dancing around my house screaming the lyrics to 22, wanegbt, I knew u were trouble, red, all too well etc. obviously I loved all the songs on red but as a kid those were the ones that stuck out to me the most. When 1989 came out, I remember hearing wildest dreams for the first time and I was OBSESSED. For years if anyone asked what my favourite song was I would always say wildest dreams, to this day this song holds such a special place in my heart because it was the first song I called 'mine'.

Taylor is my ultimate inspiration; she is so strong and kind and is such an amazing example to me, whenever I'm sad taylor can cheer me up in a heartbeat whether that means listening to her music, watching music videos, watching her interviews, watching miss americana etc literally anything Taylor related will bring the biggest smile to my face. I look up to her and love her so much I can't even explain.

When I was about 8 or 9 my mum took me to the reputation stadium tour. It was one of the best experiences of my life. I remember the pure joy I experienced when Taylor started singing, ...ready for it? And I literally died dead. One of the standouts was when Taylor played long live on the piano, that song is my everything and I love it with all my heart. The other day I was watching my videos from the tour and reliving the memories of seeing Taylor play long live just made me burst into tears. That song is my world.

Despite being pretty young, those are memories I will NEVER forget. I remember when lover came out and watching the ME! Music video, singing and dancing around my grandmas house to any song on lover made me feel unstoppable. I remember being in school and when I would say Taylor was my favourite artist people would say stuff like "ew her music sucks" "don't worry you'll grow out of that phase", but I have never stopped loving Taylor EVER.

I remember the day I was on my way to dance driving in the car and my dad told me someone stole Taylors music and being so furious, in my mind Taylor was practically queen of the world and I felt so sad for her but looking back the re records have changed my life and I'm so proud of Taylor for turning something so negative into such a positive and emotional experience.

anyway, I remember the day folklore came out, I remember learning the lyrics to cardigan in my room by watching the lyric video over and over again until it stuck. Folklore is so special to me and my family because covid was such a stressful and dark time. Folklore gave me a chance to truly escape from the world around me and I am forever grateful for that.

Now I remember evermore coming out and being so confused that Taylor could put out 2 albums so quickly but being ultimately so proud of her. folklore and evermore are truly works of art. My favourite song out of both folklore and evermore is the lakes, I can't express how the song makes me feel it just gives me chills.

Now we're getting closer to the present day; I remember being obsessed with fearless and red tv. I am so proud of Taylor. Me and my mum are actually obsessed with all too well 10 minute version. It's my mum's all time favourite song, every time we listen to it no matter where we are we scream it like we're at a concert. I remember the day Midnights came out we listened to the album on the tv and my whole family were listening to the album together, (I have 2 brothers and 2 sisters all younger than me) my brothers don't like to admit it but they love taylor too, I have turned my 3 and 7 year old sisters into big swifties. Midnights is such a special album and I love it so much!! I remember on the first day the songs that stood out to me the most are lavender haze, anti hero, maroon and your on your own kid.

I have major anxiety and I went through a really hard time at the beginning of this year where I was bullied really badly and had to leave the school I was at. Through the ups and downs of my life Taylor has always been there. Songs like anti hero and afterglow (my fav on lover) are songs I always play whenever my anxiety has taken over. Now, a few days before July 7th, I was so excited for speak now (Taylors Version) I love speak now so so so much !! I ended up making a cake to celebrate the album release with my auntie who is the biggest swiftie as well and went to the speak now tour at my age speak now tv was such a fun album release for me it was one of the best days ever!!

Now we are approaching August 10th which is when 1989 tv was announced. I was one of the people who were so sure about the album announcement, that day I wore red lipstick, all my friendship bracelets, and had a 1989 outfit on. I was watching the Eras tour livestream and I remember when she announced it I screamed so loudly and started bursting into tears. The Eras tour movie was such a fun experience. I went with my mum, my sister and my swiftie bestie and her mum and her sisters. We had the best time and I was balling my eyes out the entire time and I remember thinking to myself how that was one of the best moments of my entire life, I thought to myself "I am so happy right now, no one can understand how much I love mom (Taylor).

I haven't been to the Eras Tour in person yet because I live in Australia but I have tickets to see her in February and I'm so excited, I have a countdown on my phone which goes down every day!! Now we're up to October 27th 1989 tv release day, my auntie drove from another part of Australia to stay with us, we were making bracelets and our 1989 tv cake all day! 1989 means so much to me and taylor killed it with her version, every song sounds crisper and cleaner and i'm so obsessed i've been listening to it every day since the release!!

Now as I'm writing this it's November 7th. Being a swiftie is the best thing to ever happen to me; it just gives me so much joy. If I was to talk to Taylor I would say how much her music has helped me with my anxiety and how much joy she has brought me, I love her so so so much she truly is mother. It is my dream to meet you Taylor! I love you so so so so so much it is truly unfathomable!" -Stella (YouTube@loverlore.13)

***

"I've been a swiftie since the Lover era, but Taylor's music has been a big part of my life since long before that. Some of my biggest memories from childhood are listening to songs from 1989 and Red on long car rides with my mom. Not only that, folklore and evermore helped me get through some difficult times in my life and I could not be more grateful for that. Taylor Swift is one of my biggest inspirations and I know she is for thousands if not millions of others, and that's just amazing to me. If I got to say one thing to her I would thank her for all the amazing work she's doing and for being such an amazing human. We need more people like her!" -Sophie

"I think that what convinced me to become a swiftie was actually taylor's music and her Eras Tour. I had always loved her but never actually declared myself a swiftie until this year.

The first Taylor Swift song i heard was probably shake it off or blank space. shake it off has always held a special place in my heart for that reason. I've always loved the upbeat style to it and it brings me so much joy to listen to the song, which is now owned by Taylor herself.

I love Taylor because she has such a kind and caring soul. She enjoys life and lives it to the fullest while also making sure other people are happy too. She brings joy and happiness to so many people in the world and it makes me love her even more. Her music is just a part of it. I love her as a human being as well.

Taylor's music means so much to me. I love how she has explored different genres, and experimented with new types of music. She is the best lyricist and she curates beautiful music. Her lyrics are just so different from others and that is what makes them so special.

Taylor's music and Taylor herself have helped me through so many things. she brings light to a dark day with her fun upbeat songs, while other days she's just there to support us through hard times. the many quotes she has said over the years are so inspirational and empowering, and those have had an impact on so many people.

Personally, my favourite song has to be shake it off or i know places. Shake it off is just such a fun song and makes me feel so, so happy when i listen to it. It makes me forget about the people who hate on others for fun. I know places was just perfectly written. the lyrics, the music, and taylor. it's just perfect. and the (taylor's version) of it is even better. The way she yells right before the second chorus is just amazing. I love these songs to the moon and to saturn.

The best part about being a swiftie is the community. We all have such a good connection with each other and everyone accepts everyone as is. Everyone is so kind and loving. I love the swiftie community so much.

If I could tell Taylor something, I would say that she is the most kind and pure person on earth, and that she has helped so many people, including myself. I would tell her that she deserves exactly what she has. that she is loved by so many people, and that she should keep on doing what she's doing." -anonymous

***

"This is definitely a core memory for me. It was a Saturday morning and I was watching CMT (country music television) with my older sister while my mom was getting us donuts and the picture to burn music video came on and I was obsessed with it, as I grew up my sister would listen to the albums and I would listen as well, I also remember the time in middle school we were doing song analysis and I brought in Haunted. I remember being teased and tormented by the boys for listening to Taylor, I apologize if I'm getting off the topic here and I'm heartbroken to admit I stopped listening to Taylor because of this I came back because of Reputation and I'm so happy that I did I love Taylor so so much she has made such a huge impact on me and my life." - Nate

***

"I became a swiftie when I was 7 years old in the 1989 era and I also went to the rep tour as well. I stream her songs and evaluate her lyrics all the time. She helps me out unknowingly when I'm struggling with hard times. My favorite song is you're on your own kid because it comforts me a lot. I love her so much." - Seunga

**

"I was 13 when I became a swiftie and I'm 16 now. I literally love all of her albums and it would be my dream to ever see her in concert. I became a Swiftie when a friend showed me the Miss Americana movie, then I started listening to many songs (especially from Reputation and Folklore) and I started to follow every news about her music when she announced the re-recordings.

I love Taylor as a person because I think not only she is great at everything she does and it's always a pleasure to discover a new song or a new music video from her but also because she seems like a kind, generous and incredible person with values and she fights for what she thinks is right and she inspired me a lot (as a person and as a songwriter).

Her music does not only fit every mood swings I have but also it makes me feel comfortable: when I'm listening to Taylor's music, I'm in my own world and no one can hurt me. My favorite song is probably Cornelia street because it is powerful as hell and I must admit I have a thing for breakup songs.

I love being a swiftie because not only Taylor is always doing so much for her fans and giving us news and things to be excited about all the time but also because the swiftie community has become my safe place too as people are so kind and support each other in everything they do! Taylor, if there's something that I could tell you if I was in front of you is thank you for everything you've given me, I was enchanted to meet you and never stop believing in yourself." -Ariadne

***

"I first became a Swiftie from when my cousin came to stay with me and she played Blank Space. I absolutely FELL in love with it and after that I started listening to you more and more until I became a HUGE Swiftie. My favourite song of yours and just in general is Betty! Betty is just so amazing because it's part of the folklore love triangle and I LOVE the folklore love triangle and when I heard Betty like blank space I just fell in love with it and I love it so much!!! I love being a swiftie so much!!! I would say the best part for me is knowing that my favourite singer is the LITERAL BEST PERSON IN THE ENTIRE WORLD!!!" -Eva K.

***

"Dear Taylor, when I was 6, I remember my cousin getting a 1989 cd for Christmas one year. I would always beg her to listen to it. Fast forward 9 years and here I am with piles of friendship bracelets and shelves full of vinyls. You forever changed my life. You have gotten me through all the hard times. I would never be where I am today if it wasn't for you. I hope you have the best birthday in the world because you truly deserve it! You ARE the music industry. I love you to the moon and to Saturn." -Carly

***

"I love Taylor Swift to the moon and to Saturn. I became a swiftie about last October near the Midnights release. I'm a newer swiftie but it doesn't mean I love her any less. I had always respected Taylor as an artist but I really branched out into her music around midnights. My best friends are also swifties and they helped me explore her discography! I have so many posters and flags of her in my room it's wild. My all time favorite song ever is All Too Well 10 minute version, Taylor's version, from the vault. I know that it is popular but something about that song makes me cry.

I am a dancer and each year I get a solo for competitions. This year my solo song is paper rings. This is my absolute favorite solo that I have ever had. I spent $300 on custom tap shoes to match the song! My dream is to finally go to a Taylor swift concert and maybe even one day meet her. Miss swift is the number 1 artist in the world but I still feel like she is so near and dear to my heart. Taylor if you are able to read this, just know that you are my everything. Thank you for bringing this world happiness!" -Quinn

**

"My being a swiftie started when the red album came out. I loved we are never ever getting back together. That was my absolute favorite song at 8 years old. I would watch the music video over and over. when 1989 was announced it became the first album i ever bought. I had the cd, and I paid for it on apple music. I loved 1989. I would watch the blank space music video 100 times a day. IWYW was my alarm, and I would wake up to it everyday. Being a swiftie is the best part of my personality. Thank you taylor!" -Kendyl

**

"I always say Taylor Swift saved me. I started listening to Taylor during the 1989 era. I would always request to listen to Shake It Off in the car, or have a

Taylor Swift dance party with my cousins. Eventually that turned into more and I started to listen to her other albums. I remember getting into fights with my sister over which lyrics to Love Story were the right ones (I was right) During lockdown Taylor was one of the main things that got me through it. She was like my best friend that didn't even know my name. She was there for me when know one else was. She got me through the good days, and the bad.When Midnights came out I was obsessed. I would play it on repeat 24/7.

April 1st 2023 was one of the best days of my life. I went to the Eras tour this day, and even though I was in the nosebleeds I still BAWLED my eyes out when she came on. It was surreal seeing my favorite person in the whole wide world in the same room as me and breathing the same air as me. I had to use binoculars to see her clearly but it was worth every penny. If you were to walk into my room the first thing you would see would be Taylor. If you turned your head left or right you would see posters, CDs and Taylor magazines all over my walls. If I met Taylor I would tell her how proud I am of her, and how she has gotten me through so much, even though she doesn't know me at all. Taylor has truly changed my life for the better!" -Ella

***

"My mom was a swiftie before I was even born, and I became a swiftie around 1989 era and my first concert was the reputation tour! I believe the first Taylor Swift song I ever heard was Our Song, which fun fact, was one of my Eras Tour surprise songs! I love Taylor because she is such a great role model, she works hard for what she wants and carries you through every stage in life and she has a song for every occasion.

Her music means the world to me. Sometimes when I hear my favourite songs I cry because I love her music too much, the lyrics too much and because I am so grateful to be a fan of hers. Taylor's music has helped me through peaks and valleys. I mean she has been there for me since I was 5. I have had too many instances of when her lyrics have helped me. One of my favourites is when my friends and I were at an amusement park and I was scared to go on a certain roller coaster so while the huge drop was coming I was singing Shake it Off to myself, lol.

What is my favourite song and why? GETAWAY CAR!!!! I love it because it is such a lyrical masterpiece. But, when I was six watching the performance, the Why She Disappeared poem before the song and then before she came out and said " In the death of her reputation, she felt truly alive" That was one of the best moments ever. The best parts of being a swiftie are being able to look for easter eggs, becoming a clown 6 days out of 7, and reacting to new music and vault tracks. If I could tell Taylor something, I would tell her how much she means to me and I would ask her what is her favourite bridge she wrote and why!" -Julia

***

"When I was really little I used to listen to Taylor Swift. All I listened to was Shake it Off and Look What You Made Me Do but I tell you those songs shaped my childhood; as I was cleaning my room I would listen to those 2 songs on repeat. Then after those got out of the queue I listened to ME! I was amazed that Taylor actually had more music. It made me so happy I listened to the rest of the Lover album but really only loved ME!. I was scrolling on YouTube shorts one day and I found my friend lip syncing to this song that was like "our song was a slammin' screen door" and I looked it up and found Our Song I LOVED it I started listening to the rest of her albums and here I am a year and a half later a swiftie. The reason I love Taylor is because she really pays attention to her fan base which really matters. Each of her different albums/eras have a unique feel to them, a little bit of everything for everyone. Right now my favorite song is Picture to Burn. I really think her debut album is underrated and that song is an absolute banger. My favorite part about being a swiftie is how it feels like we all just know each other. We trade bracelets and obviously love Taylor." -Emily

***

"I've been a swiftie for as long as I can remember. I grew up on country music so I would hear her songs on the radio. When I was around 4 or 5 years old, I loved dancing around to WANEGBT and IKYWT.

Over the years following that, I started hearing more of her popular songs and became a bigger fan. It wasn't until quarantine that I sat down and listened to her full discography. Shortly after, folklore was released, and it was so exciting to experience that album drop at the same time as everyone else. I listened to her music 24/7 and memorized all of the words to her songs. My favorite album of hers is reputation. I love every song on it so much, especially Getaway Car.

Taylor has been such an inspiration for me. When I was a kid I would write breakup songs (despite never having been in a relationship) because I wanted to be just like her. I still write songs and have a dream of becoming a singer-songwriter. In addition, Taylor has helped me through some rough times. I struggle with anxiety a lot and music really helps, particularly Taylor's. When I need something to cheer me up or just need to have a good cry, I can put her music on.

If I could tell Taylor something, I would thank her for making beautiful music and being there for me when no one else was. She's been a huge part of my life for so long and I am so incredibly grateful." -anonymous

***

"Wow. The REAL Taylor Swift might read this! Well Taylor we love you so much. You've taught us to love ourselves, to not care what others say, to know your worth, to know that you're not alone because someone is dealing with the same thing as you whether it's bullying or something else, and most of all.... You taught us that there will be drama and there will be people trying to ruin your "reputation" hahahahahaha see what I did there. Anyways there will be people who aren't cut out to be real friends but you will find your people. And Taylor, thank you so much for that. All of us swifties love you so so so so so much and I couldn't imagine a life without the talented, most gorgeous, Dr. Taylor Alison Swift!" -Brooke

***

"I remember the day all too well. I was sitting in a class where one of my not yet friends had to sing a song and she sung love story. I was instantly interested in the song and I went home and listened to it and saw the mv. I also saw the mv of you belong with me, blank space and bad blood, the songs becoming my instant favs.

I was later paired up with her in class and we talked a lot. The fun part was that she was also a newer swiftie. We celebrated the release of Midnights, SNTV and 1989 TV together!

Discovering Taylor is the best thing that happened in my life, not to mention the sweetest people I have met online in the swiftie community. I have to admit that long story short I would not be here today if it wasn't for my swiftie bestie." -anonymous

***

"I've been a fan since Red but I was hardcore during 1989, I even went to the 1989 World Tour! Your songs have inspired me so so so much! My favorite song of yours is Betty! It's such a beautiful song and I'm so glad I heard it live. I was at your June 17th show in Pittsburgh! I love you so much and you're so inspiring! Thank you for being you Taylor." -Callie

***

"Being a Swiftie has been an incredible journey so far, going to the film, waiting for album drops and even getting tickets to the eras tour has all been amazing. Taylor's music means the world to me and it makes me feel like I'm not alone in anything really. My older sister actually made me a Swiftie along with the help with one of my friends, it was my sister's idea to go to the Eras tour and if we didn't get tickets that day I don't know what would've happened. I've only been a Swiftie for 6 months but they have been incredible ones!

PS. Thanks Evelyn for making me that playlist!" - Merryn

***

"Taylor came to me at a point in my life where I was lost. I was lonely, I had no friends, I lacked any form of confidence and to be honest, hated myself. But when I found Taylor, and her music, she helped me through the toughest times in my life. And I'm still going through a lot of things right now in my head, and Taylor is the reason that I am currently alive, genuinely, she has saved my life, and I hope one day I do get to actually tell her what she means to me. She is everything to me. Taylor, thank you for everything you have done for me, and for the world, you really are the music industry, you are a force. I love you to the moon and Saturn" -Kara T.

***

"I became a swiftie on 12/16/22 and my fav song is endgame and my fav album is REP. I really love Taylor cause she makes me happy when others can't!" - Hannanah S

***

"I remember that, when I was little, "Shake it off" came quite often on the radio and I loved it. However, for some reason, I never actually searched Taylor's name to listen to other songs by her. Then, one day 2 years ago, a song called "All to Well 10 min version" showed up on my page. Out of curiosity, I clicked, listened to it and I loved it so so so much. And when I realized it was by Taylor Swift, I was literally so surprised! Since then, I kept putting her songs on my playlists whenever I discovered them. But the moment that made me a true swiftie was this summer when I was watching a YouTube video of a "Speak Now Taylor's Version sleepover". I was so astonished by the swifties' reactions and ability to hear so many differences between it and the original (and Taylor's lyrics), that I immediately started to research. What are her album's names, what awards did she receive, how old is she, and all that stuff. Afterwards, when I considered myself knowledgeable enough, I listened to all of the songs on all of her albums in order, and my reactions were basically: "Why didn't I search her music earlier???", "This song is a masterpiece", "This album is a masterpiece", "How does she write so painful and relatable lyrics??", "I'm in love". And that's pretty much when and how I became obsessed with Taylor Swift.

Before ending, I would like to tell Taylor a message, if she ever will see it: Thank you so much for everything you do. Your music has always been there for me, no matter what I am going through. If I am happy, I have "Wonderland" and "Dancing with Our Hands Tied" to dance to. If I am sad, I have "Nothing New" and "You're on Your Own Kid" to relate to. If I need comfort, I have "Right where You Left Meand "The Lakes". If I need to smile, I have "I'm Only Me When I'm With You" and "The Other Side of the Door". And, forever always, I have "Timeless" and "Afterglow", which are my favorite songs of all time. I love you, and you will forever have a place in my heart." -Maya V.

***

"I became a swiftie because my dad is in the radio business and he gets to meet her, play her music on the radio, go to concerts, and much more. When I was 12 years old, he gave me a Speak Now World Tour award in a frame with a handwritten letter from Taylor. I thought "maybe I should listen to her to see how it goes. Long Story Short (see what I did there) I'm in love with her!!! From Red to Lover to Folklore, I love it all. I went to the Eras Tour on May 5, 2023 (Nashville N1) with the Speak Now Taylors Version Announcement!!!! So from getting that Speak Now award to seeing Taylor live and her announcement that she gets to own Speak Now IN PERSON, it really changed me.

The first Taylor Swift song I ever heard was Look What you Made Me Do. This song has grown on me. The first time I heard it I wasn't a fan to be honest but, as I listened to it more I definitely love it now.

I love Taylor for who she is. Her personality, Her persona, the way she treats her fans, all of it. I love the way she laughs, the way she is so silly and funny, and how kind she is. She is not your typical superstar, she's more than that and everything a Swiftie could want.

What does Taylor's music mean to me? Her music is calming. It gets people through hard times, celebrates success and way more. Her music is inspiring. From You Belong with Me to You're on Your Own Kid.

Taylor's music has helped me so much. My dad had prostate cancer 4 years ago and it was really hard on me. Lover specifically soon you'll get better) and he got cancer free but this may he got throat cancer. Songs that didn't even relate like Exile, Midnight Rain, and So it Goes... got me through another hard time with my dad. He is Cancer Free now and happily living his life!

The best part of being a swiftie is keeping up to date with Taylor, seeing what she's doing, what she wears, and who she goes out with, most importantly, who she's dating haha. I love watching the Eras Tour every night and screaming every word and just watching Taylor grow and grow.

If I could tell Taylor anything, I'd tell her that no matter what the music business tells you, you are enough. You are not better than anyone else, no one is. Just keep pushing through the hard times and your achievements will come through. And that I love her of course."

-Naomi S. (YouTube@naomiischandler)

**

"Growing up, until class 5, I was that girl who was friends with everyone in my school. The young, talkative and cheery girl who would snag every opportunity she got to make friends, to sing, to dance, and to be happy and make people cheer up. When I got to 6th grade, we had to move states. Over 700 miles away from my home. A new place, a new school, a new culture, and new people.

I spent 3 years in that place, which I would say were probably my worst. What would a 10-year-old expect at a new school? With new friends, new teachers, and new classes, my new school was nothing of the sort. I spent those 2 years getting bullied, for not knowing their language and for being a "teacher's pet". Some kids would tease me, laugh at me and a girl even hit me. If the kids weren't enough, the teachers too were like that. During this time I got distant, quiet, and sad. The girl I knew just a year ago was gone. I tried to find things to do at home just so that I wouldn't have to go out (a lot of it happened during COVID-19). The day that I found Selena, now looking back at it, was the best thing to happen to me. I immediately fell in love with her, her music, and the person that she is and it brought me happiness that I'm not alone.

I found out about Taylor all because of Selena and the day I did, I knew that I wanted to be just like them. I was assured that I had found my role models. Taylor has helped me to learn how to express my emotions. I have become a very quiet and introverted person now, and Taylor helped me to express my emotions through poetry. I even participated in a national poetry contest. This was my first time writing a poem and surprisingly, I was in the top ten national winners. Ever since then, I haven't looked back and I try to write as much as I can, Taylor's songs inspire me. I've been a Swiftie for about just 3 years now, but getting to know her, her songs, even her best friends, and this incredible family that we have, has been life-changing. I'm making friends from across the world. We laugh, we talk, and we come together to support our mom. Going to the Eras Tour movie, trading bracelets, making new friends, and hearing my mom, who saw and heard Taylor for the first time, compliment her was one of the best things I've ever experienced. I loved it so much that I'm going again with my friends. It doesn't even feel like Taylor is just some person on the other side of the world, or should I say The Other Side of the Door hehe, she is our mom, our sister, and our best friend. I don't know what the chances are that you're going to see this, but if you do I wanna let you know, thank you for this. Thank you for saving me from falling into a pit of my own darkness, thank you for making me and millions of other people like me feel seen, and thank you for giving me this family of the most amazing people who build each other up and love each other. Truly thank you for everything that you have done. We are having the time of our lives, with you." -Kavya S, India

***

"I started listening to Taylor in 2018. I was one of the many 8-year-old girls who loved Shake It Off. Then one day, when I was 9, I heard Ready For It on the radio and fell in love with the song. I didn't know what the name of the song was at the time but I assumed it was called "In the middle of the night" because of one of the lyrics. So one day, I looked up that title so I could find the song and I clicked on every video result until I found the correct one (Ready For It) and that was my favorite song for a while in 2018. I also discovered songs like LWYMMD, Blank Space, Bad Blood, Delicate, and End Game. Those were the only songs I knew for a while, and Taylor had been one of my favorite artists starting at that time. Then in 2019 I saw some of the Lover music videos.

2020 and 2021 was when I really started to discover more of her songs. I would always get Taylor MVs on my YouTube recommendations so I watched them. I discovered hits like You Belong With Me to deep cuts like Cornelia Street. Sometimes I would also put Taylor on shuffle on my Alexa device and would discover new songs like Getaway Car, I Knew You Were Trouble, AYHTDWS, MAATHP, Picture To Burn, etc that way. I was even a Cruel Summer and All Too Well stan before they got popular. I was just a normal Taylor fan and listener for a while, until Midnights came out. That album changed my life because it's what made me an even bigger Swiftie. I started to get lots of Taylor related videos on my YouTube recommendations and learned a lot of new things about Taylor and then decided it was time to listen to her full discography in order. So I did, and discovered even more new songs, including Long Live, which is now my #1 stan song. I also watched the rep tour movie and Miss Americana for the first time. I also sometimes tune in to Eras Tour livestreams, have seen the Eras Tour movie in theaters, always make TS bracelets, have a Taylor fan page, am asking for Taylor merch for Christmas, and she is my most streamed artist." -Isabella, age 14

***

"Hey Taylor! I just wanted to express my

gratitude for your music and amazing talent. Your music has truly helped me thro some of my toughest patches of life and I'm ever so thankful for you. You've come so far and made such wonderful things, there are some songs you've written like "soon you'll get better" that I cannot listen to without getting emotional because of how significant they are to me. Being a swiftie is definitely a big part of my life. I became a swiftie during the 1989 era when I was 5. I remember coming home from a long day listening to shake it off in the car with sticky toddler hands. I also remember playing bad blood for the first time in my brother's closet when he was only 4 and explaining it to him. I have so many special little memories that I will never forget that are centered around your songs like crying to you belong with me with one of my closest friends when i knew it was the last time i would dance with her in the same school. These things I remember and they fuel my fire of admiration and love for your music. How will I ever repay you for the changes you've made in my life? I know we have never met, and we probably never will, but just know that I'm so proud of how far you've come, and all that you've accomplished, keep on doing what you do." -Ina C.

***

"Okay, so my story of becoming a Swiftie is kind of weird. It started in late April of 2021, right after Fearless (Taylors Version) came out. I was watching YouTube and clicked on a video by Jubilee titled 6 Taylor Swift Fans vs 1 Secret Hater. I had never really been into Taylor, I liked some of her songs, but at the time my favorite musical artists were Lady Gaga and Melanie Martinez, and it had never really crossed my mind to

31

listen to a Taylor album. But, as I was watching, I saw how all of these people were so passionate about liking Taylor, and it seemed like her albums were all so cool and different. I was so interested in the stuff they were talking about, that I decided to check out a song or two that I had never listened to. I went to her YouTube page, went to released, and clicked on the album titled Red. I decided to listen to the song Red because that was the title of the album. And when I tell you I fell in love, I mean I fell in love. I was so fascinated by the way the song was composed and I loved it so much. Especially the post-chorus where the re-e-e-ed plays in the background. I decided that night that I would listen to all her albums in order. Except, I didn't start with her self-titled for some reason because I didn't want to? I'm not really sure honestly. But, I started with Fearless, not Fearless (Taylor's Version) though, because I didn't understand that was the actual version I was supposed to be listening to and everything that happened with Scooter Braun. I remember vividly listening to the regular version of Fearless, not the deluxe either, listening to Speak Now, again not the deluxe, listening to Red, actually the deluxe this time, listening to half of 1989 and Reputation for some reason, listening to Lover, then folklore, and not evermore. Again, I don't know. But over time, I listened to every song of hers, and I love them all so much. Taylor and her music have gotten me through really high highs, and really low lows. I've listened to her music every step of the way, learning about every single thing there is to know. I got so excited for Red (Taylors Version), and I can't even express to you how happy I was for my first listen of an original Taylor album with Midnights. And then, I've also gotten to listen to Speak Now (Taylors Version) and 1989 (Taylors Version). My favorite album is Reputation, but Speak Now was also my favorite for a long time, as well as folklore and Red. I love Taylor because I think she's such a sweet person, she can sit down and write an amazing song that hits people in the heart, and her music and journey are phenomenal. I've had a magical time listening to her albums and feeling everything I've needed to and really just stepping into those different worlds of stories because that's really what they are. I have a lot of favorite songs by Taylor for a lot of different reasons, but my main ones are Say Don't Go, You Are In Love, Don't Blame Me, happiness, and The Archer, but I love every single one of her songs so much. The best part about being a Swiftie is really it keeps me up to date with pop culture and I can really just connect with her songs on a deep level and get so excited with every new release. I remember my mom used to play Blank Space in the car for me all the time because I loved that song as a little kid, and I remember thinking Shake It Off was two different songs after the Hey Hey Hey part, for some reason, and now knowing so much about her and all of her songs and being such a big fan. It's just so special. If I could tell Taylor one thing, I would say there are so many people who love her, there are so many people who are proud of her, and she is the most amazing and talented person on the planet. I also went to the Eras Tour, and it was the best moment of my life." -Sam M.

***

"Hi, I'm a huge Taylor Swift fan from the Netherlands. I'm only 12 years old and I have loved her since the 1989 album came out. Since then I became a huge fan. I loved all of her video clips and music. I'm even going to the Eras Tour in Amsterdam! I also went to the Eras Tour movie. I would love to meet her in real life. She is so sweet and nice. I love her." -Ela

***

"When I was 3 my mom loved her so we would play her music in the car all the time and I would listen to Bad blood, Blank space, and Shake it off all the time when I was younger instead of a lullaby my mom would sing me Blank Space. Also later on my mom would play Haunted, Back to December, and Enchanted a lot. It wasn't until recently I started listening to the other albums like Red, Folklore, and again 1989 and I've been a huge fan since I was 3. My favorite songs have to be Blank space, 22, TLGAD, and Betty." -Marisa

***

"I'm a 16 year old boy and I live in France. I have been a swiftie for almost four years but I have known her unconsciously since my childhood. I have known a lot of songs by her when I was little like Love Story, Shake it off, Blank Space, Wildest dreams and I knew you were trouble...but the first song I have ever heard from her and is very special to me is Begin again. Time passed by, I realized that a lot of songs in my playlist have the same artist's name. I looked up and it was Taylor Swift, I didn't really know her at the time so I searched for some of her songs and I loved them ! At that moment I listened to her albums non-stop and became a fan.

It's super great to be a swiftie, there is a lot of content, albums to discover and especially now where we have the Eras Tour, the re recordings and all that! The best part about it, for me, is really the amount of content we get ! I mean, Taylor, you can take a break if you want !

I love Taylor, first for her music which is awesome and really tell stories (it's something I absolutely love), second for her achievements, she is really a great performer, songwriter and activist, she doesn't fear to be judged and do what she thinks is good which I respect a lot, and finally her personality, I have found that she is really sweet and careful.

Her music is my daily dose of imagination. I listen to her when I go to school, during breaks, at home... For me, they are my library. Every time I play a song I make a story in my mind. I have made a lot of mental stories on a lot of songs ! It helps when I feel like my life isn't going in a nice direction or I just need the feeling of escape.

My favourite song is either seven, because I love the storytelling who looks easy but is really deep and the melody which I mesmerising, or either illicit affairs which is very important to me, it's a kind of "my song" type, I have made a whole more about it and I have cried listening to it while dreaming so many times!

My favourite albums are red (Taylor's version), folklore and evermore. Their songwriting always leave me speechless, they are all a unique universe that I cherish!

If I could talk to Taylor, I would say that she helped and still helps me in my daily life with her amazing songs that are not worthy of this world (honestly) and that I hope that she is alright and healthy in her life. I will encourage her to follow what she feels is good for her." -Ilya

**

"Hey Taylor! I love you to the moon and to Saturn, and I'm so happy I found your music! I stumbled upon you while looking for some new music choices, and I'd heard of you before but never listened much. The first sound I ever listened to was Never Grow Up, and it's still one of my favourites that makes me cry a little bit. Thanks for being your amazing self, and continue to write amazing songs!!" -Adalene

***

"I got my 1st Taylor record on my birthday. (february.) The record was 1989. BUT I recently got 1989 (Taylor's version.). My top 3 albums are 1989, Reputation, and folklore. I went to the Eras tour, (outside of the stadium.) the movie, and own a lot of merch! My favorite Taylor song is either Mr perfectly fine or don't blame me. I own 4 Taylor records and 1 CD. Have fun and stay safe swifties!!" -Henry, age 9

***

"I became a swiftie by listening to sparks fly 3 years ago with my mom. I really enjoyed that song so I listened to another one of her songs which was we are never getting back together then I listened to cruel summer, which is one of my fav songs by Taylor." - Courtney

***

"Dear Taylor, your music has had a BIG impact on my life. You have written so many songs I can relate to. These songs include: Tim McGraw, You Belong With Me, Dear John, august, and many more amazing works of art. I know you will continue to lift my spirit with your amazing lyrics and vocals! Thanks so much for being an important person in my life! It's an amazing thing to hear your songs when I'm in the car, listening from my phone, or on my vinyls and cds. A big thanks to you, Taylor." -Robert

***

"I became a swiftie in 2022 when she released Midnights. At first, I only listened to that album, but when I found out about the others, I listened to them right away. What I love so much about her music is how she's able to play with the words but it still looks and sounds cool. Every time I have a hard day, I put on her music. She is so calming. My dream is to go see her in concert one day." -Aurélie, Canada

***

"I have been a swiftie since third grade. Every time I'm in the car, I always put on Taylor as soon as possible, making my family listen to her, because she's just so perfect. I have made tons of bracelets, her wonderstruck perfume smells enchanted, and I have all of her albums on CD! I would love so much to personally meet Taylor! I'm very excited to go to her concert in 2024! It's the only thing I ever think about, and I just know it will be a wonderland. (Ay, ay)" -Bella

***

"One day, I was scrolling through YouTube when I found the song Love Story and absolutely fell in love with it. So I started listening to Taylor's music, and was fascinated by how amazing her and her music is.

Fast forward to now, and I can't live without Taylor or her music. It has helped me through every stage of my life. Whether I was a teen, going through a breakup, or whatever else, Taylor would be there for me. If you're reading this, Taylor, then thanks for being you. May you continue to make music and inspire young souls." -Nene

"Dear Taylor, I don't know if you will see this but I want you to know anyway, that you saved my life. I became a swiftie in a really dark time and your music is what helped me. Having something to look forward to, whether it was a new release, the Eras Tour, or something else, I always looked forward to seeing you. You've guided me through life, and continue to do so. I think I speak for all swifties when I say, we love you, Taylor." -anonymous

***

"When I was little I heard Debut and loved it so much. I loved picture to burn.(now that I'm older my favorite debut song is Tied together with a smile.) I kept following Taylor and listening to her music through every era. I have bought merch and all that jazz as well. And survived all the droughts. I love them all, but Folklore is my favorite album. I just relate to it and I love it! It was great to have during covid. I will always defend Taylor. She's so awesome and I always know that if I'm having a terrible day, I can listen to Taylor and it will make my whole day. Love is a strong word but I can confidently say with a huge smile that I LOVE TAYLOR ALISON SWIFT!!!" -Maeya W.

***

"I am a swiftie but this is how it all started. So I just scrolled on YouTubeshorts, but then came across this channel called wonderland.13. After watching a few of her shorts I decided I want to learn about her. I learnt things such as birthdays, cats, albums and many other things. Then after school I listened to my very first song, "Tim Mcgraw." I listened to it a few times and then moved on to listen to the whole debut album.

After I listened to all her albums and eventually I loved her music and then considered myself a swifte! After my "swiftie graduation" I woke up early to listen to 1989 taylor's version. So because of wonderland.13 and taylor I am a swiftie so thanks to them I am a swiftie today!" -Samantha

***

"Taylor, one of the things that speak to me the most about your songs is your lyric writing and the way it encapsulates simply the most complicated of feelings, it is something truly I cannot begin to understand how you do. In almost an ethereal way, having your emotions that are so deeply felt being shined through the light of your songs, being able to relate to your songs has made me and so many others love your songs even more. It has healed me in so many ways I cannot describe, things that have happened that have been soothed through your music and I am sure for many others too. My personal favorite song: Daylight. This song may not be a popular choice, sure, but it is my favorite because of the beautiful lyricism, the outstanding way it serves as a last track. A metaphor almost for love, in some ways, and most importantly the sweet message that comes out of it all: 'you are what you love' instead of being defined by what you hate. This song has just been one of my absolute favorites and I feel so lucky to just listen to it on repeat.

I became a swiftie because of my friend who was a big swiftie since she was around 13. She also went to rep tour which is amazing. She has known me literally since I was 3 days old. I am truly blessed that she did introduce me to your music around before the first lockdown... Ever since then I have fallen in love with your songs, I started playing them on the piano and I uncovered the hidden beauties of your melodies and everything else about them and I think it's just amazing how many beautiful things people can discover through the interests of their friends. We are both attending the Eras Tour next year and I feel so incredibly fortunate to be able to see you sing live.

You are honestly the sweetest person ever and I hope that you know how much everyone loves you, a lot of things about your personality are extremely comforting. I think about it a lot, I have listened to a lot of artists and albums and songs, but of course I think the thing that inspired me the most to write songs myself was you. Your dedication. Your abilities and your style to write and your songs that are just purely magical pieces. There is so much more you have done for me, some things I can't write all down, but I hope you know how much you have done for me.

Thank you ever so much Tay, I am eternally grateful for you." -Divina K.

***

"So I was a fan of taylor my entire life but I wouldn't consider myself a swiftie up until about 8 months ago. I found out I was moving across the country and Taylor's music is one of the things that calms me down. This past summer after I moved I went to spend time at my grandparents house and when we got back home my mother surprised me with Taylor Swift Eras Tour tickets for November 2024!!!!!!!!!! and that just made me feel 1000% AMAZING cuz anytime I feel defeated or down or missing my friends back home I listen to Taylor and sing and dance my heart out and think about how in a year I'm going to see her in person and right away I'm always feeling better. Also, my sister is 7 years younger than me which means I was an only child for quite a long time and wanted a sibling so badly. When she was born I was ENCHANTED to meet her and I always sang that song to her and she is now 6 years old and a big swiftie enchanted is her fav song ever we love singing it together and at the Eras Tour movie we had the theater to ourselves and she made sure to find me to sing enchanted together. Taylor has really made a huge impact in me and my family's life. also one thing i want to tell talor is that i love how she is always caring for her fans i love how she is adding more shows in the us and canada so more fans can see her im going to one of the added shows in the us i also hope she knows how much her music ha impacted not just swifties but also the world!!!!!! and has inspired young girls like me and my sister!" -Arial

***

"I have loved Taylor Swift for so long and it first started when the original red was on the radio. I fell in love with all the songs especially I knew you were trouble. But I was young at the time so I didn't have any music apps. So the real swiftie journey started when Red Taylor's version came out and it was on the radio. I immediately started listening to her on Spotify and now I can't stop. When The Eras Tour Film came out I immediately got tickets for opening night. It was the best experience I've ever had in my life before. Just being able to sing, dance, and see all these people come together. It was so amazing and I hope I get to do that again someday. I have loved following Taylor's journey and seeing and listening to all these songs and all these amazing things happen to her. Taylor has been such a role model for me and I know people say this a lot but she did save me. Her music was so lifesaving for me after my dad died and I am just astounded with her music. Her music is so relatable for me in many ways and it continues to make my day even when I'm sad. I am from Oregon and I couldn't go to the Eras Tour but I am so happy that she came out with the film because even though I haven't see her in concert going to the film will forever be in my memory." -Kiera C.

***

"The first Taylor Swift song I listened to was Love Story in the spring of 2009. I was sitting in the dining room and the radio was turned on and at first when the song started to play I thought I was listening to Wake Up by Hilary Duff. But it turned out to be Love Story by Taylor Swift!

Me and my siblings became fans of hers after that and then we once watched the music video for You Belong with Me.

I was a normal Swiftie between 2009 and 2017 loving her hit singles like 22 and We Are Never Getting Back Together. Back in February 2015 I also used to sing along to Blank Space and Style.

But then in mid April 2019 I was on CNN and I saw an article headline that read that Taylor was going to release a new single. That single ended up being ME!

After listening to the single I became a die hard Swiftie and between April and August 2019 I went down a rabbit hole of Taylor's music catalog and I discovered a few songs that I liked like Gorgeous, Welcome to New York and State of Grace! (Till this day I still am discovering other gems that I never heard before like Don't Blame Me and This is Why We Can't

Have Nice Things)

Then she released her album LOVER and since then I have been obsessed with her music!

Finally I just want to say that as a guy I love that a woman is leading the music industry and that she is enjoying her explosive popularity!

Last but not least even though I haven't met Taylor herself I just want to say that I'm proud of being a Swiftie since way back. I'm a Fearless Swiftie since I became a fan of hers during her Fearless era!" - anonymous

***

"I write this as I listen to your first ever song, Tim McGraw. I'm literally OBSESSED. Like, how did you write this... AS A FRESHMAN? I'm a freshman and I could never. And you've only gotten better.

I became a Swifite thanks to Back To December. I've gone through phases of being obsessed with different songs (it's Tim McGraw right now), but I love all of them. You're a storyteller, and you always have been from the very start with Tim McGraw. My favorite album of yours is Red. Taylor, if you see this, I love you." -Izzy

***

"I've been a swiftie probably since 2021(?) maybe like This Love (tv) song release and that song was the 1 (wink wink) that made me a swiftie.

The first song that I heard of Taylor is... I don't actually remember, probably like WANEGBT or LWYMMD. Taylor's music has meant a lot to me, is helping me to get through many situations and I feel like Taylor is singing them to my ear whenever I put my headphones on.

My fav tay's song, I have been saying for a long time that it is Gorgeous, but it's actually a hard decision cause my fav song changes like every month but i just don't accept it but right now it's like Gorgeous or "Is It Over Now?"

I love being a swiftie, it's so fun! It's always fun solving the Easter Eggs (i'm not saying that i'm good at it) but it was so fun when I saw the I Can See You MV and saw the "1989tv" sign at the end, i felt like i did something for the fandom HAHA.

I went to a mexico city concert, it was august 27th! it was so cool, it was SUCH A THERAPY SCREAMING THE LYRICS TO THOSE SONGS it was so cool! my surprise were Afterglow on guitar & Maroon on piano

If i could say something to Tay rn it will be; "even though you don't know me, i do know you, not like if i was your closest friend, but i do know you to know that you are the sweetest person that could exist, the kindest, the nicest, etc. Thanks a lot for your songs and for all the things that us, swifties, will learn & learned from you. I hope that you'll return to Mexico someday :) it will be great, we loved seeing you. I'm so thankful for all the things that you've changed for me for the better, I know that you will still change us for better.

Also: PLEASE RELEASE REP TV SOON OMG. I will be such a clown if she announces rep tv before the publishing of this book." -Emilio (@GorgeouSwift_13)

***

"I've been a swiftie all throughout my life, and Taylor always lifts my mood. when I was little I would always listen to 1989 and red, but I didn't listen to any music except for the radio until around when red tv came out. I started becoming a swiftie again and I've become such a big swiftie. I love the friendship bracelets, I love her music, I love her different music styles, vault tracks, puzzles, and easter eggs. most of the swiftie community is so sweet and i love taylor so much." -Maeve

***

"Where do I even start? Sitting in the car driving (not getting lost) in upstate NY in 2014-2015 ish. My parents would turn on the radio as you do on LONG car rides far from home and songs would come on but one would always come on that I loved. It went along the lines of "hey hey hey, just think while you've been getting down and out about the liars and the dirty dirty cheats of the world you coulda been getting down to this sick beat". I would dance in my seat and learned all the lyrics by heart. At this point my parents decided that if I liked this then we could try listening to other music by a woman named Taylor Swift.

They didn't know much about her, but they played her music anyway. Songs like "Blank Space", "Wildest Dreams", "I Wish You Would", "Style", "All You Had To Do Was Stay", and more are associated with the smell of rest stops across the east coast in the best way possible. Because of my mom's job, we spent so much time on the road and 1989 brought a spot of joy in not very fun conditions. For about four years the only thing I listened to was you. I lived, breathed, ate, slept, cried and smiled to 1989.

It was the summer of 2019 and I got in the car coming home from a friend's house when I got in my little brother handed me a cd. It was pink and blue and had beautiful cursive writing that read "Lover". Inside was Taylor's very own diary entries from when she was a kid and as she grew up. I never had and and still to this day have never felt more connected to anyone ever let alone one of the most famous people ever. Now all I listened to was Lover. I LOVED Lover.

Somewhere around the summer of 2022 I decided that I was just "too cool" for Taylor Swift. I searched far and wide for something that made me as happy as your music but I couldn't. You might say the music I was looking for was the music I had. But I refused to be just another "Basic white girl" like everyone told me I was.

But late September early October 2022 comes around and I'm hanging out with one of my current best friends for the first time and I ask her "when was your Taylor Swift phase?" And she replied "NOW!" She continues to go on about her whole swiftie journey and I just nod along but after that I go back and I listen to all of the songs. I made a challenge where every week I listen to a different album so hear and mesmerize all the songs. Let me tell you I was OBSESSED! I had finally given folklore and evermore the appreciation that they deserve. The past couple years I had struggled with extreme anxiety and songs like the lakes, this is me trying, mirrorball, and tolerate it made me feel less isolated. And after feeling freed by those songs I was able to relate to long story short.

Taylor you have changed my life 3 times. Brought joy to boredom, connected me to something, and freed me from isolation. And I can't thank you enough!" - anonymous

***

"I was honestly too young to remember the first

time I heard a Taylor Swift song. It was probably Love Story, though I would have been three years old when it came out. When I was little, I had the whole Fearless album on my little IPod and would listen to it on repeat. But, the first album that really made me a Swiftie was Lover. I was having a really hard time when it came out, and it helped me to get through it.

My personal favorite song is Nothing New. It's such a beautiful song, and it introduced me to Phoebe Bridgers. I got to hear it live in Nashville, which was an amazing experience that only made me love the song more. My absolute favorite part about being a Swiftie is the sense of community. When Speak Now (Taylor's Version) came out, my cousin and I stayed up all night so that we could listen to it for the first time together. We stayed up dancing and singing along to all her music, it's an amazing memory. If I could tell Taylor anything it would be: thank you so much. Your music really, really helps people." -Lily

***

"I guess I've been a swiftie for as long as I can remember. My mom started listening to Taylor back during debut, which came out the year I was born. And since she always listened to Taylor, I became a fan too! We talk about her all the time, and went to the Eras Tour and Eras Movie together! I can't thank her for much, but I will forever appreciate her introducing me to Taylor.

As for why I love Taylor so much, it's sort of hard to describe. Obviously, she's a great singer vocally, especially her range!! I love when she hits low notes, or when it gets high-pitched and breathy. But I think the thing that's made me love all of her songs is the way that she can convey emotions. It feels so reassuring that someone, or several people, are feeling the same way I am. And, it doesn't matter if I've ever felt those emotions, because Taylor is so good at songwriting that I can understand those feelings. This, too me, is what sets her apart from so many of the other singers in the industry.

I definitely have to talk about my favorite song here, because it doesn't get enough love from the fandom!! My all-time favorite Taylor song is "ivy". I think that it's the most lyrically beautiful song. If poetry was music, "ivy" would be a prime example. And the story is so complex and interesting and can be interpreted in so many different ways... I just can't get enough of it.

I love you Taylor!!" -@midnight_rain on YouTube

***

"One of my friends had a bit of something to do with convincing myself to become a Swiftie but it was also when I learned more about Taylor and started listening to more of her songs. The first song I heard from Taylor was the one and only iconic Love Story when my friend was doing karaoke.

I love Taylor for the person she is. Her music means everything to me as a person can't live without music in general but when it comes to Taylor her music feels as if I am finally heard or when I am unsure about how I feel it's like she helps me understand more about how I may feel. Another way Taylor's music has helped me is by dealing with emotions or basically whenever I was going through something. The best part of being a Swiftie is having our secret language and how interactive it can be like when there was this whole puzzle for 1989 TV.

If I could tell Taylor something it would be thank you. Thank you for being the kind of person you are that many people can look up to and for showing that things we want to achieve in life are possible. I love you so much and you have made a big impact in my life. Being a Swiftie is seriously one thing I will never regret and even though I haven't been one for long all I can say is "I had the time of my life fighting dragons with you."" - anonymous

***

"I've been OBSESSED with Taylor and her music since I was a little girl. It all started when my mom introduced me to Taylor's album called "Fearless" (I'm sure you have heard of it haha)! About 4 years later, my parents surprised me with tickets to the Reputation tour!! That was a LIFE CHANGING experience for little me! I remember when I was in elementary school, I was know as "The Ultimate Swiftie"! (No joke, ask any of my friends.) My favorite album is folklore, and my favorite songs are "The Lakes" and "Seven". My favorite re-recording is 1989, I have to admit my inner child was SCREAMING! If I could say one thing to Taylor, I would say "Thank you so much for being you and never giving up on music." If it wasn't for her, I wouldn't be where I am right now." -Fiona

***

"I have not been a Swiftie for that long. Only about a year and a half. But even in that relatively small time period, that was enough for Taylor to grab my heart. When I was 9, my father showed me the music video to her song, "Mean", from Speak Now. I absolutely loved it! At the time I was going through some bullying from my cousin, so this truly did block out the voices.

My favorite lyric was, "Someday I'll be big enough so you can't hit me.", because it gave me confidence! I do however regret not becoming a Swiftie during this time. I could have discovered her amazing music years ago, but I simply did not know how the internet worked. Regardless, this amazing and nostalgic song will forever be in my memory! Thank you so much Taylor.

The Midnights era was when I became a Swiftie. I was still going through hardship during this time. Around October 25th, when I was in the car, I heard my mom talking about the new album and I got curious. I went onto Spotify and listened to the album front to back. Every song was just a smash. It resonated with me so much. I was also holding back when Dear Reader ended. I didn't even have to listen to her other albums, I was instantly. After that, I listened to her hits such as Shake It Off, You Belong With Me, IKYWT, WANEGBT, and more. One that stuck out to me was her song from Lover, "ME!" It gave me so much happiness! It was my favorite along with Dear Reader at first. I listened to her other albums and instantly got new favorites. Near the start of 2023, I declared myself a Swiftie. Thank you Taylor.

It isn't only her music that is awesome, it is also being a Swiftie yourself! The easter egg hunting is so fun, anticipating seeing her at award shows, something about waiting for her re-records to release at Midnight with other swifties and claiming vault tracks is simply a whole fun within itself, and being jokingly disappointed a surprise song was taken. These all make me smile. And Taylor isn't just a singer-songwriter, she is an entertainer! Seeing her at the Eras Tour that Friday Chicago Night was the best day of my life!! Thank you

Taylor.

I do have new favorite songs now different from when I first became a Swiftie. But one that has always stayed the same and never changed is Dear Reader. It shows a high level of vulnerability and advice. But the best part is that the advice isn't perfect, and that's good. This has resonated with me the most out of all of her songs, and it is so underrated! This song is a masterpiece and helped me get up from the floor I've been on for years after tripping and I couldn't get up until I discovered it. Thank you Taylor.

To me, her music means so many things I simply could not describe enough with words. It is something that has to be felt and heard to truly understand. It includes heartbreak, regret, grief, revenge, anxiety, depression, and vulnerability. But it also includes love, happiness, gratitude, and appreciation. Taylor's discography means so much. However, it has to be felt to truly understand. Thank you Taylor.

It isn't just her music that I love, although it is a huge aspect. She herself is also why I love her so much. She is so kind, inviting her fans to her house and baking them cookies! She even takes time out of her day to go onto social media and like her fans' posts. She is boosting local economies in every city she performs at and stands up for women's rights. Taylor is an excellent role model for little girls and boys all over the world! Thank you Taylor.

My message to Taylor: Happy Birthday Taylor! Just know that you are awesome! Your music and entertainment is top notch and you are so important to us Swifties. Keep doing what you are doing and keep killing it!" -Lizbeth C.

"Since I was 6 years old I have loved Taylor so much because my sister Colisa would play her debut and fearless album and they are my favorites. I love being a swiftie because it inspired me and just listening to Taylor does. I even made my own solo for a dance competition on suburban legends! Love you Taylor and happy birthday." -Ella

"My older cousin (one of my closest friends) has been a swiftie for as long as I can remember, she always talks about her at family events (and has been known to play her music videos for the family) and I've always supported her ofc, but then I became a swiftie.

So most of my family assumes that it's because I want to be like her, and it's not that I don't, but in the end it was my other fandoms that led me to being a Swiftie.

I, if nothing else, am a fangirl. I obsessed over fictional characters and there relationships, story arcs, and really anything. There's one in particular but several fandoms where I would make edits of the characters, or add Taylor's songs to ship playlists. And it was so fun. But I was hesitant to call myself a swiftie, I was relatively new to the fandom and the last thing I wanted was to be labeled as fake, especially when some people had been fans of Taylor's since day one.

I also was afraid of being compared to my cousin, not that I don't love her, but we're different people and I didn't want to be thought of as a "copycat".

But really? At the end of the day it doesn't matter. I love Taylor and her music. It makes me feel things and it helps me, and Taylor is just such a great person.

My favorite's have to be Gorgeous and Paper Rings, Gorgeous bc it's just such a great song, and Paper Rings is one my friends and I all love, I have a vivid memory or singing it with my friend in class, and laughing about how I got it stuck in her head and now she couldn't focus. My first song was Shake it Off. I remember when I was younger (and this was before I was music obsessed) we had family karaoke and I was asked to go first, so I asked my uncle to play Shake it Off and I just remember having so much fun singing it.

If I could tell Taylor one thing, it would be that her music really helps people. I can speak for myself, and a lot of other people when I say that her music has improved my life, it just makes me happy, makes me feel seen, and safe.

For the most part, the Swifties are a great community (I'm a Pinterest Swiftie so it's very chill :)) and I love to see everyone else's opinions on songs, and I just love how we all want what's best for her.

So while I became a fan with fictional characters in mind, I've found a real life interest to make me happy. Thank you Taylor" -Josie

***

"My first memory of listening to Taylor Swift is when me and my cousins put on a dance show at a sleepover. I was 5 years old and You Belong With Me came on and I LOVED it. I think Love Story also played as well. When 1989 came out and I was still just in school and I had memorised all the words to You Belong With Me, Love Story, Fearless, I Knew You Were Trouble, 22, We Are Never Getting Back Together and probably more but I wasn't really a proper fan of Taylor. Then I heard 1989 for the first time and my life actually changed. I LOVE LOVE LOVED every single song from 1989 and I would dance my heart out every single day. When I got old enough to really care about what Taylor was doing in her day to day life and understand more of the meanings behind the songs it was the reputation era and I did a whole research project on the feud between her and Kanye where I deep dived into why it started (my teacher wasn't very impressed with the "inappropriate content" in my project) and that was where the real obsession began.

I think if I had to pick one thing that inspired me to be a swiftie, other than her amazing music was this video that I saw. It was something like 10 times women stood up to interviewers and it was the clip where the lady says Taylor will be going home with lots of men and Taylor replies that she won't be going home with any men that night. I felt very inspired by this strong confident outspoken woman who made such good music and I looked up more videos. I watched every music video, behind the scenes, og Debut and Fearless tour vlogs and a bunch of compilations of funny moments from interviews etc and that was where it began.

I love Taylor because she is a genuinely good person who has had so many people against her in her life but has stuck through and always kept that happy energy. She is a kindhearted smart person who inspires me every day and I don't know where I would be without her music and just herself. Whenever I have a big essay or homework due I either put one of her tours on or listen to her music and it just makes everything seem okay. From her incredible songwriting to her angelic voice and hilarious personality Taylor is such an amazing iconic inspirational woman who I look up to every day.

When it comes to a favourite song it is hard to say just one because there are songs for any and every mood that I could ever be in. If I had to pick one favourite from each album they would be, and this is very very hard, Should've Said No, Mr Perfectly Fine, Mine, All Too Well 10 Minute Version, New Romantics, Dress, The Archer, this is me trying, marjorie, You're On Your Own Kid.

I love being a swiftie because of how supportive MOST people in this community are. We all have common interests and as soon as I find out someone likes Taylor I just immediately feel comfortable and happy. I love having debates about different songs with my friends and getting excited about the same things.

If I had one message for Taylor it would be this:

Dear Taylor,

You have helped me in so many different ways and I am so so grateful you make music. I wouldn't have made it through many hard times in my life without your music. You are somebody that I look up to as a person and you are one of the biggest inspirations I have, not only as a songwriter but as a woman. You are hilarious, kind, smart and creative, you bring so much joy and excitement into my life and I can't wait to see what you do with the rest of your already amazing life. If we should be defined by the things that we love then I would happily be defined by you, I am so so proud of everything you have been for and done not only for others but for yourself. I hope that I grow up to be half the woman and person you are. Please continue doing what you love and making music, you were and are such a big part of my childhood and journey as I grow up and

I honestly don't know where I would be without you. Sending lots of love and applause your way!" -Bridie

***

"I loved bad blood as a kid, and when I got to go to the reputation tour, the obsession of her music and demeanour started and never stopped.

What was the first Taylor swift song I ever heard? That's hard, probably welcome to New York. I love her songwriting and how she writes music, her personality and hard work. How relatable she is as a person and as an artist. She brings me happiness from the darkest places.

What does her music mean to you? An escape. To laugh, to cry, to dance. The way it helps me understand my feelings, some things can't be put into words .

Favourite song and why? Haunted. I LOVE pop rock and screaming this song gives me life.

The best part of being a swiftie is the fandom.

What I would tell Taylor: Your music is a constant source of solace and inspiration, you're like a superhero with the power to capture complex emotions and experiences and put them in beautiful songs. Sometimes it's like you read my diary. It is difficult sometimes, and lately I have been down and your music has become a lifeline for me." -Delilah C. (@DELILAHVEVO on YouTubeand @delilah.cross3 on tiktok)

***

"I became a swiftie only a couple of months ago because my friend introduced me to her music, which I'm very thankful for because my life has been better with Taylor in it. The first Taylor Swift song I heard was probably Shake it off when it became very popular.

I love Taylor because she makes amazing music, she supports different charities and causes and Taylor has paid people insurance money or hospital money. Taylor is one of the most inspirational women in the world. Taylor's music has helped me feel happier just by listening to her gorgeous music. Some of her songs remind me of my childhood.

I don't have a favourite song but I currently love the last great american dynasty because I just like the story and how Taylor turns it into a song. She really is a Mastermind.

I think one of the best parts of being a swiftie is all the other swiftie's because I think even though I have never met all the other millions of swifties I feel like I could be friends with them just because of Taylors music.

If I could tell Taylor anything is

1. I would say that I love her and I would tell her how much I appreciate her.

2. I would tell her I have 2 friends who were born on 13th of December." -Holly

***

"I became a swiftie because of my best friend, Jenny, who is a super fan. We lived and worked together for a year and a half and she would play a lot of Taylor. Growing up, I liked the Taylor songs I heard on the radio, but for some reason never listened to a whole album of hers. I mean We Are Never Getting Back Together got me through a tough break-up! I listened to the YouTubevideo multiple times every night for at least like a month or two. In addition to hearing more of her other songs through Jenny, I also went to one of the 1989 concerts in Orlando. It was the one where she was Olaf!! After that, when Reputation came out, I was aware of it and listened to the album and liked it. But oddly enough, it wasn't until Lover came out that I became a true obsessed Swiftie!! I know that album like the back of my hand. I was also engaged when it came out and got married early November in 2019, sooo the timing could not have been better!!!

The first song I heard was probably something pretty generic (as in one of her popular songs) on the radio like Love Story or You Belong With Me. Could it have been Our Song?? Maybe?

I love her because she's just sooo amazing and relatable. She stays who she is and it makes her soo real and genuine. She can be classy as hell and dressed to the nines, but she's still Taylor. Also love how she advocates for women and isn't afraid to stand up for what she believes in and for what is right!! Her awkward moments make my heart melt as a fellow awkward human myself.

Her music is the background of my life nowadays. In high school, I was really into emo and punk rock. I didn't listen to girls aside from Avril Lavigne. They were too whiny for me. Fast forward to now and Taylor is by far my most listened to artist. There is a song for every occasion. An album for every mood. Her voice is lovely and relating to her lyrics elevates her music exponentially!! Also, I am 2 years older than Taylor so that makes her very relatable as well.

Her music has gotten me through tough times (ex. Breakup) and made me feel normal as in relating to her lyrics. Its also helped put my daughter to sleep. Idk why, but I sing Dress to her most often followed by Almost Do and a bunch of others.

Picking a favorite song... how though, with her discography?? For a looong time it was I Think He Knows. Recently, hmm. I would have to say Almost Do.

I love being a swiftie because of the Easter Egg Hunting and breadcrumbs she leaves. The endless speculation.

If I could tell her anything, I'd tell her how awesome her songwriting is. How wonderful it is to be able to relate to her and know you're not alone in feeling sad/mad/heartbroken/in love/etc. How happy I am to have truly listened to her music. Everything I think of sounds so cliche!!" -Jil

***

"I started listening to Taylor Swift in 2012. I had a little playlist with maybe 30 songs on it, and I would listen to that every day. My very favourite songs on that playlist were I Knew You Were Trouble and We Are Never Ever Getting Back Together. I noticed that they were by the same singer, I've loved listening to Taylor ever since!

Two albums that are really special to me are 1989 and Midnights – 1989 because it is the first album that came out while I was a swiftie, and Midnights because it's the most relatable album. I love all of her music, but my favourites at this very second would have to be "Slut!", Haunted, Dear Reader and Gorgeous. Two songs that have really resonated with me are Tied Together With A Smile and You're On Your Own Kid. I love that the way I feel about myself was put into two beautiful songs.

I love being a Swiftie because I can connect to people through my favourite thing – music! It's like I have millions of friends who I can dance with, sing with, and dress up with, even though it's all through the internet. I love having the excuse to dress up and make friendship bracelets, bake cookies and celebrate, and have a party on a release day!

If I could say one thing to Taylor, I'd thank her. I'd want her to know how much her music has impacted me and people around the world. I hope she knows that she's appreciated and that her hard work and dedication has payed off. Her songs are amazing, and it shows her talent, and I hope she knows that!" -Charlotte

***

"When people ask me why I love Taylor Swift, why I became a fan, the answer is a long and complex one. I have been a Swiftie since 2006 and my love for her hasn't faded at all throughout the last 17 years. I was 8 years old when I found a video of Taylor performing Tim McGraw at a small stage in Nashville. A few months later, her debut album hit shelves and I picked up my copy. I immediately fell in love with every song. My favorite song being Cold As You. I loved the complex lyrics and beautiful bridge the first time I heard it. To this day, Cold As You is my favorite song of all time.

In 2009, my mom surprised me when I got home from school on a Friday and told me that we were going to see Taylor Swift at Country USA in Oshkosh, WI. I was so excited and immediately planned my outfit. Sparkly sunglasses, my LEI Taylor Swift shirt, and rhinestone jeans. I had heard rumors of the Tea Party and I dreamt of the day I could meet Taylor. I didn't get picked for the Tea Party and was a little bummed out. All I had wanted in my 11 year old life was to meet my role model. The show was general admission and as an eleven year old, I couldn't really see much but I got to hear her, which was the important part. It was such a beautiful day! I performed Love Story at my school talent show that year and wore a white dress. I also memorized the movements in the music video so I could incorporate them into my performance. I felt so proud of that moment.

In 2010, I was starting middle school and battling a lot of bullies. Speak Now came out at the perfect time in my life. That album got me through some very rough times and became the escape I could go to after a hard day at school. I started playing guitar and writing songs like Taylor but, unfortunately, it didn't stick with me. Middle school got a lot harder in 2011 when I lost my grandpa who lived with me my entire life. I missed 2 weeks of school and came back just in time for talent show auditions. I auditioned with Never Grow Up and made the teacher cry. I got a spot in the show and immediately started rehearsing. Words cannot describe to this day how much this song means to me. I also got to go to Nashville for the first time this year and go to the Country Music Hall of Fame. I was so excited to see artifacts from Taylor Swift and get merch. I had a great time and loved every minute of it.

Fast forward and I was beginning high school in 2012, right before the release of Red. High school felt like a relief. It was big and I had a place and could be myself. I was free from bullies. I joined choir and theatre and truly found my happy place in music. Red came out and I immediately started learning all of the songs. When The Hunger Games movie came out and Safe and Sound was HUGE, I auditioned for my first high school talent show with that song and got in. So another one of Taylor Swift's eras became a significant part of my life.

When I was a sophomore, I went to school on the first day and found out our choir trip was going to be in New York. That was in 2013. I had no idea how significant New York was going to be to Swifties. 1989 became an anthem to everyone who loved New York and everyone who embraces their wildest dreams. I heard about Taylurking and Swiftmas and tried for months and months to be noticed by Taylor and Taylor and Taylor Nation. I was never noticed but sure had a fun time trying. My dream was still to meet Taylor and thank her for everything she's done for me. 1989 was the Taylor album that got me through high school.

Taylor was getting so much hate in the years I was in high school. I always stayed a true fan and stayed by her side. I didn't like any of the people that were bullying her so I didn't care what they had to say. Taylor has gotten me through so much. I graduated in 2016 and longed to see Taylor again because I hadn't been to a concert of hers since 2009. My parents could never afford to go to another one of her concerts and she rarely came to Wisconsin anymore. When I went off to college, a new album was announced, Reputation, and it seemed dark and mysterious. An epic return after her hiatus. I was so excited! I became obsessed with Look What You Made Me Do and black sparkly clothes. Since I was a college student who heavily focused on school and had no job, I was unable to go to the Reputation tour. I was so sad. Reputation was an album that got me through a lot of college drama and a lot of decision making. I spent my first 2 years at a small college where I was trying to figure myself out. I met my husband there, figured out my love for teaching, and made some great memories.

In 2019, I went to the college of my dreams and was fully engulfed in the education major life. It was everything I dreamed of! Lover came out that year and it really motivated me to do everything with love. I felt on top of the world. I even signed up for verified fan for Lover fest, even though there was a huge chance I may not get to go. I was sad at the fact that it was only on the east or west coast and really started to imagine myself at this concert.

In 2020, Loverfest and every other concert and major event on the planet was put on hold because of a pandemic. I couldn't work because schools were closed, I was lonely because my husband still had to work, and I spent days just sadly buying things on the internet. Then we got a cat and my life wasn't so bad. You know what else happened around the same time, Taylor Swift released a surprise album, Folklore and soon followed Evermore. These two albums brought some brightness into the unprecedented times. I loved listening to these albums everyday! It was truly a light during the darkness.

When Taylor announced she was re-recording her first 6 albums, I was so EXCITED! I would get to live all of those eras again! In 2021, she started this process with Fearless. I could wait to be 10 again listening to Fearless for the first time. The day Fearless was released, I actually had no classes and could spend my whole day just listening to the beauty that is Fearless (Taylor's Version). Later that year, it was announced that she would be releasing Red next with the 10 minute version of everyone's favorite song, All Too Well. I was so excited and counted down the days until we got to hear it! I woke up at 5 just to listen to the whole album all the way through before school that day. The short film was then released and I watched it about 20 times the day it came out! I love it so much!

In 2022, the day before my first day as a teacher, Taylor won several VMAs and announced that her brand new album would come out on October 21st. I was so excited! I couldn't believe that another one of her albums was coming to me at the perfect time. My first year teaching was an up and down experience but Midnights made it a little better. My husband surprised me with an autographed vinyl and I was so happy I cried. In October of 2022, she announced the Eras Tour. I registered for Verified Fan and was waitlisted. My husband also registered and was lucky enough to get a code. I took a PTO day for the presale. After 11 hours of waiting in a queue, I ended up with no tickets. My heart was shattered. I had been longing to see Taylor for YEARS. I was determined to go. In December, my husband received another email that stated he had a chance to buy 2 tickets for one day only. We applied for the tickets and played the waiting game. On Taylor's birthday, I was celebrating by watching Reputation Stadium Tour when I got the notification that we were going to the Eras Tour. I was so happy, I started crying. It was truly a happy moment! I was going to Chicago night 3 and immediately started planning our outfits and making bracelets.

In March, The Eras Tour started and I stayed up and watched every live stream to see which surprise songs she would be doing. I kept track in a notebook and anticipated the day I would be going. I also anticipated the day she was announcing her next re-recording and hoped it would be Speak Now, my favorite album. On

May 5, she did exactly that, in Nashville.

Finally June 4th came, the day of my Eras Tour experience! I woke up at 5:30 so we could leave and be in Chicago by 8. I had a full day ahead of me! We went to All Too Well sandwich shop which was, unfortunately, closed due to being sold out. So we ate at the stadium. We got there around 3 and exchanged bracelets in the parking lot, talked to other Swifties, and had a good time. Taylor went on at 8 and it was the most beautiful and euphoric experience I have ever had! I stood, danced, and sang for the entire 3.5 hours. During surprise songs, Taylor even pointed out how a lot of us were performing along with her and how she thinks we are probably tired. Our surprise songs were The Moment I Knew and Hits Different. It was a beautiful night.

It's been 5 months since that night and I still look back at the pictures and videos and can't help but smile. It was one of the best days of my life. I would go back again in a heartbeat.

Thank you Taylor Swift for being such a huge part of my life for so long and for truly helping me find a passion and something to look forward to! You've been a role model for me most of my life. Everything I did with confidence, was with the confidence I got from you. It's been a true blessing being a Swiftie for 17 years. Here's to 17+ more!" -Lilly D.

***

"What convinced me to be a Swiftie? By choice, I decided to listen to some Taylor songs, and I just kept going on until I got hooked. It's pretty simple compared to other people but it's the truth.

What was the first Taylor Swift song you ever

heard? Shake It Off, definitely. Such a classic you'd hear anywhere.

What is your favorite song and why? Mine is "betty" off folklore. It has always had such a special place in my heart. Beautiful tune, one of my favorite performances, a unique male perspective...it's just really special and I can't explain it better than that honestly. It's just my favorite.

Why do I love Taylor? She has done so much for me and so many other people. I know a girl who enrolled in choir because of her and how beautiful she sounds. Cheesy as it sounds, it's truly lovely to know she inspires others." -Summer

***

"I have recently become a Swiftie but have a long history with Taylor. When I was little right around when Speak Now came out I can remember my grandmother singing Never Grow Up. It is probably the best memory I have with her. When I was about eight or nine I really loved the Reputation tour and I really wanted to go. I did not end up getting tickets and I kinda lost interest after my parents said no. I kinda still listened just not as much. Last year I stumbled across a video of Taylor being so kind to children in the hospital and I loved how kind she was it made me so happy to see that there will still amazing people in this world. When Midnights came out I really started to listen especially to Your On Your Own Kid .This year I lost my grandfather and Taylor really helped brighten my day and her music has helped me get through it. I love Taylor and she is just so encouraging and brightens my day." -Ellen

***

"I became a swiftie during the album 1989 and to this day that album is still my favorite. I had first heard the song shake it off in a store and I decided to give her a listen and I fell in love with it." -Ava

***

"I am an Indian Swiftie who loves her. She had said in an interview that she thinks Indians don't like her music but the truth is that we love it.. Her concert movie has become a blockbuster all over India. I just saw the movie and I am mesmerized; I hope to see the concert someday.

I became a swiftie in 2022 and I am so grateful that I have heard her songs. I heard Cruel Summer for the first time and I was so happy to hear it. I searched for her on Spotify and started listening to her. Her music has helped me in tough times as well as in pleasant times. Her music is comforting to me. Today I am one of her biggest fans who has been included in the top 1% listener of Taylor. My favourite album is Reputation and I am so excited for Reputation(Taylor's Version). I love you Taylor." -Tanushree

***

"I was only 3 or 4 years old when my parents first started playing Taylor's music around the house every once in a while, but never really got into her music or any kind of music because I was too young to understand. Fast forward 3 years later, I start getting into 1989, which is when I really started to enjoy her music and listen to other songs from other albums she had. I listened to all of her hits in the beginning including Shake It Off, Bad Blood, Wildest Dreams, Style, Blank Space, We Are Never Ever Getting Back Together, I Knew You Were Trouble, 22, etc.

Fast forward another 2 years and we have Reputation, which I barely ever listened to because my parents didn't think it was appropriate for my age. After that, I faded out of it. I had stopped really listening to her when Lover came out, and never picked up her music again. She was on my playlists, but I didn't listen to her as often as I used to.

And then Midnights came out, and I saw all the headlines about what had happened when the album came out. The kind of stuff like how all of the Swifties broke Spotify, and how she had already had number 1's like Anti-Hero. So I started listening to that album, realizing that I really liked it. Then, I started to listen to all of the other albums to see what they were like, and see how much her music had really changed throughout the years. And then the obsession with Taylor started.

After that I could never shut up about Taylor and how amazing she was! Long story short, that's how I became a Swiftie!" -Sophia

***

"I heard about Taylor as the Eras Tour was starting up. Since then I have loved her.

On Sep. 11, 2023, It was my 12th birthday. I had a Taylor Swift theme birthday party and invited some friends over for a sleepover. We watched the Rep. tour, made shirts, made bracelets, got some temporary tattoos with song lyrics and 13's. It was the best birthday sleepover of my life.

In October me and my friend went to the Eras tour movie! It was the most amazing thing and I appreciate Taylor so much for making a movie on her tour! People like me who haven't had a chance to go to the actual tour, the movie is an awesome alternative.

Recently I ordered the 1989 TV CD, and it is the first of many Taylor Swift CD's that I hope to own in the future. I have all of your merch in my Christmas list. Taylor, I hope you read this. If you do, I want you to know, You make me smile. You make me happy. You are pretty. And you are an amazing artist." -Izabella N.

***

"The first time I ever heard from Tay was in 2019. When Lover came out I saw Lover on Spotify, I started listening to her. I have been a swiftie since that day. Today she became the most streamed female artist in Apple Music history and in Spotify too." -Rosana

***

"I love Taylor Swift so much and I've been a swiftie for almost a year now, after listening to the Midnights album when it came out. I remember listening to Anti-Hero when it became really popular, and soon, it became my absolute favourite song! I would play it in my room over and over again. During mid-December of 2022, me and my family went on a holiday to Thailand. I was scrolling through my playlist at the airport when I found a song suggestion for Bejewled, I downloaded the song and also loved that song so much that I was listening to it on loop for almost the entire filght! At this point, I didn't know that Midnights was a new album, I just thought that these two songs were singles that had been released a long time ago.

Coming back to the UK, we found out in Thailand that our flight was delayed for an hour, so we spent that hour just roaming around the airport. I remember waiting in the terminal on my phone, when I saw on Spotify that she had released the album a couple of months ago. I randomly thought to download the entire album, not thinking I would listen to it at all, however, on a 13 hour flight, I didn't have anything else to do, so I decided to listen to it. I listened to Lavender Haze, Maroon, and Snow On The Beach, and thought about how she's a musical genius. I had a really bad phobia of flying at the time, and her songs made me feel so much better.

Months passed and that was when I realised that she had so many more albums. I decided to listen to reputation, then Lover, and then 1989, and really liked these albums so much. I then decided to listen to Red (Taylor's Version), and loved so many songs on there, especially All To Well (10 Minute Version), Girl At Home, State Of Grace, We are Never Ever Getting Back Together, and 22. Weeks later Speak Now (Taylor's Version), was released, I listened to it and immediately loved Long Live and I Can See You.

I came across something called "Swifties" on Google and decided to search for what it meant, I realised that it was the name for Taylor Swift fans and immediately after that, I decided to call myself   a swiftie. I love every single song of hers, but I think the Reputation is my favourite album. Unfortunately I wasn't able to get tickets to the Eras Tour next August but I did go to watch the movie and it was definitely the best thing I've ever gone to watch! Everyone there was singing and dancing to all her songs like it was a real concert." -Bhavi, age 13, UK

***

"Dear Taylor,

I was around 6 or 7 years old, and my crush (who was also my friend at the time) had a soccer game I was attending. I wanted to cheer for him because I cared and loved him. He told me to shut up, as I was embarrassing him in front of his teammates. I went home crying and remembered your song "Love Story." I know it may be about love, but my heart felt it was a heartbroken song. I listened to it repeatedly and fell in love with you, your music, and your lyricism." -Izzy

***

"Hi Taylor! I'm 11 years old and the first time I heard you was at the red tour inside my mum's stomach and it all started since then I love you so much you've helped me through things not even a mental hospital could." -Noah

***

"I first started listening to Taylor when I was in 6th grade. I was going through a really rough time in my life transitioning from elementary school to middle school. That same year I had surgery on my eyes to help my usher syndrome, and I got diagnosed with anorexia, anxiety and depression. Taylor's music saved my life when I was at my lowest points. I listen to her every day and she's my favorite person ever. I went to the Eras Tour night 2 in Minneapolis. I cried the whole night. It was the best night of my life. I'm so thankful I get to go to Miami to see her in 2024. Taylor, if you're reading this please know how much I love you and how much I want to meet you someday." -Aliyah, age 15, North Dakota

***

"In 2014 Taylor had just released 1989. I had already listened to her hits like love story and you belong with me but there was something about this pop masterpiece that my 4 year old brain loved so much. I was (and still am) a wonderland stan. I can't count how many hours I spent playing with my American girl dolls and that song on repeat in the background.

After that, I took a deep dive into her music and fell in love with Red. 1989 and Red were on repeat. Then Taylor released Reputation. I WAS IN LOVE. She is someone who I have always looked up to and her releasing rep just made that more clear in my mind. Because I was so obsessed my parents wanted to do something special for my soooo...... THEY BOUGHT ME TICKETS TO THE REPUTATION TOUR.

I had the time of my life. It blew my moms mind and mine too. Never once in my mind had I ever seen something that incredible before. That's why going back to the Eras Tour (especially during the rep era) makes me feel the way I did during the reputation concert." -anonymous

***

"All I can remember of me first listening to Taylor is in the 1989 era. I was so obsessed with Shake it off and ended up becoming a swiftie along with my sister and mom. I've loved Taylor since I can remember and I have never stopped. I could've heard RED on tbe radio of my mom playing it but I don't remember that. I've been a swiftie for a while now (basically my whole life) and don't plan on stopping!" -Sarah

***

"In 2014, at Four years old, I remember my parents holding the phone up so I could watch the Shake It Off music video. I have loved every moment of being a swiftie; but when the song Anti-Hero came out, I realized that celebrities and people are not perfect. I had been dealing with self esteem issues for a while, as most teens do. The song got me through some of the hardest times that I have had... and after watching the Miss Americana documentary as well, I now understand that it is not just me. I want to thank the most amazing singer-songwriter for giving me more confidence in myself and my image. Without it, my life would have went down a worse path. I am and will be forever grateful for you, Taylor Swift. I hope you know that you have helped and saved millions of lives around the world by being the person you are. Thank you a million times, and have the most incredible 34th birthday ever." -Alexa H.

***

"I am a swiftie because I fell in love with Taylor's music, lifestyle, personality, and just every part of her life because of my amazing older sister. I used to not recognize who Taylor Allison Swift really is. It's not just her music I love about her, it's what she does and how she treats her fans. She is the kindest person ever and I could not say that enough about her. She cares so much about us and adores us. My sister started playing miss Americana and the heartbreak prince which turned into all of the lover era. Then I started to love her music. I finally listened to more of her songs and soon enough knew every lyric to a ton of her songs. Then I had the biggest hardest choice in the world sitting in my hands. Should I go to the Eras tour? Can I go to the Eras Tour? Would I go to the Eras Tour? Just like would've could've should've but the words all scrambled around to make sense.

Exactly Tuesday 3 days before the Eras Tour feeling hopeless my mom got me and my sister to go to the Eras Tour! I was screaming wanting to cry happy tears of joy and then the day came. I dressed as the red era and my big moment happened. Taylor Swift's big moment came and I went to the 4th night of her LA tour. I am the biggest swiftie ever to this day. My favorite song of hers if champagne problems would've could've should've Marjorie and now that we don't talk. I am so proud of Taylor swift she has come back through the hardest times in life just for us. She is truly the best person ever like I would die for this girl that I'd not even know personally but she has shared so much of her life with us swifties that I basically know her as a best friend.

And this story comes to an end. I just want to say to the amazing, great, strong miss Taylor Alison Swift, you are the definition of everything great in the world. I love you." -Isla

***

"I became a swiftie in between the Reputation era, and the Lover era. I always wanted to see Taylor live, but unfortunately, the pandemic happened.

I remember watching either the Reputation film, or the Folklore Long Pond Studio Sessions every single day, wishing I could see her in concert. I still remember the shock I felt when I got tickets for The Eras Tour in Foxborough. Seeing Taylor live was the best experience ever, she is truly an amazing person." -Ashlynn

***

"Hi Tay! My name is Lili and I've been listening to you for as long as I can remember. I've been dancing since I was 4 and 1989 was peak dance warm up music, I can just remember dancing in the car when shake it off came on, or lip syncing to blank space in warmups, and even helping choreograph my recital dance to look what you made me do because I was the biggest fan in my class.

I'll always remember when my older sister asked me to listen to Red TV with her, and my jaw dropped open and memories of a simple and beautiful time flooded me. On my own I listened to some of the songs, my faves of red stolen, and a couple vaults. And when I saw a 10 minute song I was like 'why is it so long, i'm not gonna listen to that' the next week at school my friend was in music class with me and we had nothing to do so she asked to listen to music, she asked if I listened to Red TV yet and I said some of it. She said I HAD to listen to ATWTMV, and so we did. After that I fell in love with you, and that song specially. Me and that friend became best friends and that was OUR SONG!! I barely listened to anything other than ATWTMV and I mostly listened to that song with my best friend, but when midnights came out it again changed my life but in a much bigger way. Again my sister asked to listen to the new TS album with her, but this time I said yes. It was an amazing song, after a beautiful song, after a PERFECT song. This past year of my life has been the best, the way you've consumed my life in just over a year is crazy to me. I've always listened to you but never like now.

I know that this next part doesn't make me special but I couldn't get Eras Tour Tickets, and that ripped and is still tearing my life apart. When the tour was announced I was sure I could go, my dads boss has great connections to MetLife Stadium and can almost always get us tickets to shows there. but what I wasn't aware of was how many other lives you changed. When it became clearer that my dad's boss wouldn't be able to get tickets, the downhill started, sure my sister liked you too, but not like me, and she admits that she'll never know what it was like for me the next 6 months. With almost all my friends dropping thousands of dollars last minute to see you, money that we didn't have, and you playing my favorite song in the acoustic set the night I was supposed to go, it got hard to cope with. It's pretty much calmed down, but it pains me to know that my dreams of seeing you, at a concert, or even meeting you, are probably never gonna happen with chances becoming slimmer every second.

The moral of the story is I really really love you, which doesn't make me any different from the next but you should still know that I really love you and I thank you for everything you got me through (and put me through over not getting tickets haha!) the lessons you taught me, helping me enjoy my life and feel like i'm living a movie, or helping me crying in my bed about the people i've lost along the way. happy birthday to you Taylor, thank you for not only changing my life but 100s of millions of peoples, your legacy will be forever and always." -Lili

***

"I've been listening to Taylor's music since I was 4 years old and I'm now 13 years old. As you can see, I've been a swiftie longer than I haven't which I'm so pleased with because she deserves all her fans and more. I remember the exact time I listened to my first Taylor swift song-I was driving in the car with my brother and Dad and 'Style' from 1989 came on the radio. I was fascinated by how mesmerizing the music was and in took me to a place I'd never been. I wish I could be in that place all the time, but life happens, and my life had some unfortunate turns but I'm grateful that I can be here in this decade with my family to listen to Taylor's music.

Around the time 'Lover' was released I started researching all about Taylor swift, her music and backstory. I found out about some amazing things she had done and some bad times she had went through which I'm a bit glad about not gonna lie, not because she had to go through them but the fact, I found someone I really cared about who could relate to me. Taylor's music has gotten me through some pretty dark times in my life, so Taylor I don't know what I'd do without you and your music.

This year I went into 7th grade which is high school in Australia, and I don't want to go into too much detail, but my friends left me out a lot. They were nice but it's obvious they didn't want to engage much with me. Also, I was in none of their classes and my class... I'm pretty sure none of them wanted to be seen dead with me because they had barely said 2 sentences to me since the start of the year. When I had gone through my Taylor swift 'Researching Era' I had come across an article talking about how the phenomenal Taylor swift was also alone in middle school JUST LIKE ME!!! Taylor swift was the kindest, most honest person I had ever met and all I wanted to do was meet her.

Another really important factor that attracted me to Taylor SO much was how she started her singing career. Becoming a singer-songwriter is one of my biggest dreams and I was also really inspired on how Taylor started her career, so I begged my parents to buy me a guitar and tried to force myself to learn guitar and songwriting. Did I learn it? No. Did I waste 3 days of my life crying and being depressed and embarrassed in my room? Yes! You know why? Because most people's lives are supposed to be good with a few bad things thrown in but it sometimes feels like mine is bad with a few good things thrown in. After that 'incident' I pretty much gave up any hope that I could be a singer until.........The Eras tour came out. I got really excited even though I knew my parents wouldn't buy the tickets, I was happy other people got to watch her and I watched a lot of many amazing Eras tour experiences on YouTube. Every time I watched one of those videos it made my day just that tiny bit better that at least someone else could enjoy seeing Taylor even if I couldn't.

Over the past years I've learnt so much about Taylor Swift and how fun it is being a swiftie. It's made about ¾ of my life better and one day hopefully I'll be the one up on stage thanking anyone who listened to my rants when I was younger and Taylor Swift for making my life 100% better with her just existing. I hope these words tell you just how much Taylor's music means to me because I have no better way of putting it.

To anyone who read this to the end, thank you so much, you've read my story better than anyone else in my life could have. I hope that in the next few years I will at least be one step closer to my dream of becoming a singer-songwriter. I love you and your music Taylor, and I know someday we'll be able to meet each other. Every time I hear your voice, it reminds me how lucky I am to be here in this world with you." -Yukthi

***

""It's nice to have a friend"

I may not have many friends but one thing I know is that I'm always gonna have Taylor. Even though she has no clue I even exist,she's basically my best friend and obviously everyone's "mother".

I so vividly remember my cousin telling me to listen to a Taylor Swift song and young me telling her "I don't like english songs" but she forced me to listen to the very first Taylor swift song I ever heard- "Everything has changed".

I swear it was love at first listen, but stubborn tween me was like "I only like artists who are kind and help people", not knowing how amazing of a person Taylor was and is.

During quarantine when all my friends started getting distant, Taylor's words of affirmation never left me. In the most rough times of my life, Tay singing "Safe and sound" always made me feel at peace. Sometimes when I seek for advice I just remember the lyrics of "Dear Reader" or literally any other lyric like "Never be so kind,you forget to be clever".

Listening to her songs in my bedroom while having a crush made me feel like I wasn't alone and this was a part of growing up. Taylor made my life so much better, to an extent that now I can't even imagine what I'd do without her music.

And you know what's the best part about being a swiftie? The people and the kaleidoscope of their loud heartbeats undercoat. I just went to the Era's Tour movie and the people were so kind to us, like no one shamed us for being too loud, or dancing our heads off. Also there are so many swiftie in India who love Taylor, like 2 couples there literally got engaged.

Also Taylor, if you ever read this, I want you to know that we love you and you don't need to overwork yourself. You work so hard for us and we appreciate every single bit, even if you don't realise it...Thank you for being there for all your swifties. Lots of love from Indian swifties who are literally insane (and lovely)" - @GoldenLikeDaylight16

***

"Hi Taylor! My name is Ceecee, and, well, you've probably heard this a million little times before, but you're my hero. I became a Swiftie one day, just to see what the hype was about and, well, it changed my life. You inspired me to be brave and strong. I've always wanted to be a songwriter, but your music inspires me the most. Every single day, you are there for me. And I want to thank you for the gift you give millions of people, the lives you've saved, and for understanding me even if we've never met. Thank you, Taylor Swift" - Ceecee

***

"I was in my late teens when I became a swiftie. I watched one reel and the audio was Love Story (Taylor's Version) and I was so mesmerized by it. So I searched for it on YouTube, and I liked it. Next day, I heard the same song and then I was suggested by Blank Space, so I played that too. I didn't focus much on that song but then, I saw one more suggestion: THE LAKES! It was the song which made me a swiftie.. That song's so poetic, so magical, I fell in love with that song when I first heard it. I was wonderstruck by the vocals, lyrics and everything in the lakes!!

That was the moment I decided that I will stream each and every song and every video by her, 'cause I felt I missed so much and I wanna cover everything now. That was the time Fearless TV and Red TV was released but not ATW short film, and literally I waited for the short film for like weeks 'cause I was so much into Taylor by then. All too well the short film instantly became my favorite music video of hers!

There are many reasons to love taylor. The main reason is that she inspires me to write poems. She's brave and she fights for her rights. She's so kind as she helps a lot of people, she is kind with her fans, she is generous and she gives a lot to charities too. She always comes back stronger than 90s trend. She inspires younger artists to fight for their rights and to get the ownership of their work. She's given heights to music in her career and tried different genres. From being a country artist to a pop icon, she's really so talented, and hardworking! Her storytelling in lyrics makes us feel connected to the music.

Her music is like therapy for me, she has songs for every mood. My favorite album of all time is Evermore. And the reason is her lyrics and her vocals.

Swifties obviously are the best part of being a swiftie, when I became a swiftie I knew very less people who are swifties, but with time, I've seen people becoming swiftie and I've known many swifties. The fandom is like you will never feel left out there, there's always someone who'll be with you. And the fans are so kind and welcoming that with every new swiftie, they involve them like they were friends from years.

If in case some stars in the universe meet in my favor and I get a chance to meet Tay personally. I would be thanking her for existing and creating music for us. I will tell her that she's my favorite and I will tell her everything I'm writing here. I will thank her for inspiring me and writing such beautiful songs!" -Aditi

***

"I am 18 years old and I wanted to write to

let you know how much I appreciate you and your music. As a sentimental introvert with anxiety, I have always loved music. I started learning how to sing from listening to Celtic Women, and the Fearless album that my parents bought when I was very young. As I have gotten older, you have inspired me to explore more of the world of music, which has helped me a lot in dance. The time and thought put into every piece of music is something that I have always looked up to. The thought behind the lyrics, annunciation/dynamics in the vocals, the music, rhythm, and chords, and even the timing of the music between the phrases is so perfectly natural and powerful. My three favorite albums are Reputation, folklore, and evermore, and three songs that I find so powerful are tolerate it, cardigan, and epiphany. I don't even have the words to describe what masterpieces your songs are and how much they mean to me. I have found that I don't need to listen to any other music artist because there is always one of your songs or albums for every mood and every time of day. I will continue to listen to and sing your songs every day and appreciate your hard work and dedication. Though I was not able to go to The Eras Tour, I get just as much joy seeing videos of the show and seeing how much you enjoy it. I will always support your creativity and hard work, and wish you the best in your career.

Side note: I am also a cat lover as I have 4 cats (crazy, I know) 2 adults and 2 kittens." -Julia (@cardigan_24) on YouTube

***

"So one day we had a road trip and we took turns putting on music and it was my sister's turn and she choose paper rings and I really liked it (I've heard Taylor

Swift before but not really knowing) and I look her up on Amazon music and I felt a connection and I start like only listening to her and becoming a swiftie and in December we were trying to get tickets and my sister got a email that she got a code and we got six tickets and ever since I've been a really really big swiftie!" -Avery

***

"Honestly, I have always been a Shake It Off kid. One time, I got a Build A Bear and named it Taylor Hearts because I was really obsessed with 1989. Once Shake It Off's popularity went down, so did my obsession. Fast forward to 2023 when Karma ft. Ice Spice came out. I saw the music video and wanted to listen to it. I fell in love. I checked out more of Taylor's discography and really loved it. Now, I have all of her CDS, posters of her in my room, and a lot of happiness as a Swiftie!!" -Emma

***

"I first became a swiftie around 2020. With the pandemic, it was hard to have stuff to do around the house. I started listening to a lot of music and that is when I really started to get into Taylor. It was so amazing to be shocked about how talented she is. I definitely am a huge swiftie and she is absolutely a big part of my life." -anonymous

***

"So 2 years ago for competitive lyrical dance, our song was Never Grow Up from Speak Now. When I listened to it, I felt like I had something special with it . I had heard it a few times before and thought nothing of it. But that time I did. I related. I felt I had just had someone help me with all my problems, they had just well gone away. So when I went home I listened to lots of her underrated songs from other eras. I related, loved, and fell in love with her.

She was somewhat different from any other artist, in a great amazing understanding, unique way. I started to know her personality, what kind of person she is. It felt absolutely amazing to have such amazing music that really affected my life and choices .My favorite song by her is Ronan (Taylors Version) because my aunt died from untreatable cancer when I was five years old. I loved her so much. It broke my whole world when I found out she was gone. She is in heaven now. God has taken care of her and I know she is at peace now.

If I had anything to say to Taylor I would say:

Dear Taylor, you are such an amazing, heartwarming, inspiring person to me. You have saved my whole life, I don't think I would be here today if I didn't start listening to that one song. I hope that you find joy, and a meaning to life, God and Jesus Christ loves you. He has a plan.

Her music brings me joy, it heals me because I have something to relate to. I don't feel like I need to give up as long as she keeps me going in life. I am so grateful no matter what. She taught me so much. I want to thank her for how she made me laugh, smile, and made me love myself for who I am." -Natalie K.

***

"Allow me to introduce myself. My name is Ceci, I'm non-binary, I use any pronouns, I'm Canadian, and I'm in my senior year in high school. I'm also autistic and one of my special interests is - you guessed it - Taylor Swift. So, today I'm going to tell you howI became a Swiftie. It is a very long, complicated story so... are you ready for it?

The first part is my childhood, also known as my Casual Fan Era. The first song I ever heard was Love Story in 2008 (when I was 2) because my parents had it downloaded on iTunes (back when that was a thing) then later on came Mean and I Knew You Were Trouble and other songs that played on the radio during my childhood. The only albums I ever listened to in full were Red and 1989 because my friend had them on CD, and 1989 was my favourite. I had no idea of how horribly Taylor was treated by the media during this time, because I was a kid, singing along to Shake It Off and playing Webkinz and Club Penguin and living my best life.

So yeah, it's safe to say i've loved Taylor Swift my entire life. even during my "not like other girls" phase in middle school where i pretended to hate any music that was "too mainstream", i was still secretly streaming Lover. but my Full On Swiftie Era really started in late 2020, when i found an edit of my favourite character (Ámbar) from my favourite TV show of all time (Soy Luna) to LWYMMD. and it was like i fell in love with Taylor all over again. I listened to every album in full, bought some merch, and my favourite album now is reputation and my favourite song is I Did Something Bad. not just from Taylor, like, in general.

Mean and Shake It Off helped me when I was being bullied. You Need To Calm Down helped me when I started questioning my gender and sexuality in a world that is unfortunately still very hostile to us. TIWWCHNT helped me get over a toxic friendship. evermore helped me when I felt like I was better off dead. WCS helped me deal with the worst night of my life. Anti-Hero and YOYOK helped me when I was struggling with my BPD and ended up losing some of my closest friends. I Can See You always makes me happy on a bad day for reasons 100% completely unrelated to me and my friends' Spider-Man fanfiction.

All of these songs, and so many more, have been my daylight in the darkest nights. Taylor is such a kind and talented and lovely person, and she was my childhood role model and is still one of my favourite people on this whole planet.

So thank you, Taylor Swift, for everything you've done for me. for all of us." -Ceci

***

"I've been a swiftie since the 5th grade. I think the first song I heard (that I remember) was Shake It Off when it was released when I was 5. Taylor's music is so incredibly special to me, it's helped me through almost every part of my life. I love Taylor because she is just so passionate and kind and just the most wonderful human being. I can't even begin to pick a favorite song, but some I really love are YOYOK, this is me trying, Long Live, betty, and Haunted." -Peyton, age 14

***

"I was around 5 years old and I don't remember much, but I do remember listening to one song. Shake It Off. I loved that song so much that I would make dances to it for talent shows. So I became a swiftie because of Shake It Off!" -Eden B.

***

"If I'm being totally honest, I don't remember how I became a Swiftie. I grew up listening to her hits as I'm sure many others did. One night, I was going down a YouTube rabbit hole & discovered the song "betty".

I was captivated by the harmonica & storytelling narrative that Taylor takes on in the song. I remember learning everything I could about the song & thinking "I want to hear more of this." Which probably explains why I'm such a folklore stan.

I honestly don't remember the first song I ever heard. Maybe Love Story? However, I vividly remember Out Of The Woods being a favorite of mine when it first became a single.   And then, of course, came the unavoidable "twenty stitches in a hospital room" meme. (Lilo & Stitch is in my top three Disney movies, just btw)

Why do I love Taylor? I truly don't know how to respond to this question because it is beyond my words. She is one of the best songwriters of our generation, if not THE best. Like most Swifties, I'm sure, Taylor's music was my first real opening to understanding my emotions. But now that I'm older, it's not just about her music. It's about her as a person. For example, on the Eras Tour, she has donated to food banks in cities she performs in. Taylor also has such a passionate, deep-flowing connection with her fans & cares about us to a great degree. There is so much more I'd like to say (her kindness, humility, confidence, I could go on) but I am unable to find the words.

Taylor's music means more to me than the sun does to the moon. It holds so many memories for me that it's impossible for me to just stop listening to her music. Not that I would ever want to stop. She's too remarkable for that.

In 2021, I was irreparably depressed. I won't delve into all the details for your sake, but so much had happened I thought I couldn't be saved. Then, I heard the lyric "beyond the curses & cries, beyond the terror in the nightfall, haunted by the look in my eyes that would've loved you for a lifetime, leave it all behind... and there is happiness." Hearing this lyric made me think about what was mine to carry & what was to be let go of. Taylor has also made countless speeches at concerts, award shows, etc that are so empowering. Her & her music helped me heal myself.

Choosing my favorite Taylor song is something I've been asked to do countless times, and it's incredulously difficult. Last Kiss, Long Live, Call It What You Want, tolerate it, illicit affairs, Better Man, Cornelia Street, I Almost Do, and right where you left me are definitely big contenders. Currently, I'm in love with Say Don't Go, Slut!, Dress, Death By a Thousand Cuts, We Were Happy, & the last great american dynasty. At this point, pretty much every song she's ever made.

The best part about being a Swiftie is probably the magic & the other Swifties!. Personally, I spend a lot of time on Pinterest & the Swiftie community over there is so sweet! They are always so respectful in addressing each other's opinions which is something I don't see a lot nowadays. Taylor is also really great at knowing what her fans are thinking. I mean, you've SEEN the Eras Tour, right? The setlist is everything!

If I ever met Taylor, I would probably break down in tears. I wouldn't know what to say! But Taylor, thank you so much for giving girls like me who felt too much at once a space to call home. From the girls who were always known but never popular, who have kept every birthday card they've ever gotten, who have a difficult time keeping friends, who are hopeless romantics, who always fit in but never fit in all at the same time, we thank you from the bottom of our hearts." -Madeline

"I'll admit I'm a new swiftie but I've fallen so hard! Going to the Eras Tour movie with my friends was the most fun I've had in a while and it was 99.13% because of your amazing songs and performance (the other .87% was because I have awesome friends that I love). I've actually watched the Ms. Americana documentary for the 13th time today by some crazy coincidence, and I always feel so proud of your growth. I know it's weird to know some random 12 year old girl cried from pride for you but she did. My bat mitzvah is coming up next March and the party is YOU themed! I'm turning 13 so it's fate! Destiny! Meant to be! I know that might not seem like a good excuse for some, but to be fair some girls have their bat mitzvahs when they turn 12. You know, because we're way more mature and less dramatic than boys? You know that all too well. Also it's March 16th, or 3/16 and 16-3= 13. I'm so excited for my party because it will showcase all of your eras! You're such a good role model and I'm so happy I became a swiftie!!

Also my friends and I dressed up as your different eras for halloween and I was red so I wore the "We are never getting back together. Like ever" shirt, and heart sunglasses and the hat and black jeans and red lipstick. My best friend was 1989 and she looked so good!! We got a bunch of compliments. One person giving out candy was a swiftie and we were talking and she was like "What's your favorite 1989 vault track?" and without thinking I was like "Maybe Say Don't Go, maybe Slut!" AND THEN I was like "Oh my god pretend I didn't say that!" because a big group of like 4 or 5 year olds were right next to me and you know, that's a conversation for their parents but then me and my friend started bursting out laughing so much we got cramps and it was an amazing memory and it's because of you and the community you've created with your fans so thank you so much! Also I don't think the little kids heard me so that's good!" -anonymous

***

"It was a bunch of different songs that convinced me to be a Swiftie, actually. I guess the most prominent ones were Cardigan, You Are In Love, It's Nice To Have A Friend, Mine and Fearless. I love Taylor for so many reasons: her music is so emotional and relatable, her personality, her values and what she fights for, everything. I've been in a bad mental space for a while but her music really helps me feel less alone and I know she loves all of us, even those she hasn't met yet. I relate to Taylor as a person a lot and being a part of the Swiftie community helps me because there's just so many other people who have gone through similar things and it's like we're all being healed by Taylor together. It's amazing to see and feel the love between us and Taylor. Some of my favorite songs are Would've, Could've, Should've, all the 1989 (Taylor's Version) vault tracks, all of Reputation, Wonderland, Maroon, You're On Your Own, Kid and more. A lot of Folklore, Evermore, Lover, Reputation and Midnights are relatable for me and it's like Taylor understands me on a deeper level than anyone else. The best parts of being a Swiftie are getting to form theories and find easter eggs with other Swifties online, supporting Taylor, and just getting to be a big fan of an artist I love. If I could tell Taylor anything, I would say that the haters gonna hate but we Swifties gonna love her. And also Happy Birthday,

Taylor!" -Evyn

***

"I have been listening to Taylor for about 7 years now. I remember the first ever time I heard a Taylor Swift song driving in my moms car listening to You Belong With me. That was probably around 2015 and I remember thinking how much I loved that song. For the next year I would listen to her on and off. I really became a swiftie in 2016. What really made me become a swiftie was my parents divorce. At the time I was 5 or 6 and I remember thinking about how happy listening to Taylor made me. I put my headphones in and from that I started to listen to her almost everyday to cheer me up and distract me from everything else that had been going on. In the past few years I've started to listen to her a lot more.

Not only Taylor's music, but Taylor herself has gotten me through so much. I've been struggling with anxiety the past year or so, and listening to Taylor's music helps me calm down. Now I get home everyday and put my headphones in and listen to her. My favorite song from Taylor changes on a daily basis so I can't choose a specific favorite since their all just so good but my current favorites are your on your own kid, wonderland, call it what you want, is it over now?, tolerate it and Betty. My favorite part about being a swiftie is literally everything but mainly clowning with each other over all the easter eggs Taylor leaves us. Another thing I love about Taylor/ being a swiftie is that I can relate to almost every song but at the same time I know that somebody else understands me because they relate to that song too. If I ever got the chance to tell Taylor something (which will never happen) it would be that she has helped me and others so much that she deserves the world. And, on the very rare chance that Taylor is actually reading this, I love you." -Aislyn

***

"Dear Taylor, I truly became a swiftie when I was about nine years old. Lover or 1989 was pretty much always playing whenever I was home. Since then, you have pretty much always been my number one artist. But especially this past year, you have felt like more than just a singer to me. I've never met you before, but I feel like you know me a lot better than most people in my life. Your music has helped through some tough stuff. You were always there for me. I feel like you half raised me. You're such an idol to me, but also incredibly human. I wanted more than anything to go to the Eras Tour but the movie made me almost feel like I was there. It was so magical and one of the best experiences of my life. I've already gone three times haha. You mean so much to me. I would give anything to meet you. I just admire how you always keep going even after all the bad things that have happened to you. You inspire me so much and remind me to keep going. You're truly a beautiful soul and I hope you have the happiest birthday." -Ruby

***

"I have loved Taylor for years now and hope that she has a wonderful 34th birthday. I have tried to go to the Eras Tour and failed but I went to the movie as many times as I could . One cool story I have is the day I bought 1989 tv Taylor announced new Eras Tour dates." -anonymous

***

"Dear Queen Taylor, I am Jasmir, one of your

fans since 2014! Happy Birthday queen!! I just wanna say you have been the most amazing person I've ever known, you're such an inspiration! My dream is to go to your concert, and I will! You're so talented and amazing that you've inspired me to write my own songs, they might see the light of day one day! My favorite album is 1989, Taylor's Version obviously!! You've helped me get through hard and special times through your songs, and your lyrics are so relatable and just so amazing there's not a word for it. I've supported you even when many people started canceling you, I'm so happy for you I'm so beyond happy for you. Whenever you're happy I start crying because I get so happy seeing you smile! I can't believe it's been 10 whole years since I've known you, and I can't wait for more. I love you so much queen, and once again.. HAPPY BIRTHDAY!" - Jasmir

***

"Dear Taylor, you have helped me with soooo many challenges. You always were there when I needed you and always at the right times. I cannot thank you enough.

I remember I started listening to you when I was 5 and my Dad would play your songs in the car. I didn't really know who you were but once I got older I did. When I was about 9 years old I became obsessed with RED and Speak Now. I went through different phases through music and it went from Taylor, Drake, Taylor, Katy Perry, Taylor. And it always went back to you no matter how many new types of music I tried.

When midnights came I was 11 or 12 and I became even more obsessed. Now that you've been on your tour my parents don't really like concerts so I haven't been able to go but I will find a way. I've watched your reputation movie way too many times to remember and the folklore documentary on Disney Plus. Right now since you've released your 1989 TV it's helped me so much, especially the vault tracks. My favorite songs that you have written are Willow, You're On your Own Kid, New Romantics, Wonderland, Delicate, Paper Rings, 15, and many more. If you're reading this I LOVE YOU SO MUCH!!!!!!!!!!" -AnaLucia

***

"I heard about the Eras Tour and I thought it would be fun to go, but I couldn't. I was super upset but I became more interested in Taylor and became a big Swiftie. These girls who started a big argument are always mean to me, and Taylor's songs help me with that (Mean, Bad Blood, LWYMMD, etc). Anyways, the first Taylor song I heard was Bad Blood, it's a special song to me because when I was younger I would sing to it all the time. Taylor's music means a lot to me and helps me through a lot. My favorite song is Enchanted because it helped me when I was sad, and just the meaning of it; and it's a great song. The best part about being a Swiftie is Taylor. I'm so glad to be a huge fan of someone who is so kind and has such great music and a great personality. If I could tell Taylor something, it would be a thank you for everything. I really want to meet her." -anonymous

***

"I honestly don't know when I became a Swiftie but I've known who Taylor was all of my life just in the past year finding out how amazing she is as a person and a song-writer. When Speak Now tv came was when my best friend was exposed to her amazingness. My favorite songs are from folklore because they are the ones that connected me with my family more. Betty, cardigan, the 1, August, etc. these are some of my dad's favorite songs which makes them my favorite to listen to with him. Thank you Taylor for everything." -Kristin

***

"Taylor has helped me in so many ways and I will forever be thankful for her. She's such an amazing role model and I'm unbelievably happy to exist at the same time as her. Taylor has a song every single experience. No matter what you're going through, there's a Taylor Swift song to help. When things get really hard for me I turned to music. And when I looked for songs that related to the situation I was in a few Taylor Swift songs came up. I went and listened to them and it was just so filling to finally have a song that related to my situation. As I listened to her music more I really liked it and before I knew it I became a full-blown Swiftie!

The very first Taylor Swift song I ever heard was Sparks Fly. I really liked the song. It was just such a cute song and it's still one of my favorites till this day. I love Taylor so much just for so many reasons. She's such a good person. She has such a good heart. She truly cares about her fans. She truly deserves the world. Her music is so amazing. Idk what I would do without her music. I probably wouldn't be here if it weren't for Taylor and her music. And I know that Taylor has had her hardships as well and it's so encouraging to see her beat her demons.

I honestly don't think I can pick a favorite Taylor Swift song cause I love them all so much. But I think if I had to pick a top 5 they would be Delicate, Tolerate It, The Last Time, Long Live, and You're On Your Own, Kid.

Those songs truly just mean so much to me.

And being a Swiftie is so fun! We all are like a family and Taylor is our mom. I have more Swifties friends than I do friends. The Swifties are so encouraging of each other and of Taylor. It's truly a great thing.

If I ever get to meet Taylor or if Taylor ever sees this I just want her to know how much I love her. I love her more than anybody else on this planet, even more than my family members. She's truly helped me so much and I'll forever be so thankful for her." -@FlamingoPink1989

***

"I became a Swiftie when Taylor started the Eras tour. I was always a fan but not always a Swiftie. When I was younger I knew some of her songs but not all of them. I know a lot about her and I love her SO much. I have never been in a break-up but for some reason I still connect with her music and I think that's hilarious.

The reason I became a Swiftie was because I realized that she actually cares SO much about her fans like not a lot of celebs care that much about their fans. Also, I have never seen another Artist play 3 sold out shows in Philadelphia (or any other state) and have thousands of fans outside the stadium as well. I have never been to a real concert of hers, I went to the Eras tour movie and I hope one day I will get to go to one of her concerts." -Rachel, age 12

***

"The first time I heard Taylor on car radio was the release of shake it off. Although I did not become a major swiftie until Midnights, she still holds a special place in my heart. Speak Now is my personal favourite album, as it is a genuinely enjoyable and loving album that speaks to me. Songs such as Sparks Fly, Mine, Back to December are amongst my personal favourites. I appreciate how this album merges country and pop, elements of her origins and her return. But Taylor isn't only 'Music'. She's also a kind, encouraging, charitable celebrity which is harder to find in any famous people nowadays. Taylor IS the Music Industry and I wish she knew how much she meant to me." -anonymous

***

"I was 1 when red came out and 3 when 1989 came out. I loved her songs. I remember me and my dad listening to songs like "shake it off" and "I knew you were trouble" and "mean" on the way to and from school in kindergarten. I've loved Taylor ever since. When I was really young my older brother cut my hair and I had a bald spot. So when my mom went to cut it to cover up the spot I asked her to give me the iconic bangs with short hair. I rocked that style for years. Then on my birthday my mom surprised me with tickets to the Eras Tour. I went to Cincinnati night 1 in a V.I.P. Suite. I was so happy. I have since then grown into a really big swiftie. Taylor swift makes me smile whenever I'm sad. My dream is to meet her because she is my idol. I want to be like her one day. She is the best singer ever. I would be honored if she ever read this." -Lauren A.

***

"I have been a swiftie forever. I love Taylor. The first song I listened to was shake it off. Yes I know it took me a long time to become a swiftie. I was at a party when someone played shake it off and I instantly started dancing. Ever since I've been a swiftie. My school has a club called Scientific Swifties and I'm in it.

It is the best club." -Genevieve

***

"Taylor Swift... I remember hearing everyone talk about her as a kid. I remember watching those original 1989 music videos, or how in love I was with the "Crazier" scene from Hannah Montana The Movie. It was all special to me, and honestly, I believe I was always meant to come to this point and become an obsessed cat-book-TaylorSwiftTheQueen person. She is the one who made me realize who I actually am. That I'm not "damaged goods" and "experiencing turbulence" is alright because it probably means "you're rising". She taught me to be kind. She taught me to love the world and people in it, even if sometimes it hurts too badly. She taught me that there is no such thing as "a slut" or "a bitch". I remember looking at the sky, tears all over my face, listening to your marvelous, orphic music. You taught me that it's alright to be a "mad woman". Taylor Swift, thank you for being you and saving my heart and my life. My Soul is forever thankful to you. You once said that you wish you could heal people. Well, you healed my Soul so beautifully, gently, softly, lovely and peacefully that you will forever be there. To protect me. And I'll protect you. Please, picture me in the trees. I love you." -Sabrina G.

***

"I became a swiftie around the lover era but even before that little me would be the girl listening to shake it off bad blood you get what I mean. I remember my first time listening to the red and fearless TV vault tracks and being so happy just listening to them all the time. It's my dream to go the Eras Tour but if that can't happen maybe this will." -Zara

"I heard my first Taylor Swift song when I was about 4 years old. My dad had played I Knew You Were Trouble for me and my sister and we loved it! Then I Knew You Were Trouble turned into Shake It Off and when I turned 12 right after I lost my dad my best friend Isabella turned me full Swiftie! I owe Taylor my life for her music. She has inspired me to try and make my own music too! I wish I could thank her for all she has done for me but I'm unfortunately very poor and live in a small town away from big cities. I wish Taylor the best in everything she does in the future!" -Annalise

***

"I was at my friend's house one night (she was a swiftie) and I was going through a lot of stuff with my depression and anxiety and getting bullied a lot at school. She told me one day and said "Hey you should listen to Reputation, it's such a good album!" I thought it wouldn't be good because I really never listened to Taylor Swift ever in my life. So I told her "Ok I'll listen to it". So I listened to it and I couldn't stop listening to her music. It was just so good!! Soon enough I was listening to every album over and over again,knowing every lyric to basically every song, learning so much about her life and her music, I was having listening party's to all of her new albums (including taylors version too!), and soon enough I became a swiftie!! Taylor has done so much for me her music has helped me through depression,anxiety, and stressful stuff in life. Ever since I became a swiftie I've been 3 years clean! Taylor I Love You So Much!" -Emma

***

"I first became a fan of Taylor during her speak

now era, but a hardcore fan during 1989, she is to be honest one of the best singers ever, and deserves the best, she also sounds really good when performing and I love how you can look back her past performances, to see how her voice has perfected over the years, I also think she is a great person to look up to, because she puts others before her, and she acts like a normal human unlike some celebrities, she always has something planned in mind to surprise us Swifties with, and I have some of the funnest times decoding Easter eggs, over all, Taylor is an amazing person, and "the haters gonna hate" but Taylor will just shake it off." -Leila

***

"Taylor I love all your music and can not stop listening to it.I love how you care about your fans so much." -Eliana

***

"Thank you sooo much for being yourself and being a complete boss. I absolutely love you and I'm so glad that I am able to listen to your amazing music. I got an amazing notification that I'm a top 5% listener on Amazon Music and I almost cried because that is such an honor. I'm so glad that you are so down to earth and you don't take advantage of your fame and that you do whatever you can so that Swifties can all have a great opportunity to listen to your music. Sadly I didn't get tickets to our show but I did stand outside of the stadium of Pittsburgh night 1. It was such an awesome opportunity and even though I didn't see anything it was one of the best experiences. Thank you so much for all that you do and keep doing so much for us Swifties. Keep on being awesome and holding up the music industry, love you so much!" -Ellie R.

***

"Dear Taylor Swift, I have loved your music for a very long time. You're an amazing singer. My favorite albums are 1989,Reputation, Lover, Folklore, Evermore and Midnights. They are all amazing but those are the ones I listen to the most. My biggest dream is to meet you and go to the Eras Tour. My mom went but she took her friend instead of me. I cried for a long time but I was happy for her. When you came out with your movie my mom took me to that and I loved it. I went twice. The first time I dressed up as Midnights then the second time me and my mom bought a dress that looked like the dress for Evermore in the movie and put flowers on it, I was gonna try to braid my hair like yours on the Evermore album cover but my hair is to short so we just kept it down. You're my #1 favorite singer. Keep up your amazing work!" -Caroline

***

"I am a late swiftie, but when midnights came out I fell in love. I started hearing more of her music and I realised she is more than just a country/pop singer. She is an independent woman who puts her life stories in her songs. She has amazing vocals and does not deserve the hate she gets. I hope that in the future she deserves more praise for her music." -Falak

***

"It all started when I was around 3 years old. My uncle at the time was a huge T-Swift fan, and I used to always hangout with my uncle because he's one of those cool uncles. My uncle was trying very hard to get me to become a fan, and let's just say it did not take long at all! Within a few months, I was a big fan and you would catch me singing along. In addition, my uncle would play You Belong With Me and Our Song on repeat! Let's say that those songs are some of my favorites to this day. Whenever we would hangout, I would yell at him to play T-Swift; preferably YBWM (You Belong With Me)! Then, when Speak Now came out I was so thrilled! I even asked my uncle to take me to the Speak Now Tour, but he unfortunately couldn't afford it.

I would watch Taylor on the CMA Awards back when she was country, and when she won I screamed and started bawling my eyes out! Then, Red and 1989 came out. Holy cow! I was OBSESSED! All I listened to was 22 and Starlight, as well as Shake it Off and Bad Blood (Feat. Kendrick Lamar). THAT WAS SUCH A GOOD TIME IN MY LIFE! My uncle went to see Taylor (you) for the Red Tour, but ya know, he didn't invite me! Then, the 1989 World Tour came a thing and I wanted to go since 1989 was my favorite album, but it was too much money. Little did I know, they were setting me up for the Rep Tour!! Yes, the Rep Tour!!! On July 13th, 2018, I went to go see the music industry. I got floor seats for Easter with my mom, and I was so close!

When she came out singing ...Ready For It?, I started bawling my eyes out as well as screaming my head off. It was honestly the best night of my life. When Taylor sang Delicate and Shake it Off, she went on this thing that lifted her up and brought her to a different stage, so my mom and I ran over there. These two really sweet girls let me go in front of them, and I was only 6 ROWS BACK!!! I was screaming, jumping up and down, it was just so awesome! I remember when the concert ended I picked up the confetti, and I still have it today! I have a T-Shirt and a book that I got. I remember I asked my mom if I could go back next time, and that next time would be The Eras Tour. Unfortunately, my family and I could not afford The Eras Tour, so I did not get to go. I was devastated and thought my life was over at that point. I was watching videos off of YT and it made me so depressed. I'm glad to see other fellow Swifties having fun though! That's the end of how I became a Swiftie, but I would like to add my favorite song and I'm gonna do it from each album. Starting with Debut (Taylor Swift), my fav song is Invisible or Teardrops on my Guitar. Next is Fearless, my fav song is Hey Stephen (iykyk) or White Horse. Next is Speak Now, and my fav song is Haunted or Last Kiss. Next is Red, and my fav song is probably Starlight or Safe & Sound. Next is 1989, and my favorite song is either Wonderland or Now That We Don't Talk. Next is Rep, and my favorite songs are Dress and Delicate. Next is Lover, and my fav songs are The Archer and DBATC. Next is Folklore, and my fav songs are mirrorball or the 1. Next is Evermore, and my favorite song is champagne problems or right where you left me. Lastly is Midnights, and my favorite songs are Would've, Could've, Should've or Mastermind. Thank you for all you do Taylor! Your music has saved me in so many ways, and all my memories are from you. Thank you. We all love you!" -Kaydence

***

"When I was five I heard the Disney princess version of shake it off and loved it a lot. So I decided to listen to the original and I liked that one even better. So I searched for Taylor Swift on Spotify and loved every single song I heard.

My favorite songs now are speak now, long live, enchanted, I can see you, and when Emma falls in love.

My favorite album as you can probably already tell is Speak Now TV. My favorite Taylor memory is going to KC N1 and seeing the world premiere of the I can see you MV." -Karleigh

***

"I have been a Swiftie since the Lover era in 2019-2020. When I first started listening to music, I had no idea who Taylor even was. My aunt had told me about her, so I decided to listen to some of her music. I remember listening to her self titled album first, and after that, I listened to Lover. I remember really liking it, so I listened to her other stuff as well and now I am a huge Swiftie! I never really expected this, but I'm forever glad it happened. When folklore and evermore came out, I didn't really like them as much, and never thought much of it.

Funny enough, my favorite album is actually folklore now! I think all the songs tell great stories and are lyrical masterpieces.

I love Taylor because I think her singing/ songwriting skills are AMAZING. Her music has helped me a lot through multiple things in my life. I also think she's an amazing, sweet person in general, between all the money she donates, how much she loves her fans, and everything she does for us, I think she's absolutely an AMAZING person. If I could tell Taylor one thing, I would tell her she's amazing and has come a long way. I am so proud of who she's become and I can't wait to see what the future holds for her and us!! (Taylor, if you see this, we love you!)" -Kaylin (YouTube@urfavkaylin)

***

"I started to like Taylor's music when I was 3 years old, listening to it on the radio and dancing to it.

I remember loving 22, We Are Never Ever Getting Back Together, Everything Has Changed, and Red A LOT. Then 1989 came out and I LOVED it so much that I went to her concert when I was 5, which was amazing.

After the concert I started listening to all of her songs and becoming a swiftie. Then when Reputation came out I listened to Delicate so much that I didn't know what lwymmd was for about a year. And then Lover came out and I was so amazed that I don't know how to explain it, but it made me feel better than I ever was.

When Folklore and Evermore were released I thought it was too country for me, but now I adore both of those albums. For Midnights it was the first time I stayed up till midnight to listen to an album and I did it with my mom, we both loved it so much. When I was 12 I went to see the Eras Tour and I have never smiled so much then that night, it is probably the best concert I'll ever see in my life. And throughout all of this I not only loved her music, but looked up to her as a role model and still do." -Adrianna

***

"I have always liked Taylor Swift, but I never called myself a swiftie before she released her album Midnights, which I fell in love with. I then listened to all her other albums (Folklore is my favorite) and became invested in the community. I love how creative she is with her song lyrics, and how kind she is to her fans. I haven't been to any of her concerts yet, but it's my dream to someday. Thank you, Taylor, for being an amazing inspiration and wonderful person!" -Liv

***

"I became a swiftie at age 3 when I got an ipod

for my birthday, it was an old family member's and it had songs already downloaded on it and some of which were Taylor's. Sparks Fly had just come out and that song was replayed nonstop for MONTHS. Then I found White Horse and So it Goes from there. I feel so glad for everything Taylor has done for us to this day. If she never sees this, I still want to express my love for her by helping me become who I am and loving me for ME!

It's been an amazing time with her from concerts to her movie (which I am renting a theater out for btw) and I have to mention my complete vinyl record collection and custom pins i've made for myself, bejeweled halloween costumes, getaway car rides, tears, and everything in between. I think that if people say they don't like Taylor they are either jealous or confused & all they are is Mean, but everyone can take something from her and find the good in life and we know All too Well she's been through Death by a thousand cuts. Cuz she is the best thing that's ever been Ours. So good for people getting together to make this for her. Debut album has been there for nostalgia and roots, Fearless for daydreams of love & family, Speak Now for seeing who's been there for me all along, Red car rides and emotional rides, 1989 getting my energy out and just having fun in general, Reputation for confidence and teenage years, Lover for well…love, folklore all my tears ricocheting , evermore for giving me what folklore didn't have enough of, and Midnights for being true to myself. So thank you Taylor, WE LOVE YOUUU!" -Gavin

***

"I'm a new Swiftie and became one this year. Sometimes people say, "it's just a song" when I'm talking about You're On Your Own Kid or Epiphany, but it's more than a song. Taylor was there for me when I needed her. I would be crying and I would put on her music and she would automatically make me feel better. That's why I love Taylor. So many people have said to me to stop being a Swiftie and that Taylor's overrated but they just don't get it. I get made fun of by my own family for being a Swiftie but that doesn't stop me from blasting Reputation at 10PM. She has a song for every mood possible. I'm currently in my Lover era and am loving it! At the moment my favourite song is Wonderland and It's Nice to Have a Friend. One thing I wish Taylor could know is that she is incredible, she deserves everything in the world and to never let anyone bring you down. She brought herself up better than ever after the K*nye W*st incident and came up strong and powerful. She is a role model. WE LOVE YOU TAYLOR!" -anonymous

***

"My mom always liked Taylor Swift her whole life (especially during the debut, fearless, speak now, time) but was never really a 'swiftie'. So I have been listening to Taylor ever since I was a baby. (I have videos of me as a baby and like toddler dancing, singing, and just listening to you all the time). I've always loved your music but never really listened to you that much until about two years ago.

Two years ago I started to listen to Speak Now and Fearless a lot with my mom since she loved those albums. Then since I thought Taylor was amazing and so talented I wanted to listen to more of her music so I obviously did. That's really how I fell in love with Taylor and her music. There is no possible way I can describe how much I love taylor but I've been through some really hard times thinking about doing things I shouldn't do to myself, but I never have and Taylor is the reason for that.

Honestly I truly don't think I would be alive today if it wasn't for taylor. She has helped me find supportive positive friends and just helped me in the worst of times to find the light in the darkness. I haven't been able to get tickets to the Eras Tour yet because of the price and how hard they are to get but I've been trying so hard and saving ever since she announced the tour. It is my dream to go and my life will be complete if I can, so let's hope I can get tickets!

Happy birthday mom, I love you so much and you don't know how much you have impacted my life and so do many others! Also you have come so far since 1989 and I want you to know that you are beautiful, strong, and worthy of all you have ever accomplished. Anyone and everyone is lucky to be alive at the same time as you and no matter how hard life gets, remember you have more than a million people behind you cheering you on. i will be with you forever and always (see what i did there haha) anyways, stay you and I will always love you!" -Laila

***

"Taylor's music has helped me through life. I've been a swiftie since I was 6, right before 1989 came out. Now she has re-released it and I have grown up from a child to a teenager. She makes life so much better and I love her endlessly." -Ardyn

***

"My best friend is a swiftie, at the time I wasn't. She kept telling me to listen to Taylor. One day I decided to turn it on and I ended up really liking Taylor. I made friendship bracelets and went to the Eras Tour movie. It was probably the best day of my life! I want Taylor to know how many lives she has shaped and how happy she makes people. She is so kind and funny. I hope to meet her someday!" -Eva

***

"When I first found out about Taylor, I was getting bullied at school. I was 9 and my mom one day, in the car, turned on "mean" and to this day it continues to be one of my favorite songs by Taylor. It helped me through a lot of things. My favorite song by Taylor is "Sparks Fly" because it reminds me so much of the sweet feeling you get when you love someone. (Sometimes I like to change the lyrics to match my crush) Taylor is amazing, and such a genius." -MJ

***

"I love Taylor Swift so much and all of her music puts me in the best mood. Not only has her great music brought me up in bad times, but her kind heart has lead a path of how to approach people in a respectful way. Taylor Swift shows revenge, kindness, positivity, and compassion towards others. She stands up for what is right, and Taylor is a big icon that I admire for her hard work and dedication. I have been a swiftie since reputation, and I will be for the rest of my life!" -Isla

***

"I became a Swiftie in 2015 and now I can't stop singing her music. My mom actually turned me into a swiftie so we were in the car and Taylor was on and my mom started singing and the words caught on almost instantly and till this day my all time favorite song is All Too Well (Ten minute version)." -Sophia

***

"I became a swiftie back when she started having issues with Scooter Braun (Lover Era) and I was going through a really hard time in my life, my (at the time) boyfriend broke up with me over text and that hurt a lot, and a lot of my friends were fake.

I turn to music when things get hard for me and Taylor was the music that helped the most. I am currently in my Reputation Era and I feel better and more confident than I ever have. I believe that people can change people even if you don't know them. Sadly she has only gone in one hour since I became a swiftie and I live in a family where those ticket prices were just not possible for me, but as soon as the Era Movie came out my parents ran to buy the tickets.

Happy Birthday Taylor, we love you!!" - @Harmony13TV on YouTube

***

"How I became a swiftie was listening to her; from the age of 5 I loved all her songs! I really liked out of the woods blank space and bad blood when I was 5-8 but then from 9-10 I liked haunted and enchanted bc those were the songs I could choose on the car radio. And now at 11-12 my favourite songs are the last great American dynasty, miss Americana and the heartbreak prince, Willow, paper rings, gorgeous, and Getaway car. I really became a swiftie recently by going to the Eras Tour movie and listening to more of her songs and albums because when I was younger I was limited to 1989 and speak now. Anyways I'm a recent swiftie but have been listening to her since 5 I love her and all her work!" -Maddy

***

"Dear Taylor Swift,

I adore you, your creativity, and your brilliant and genius lyrics, songs, and performances. Becoming a part of the Swiftie world has changed my life in countless ways. Words cannot express my gratitude and appreciation for you as a person, songwriter, artist, and everything else you are from the bottom to the top. Every day I feel like I am becoming a bigger Swiftie and I am so proud to be one. I am just so exceedingly amazed by who and what you have done and become. I cannot answer 'how I became a Swiftie' in simple words. It wasn't something that happened overnight or from a certain thing you've done. It was a process. It still is. It's learning about your achievements, your awards, your performances, your career, your defeats, your opportunities. It's understanding what you have done for everyone and for yourself and those you truly care about. It's learning your songs (playing them on repeat for hours and hours) so I can dance, sing, and relate or reflect on the people who can relate to them. It's not only seeing what you have dealt with throughout your journey, but seeing what you have done to come out stronger. You have helped so many people, including myself, get through so many days, months, even years, of varying struggles. I seriously cannot imagine life without learning about you. There is so much more I could say to you, but knowing as you may never actually read this and that your life is hopefully filled with people telling you these things every day, I will summarize what I've written into a few words:

Taylor, Thank you. You have no idea what you have done for me." -Clara

***

"On August 29th 2023 I watched a YouTube

video of people going to the Eras Tour in LA, I really liked it and wanted to go. Even though I didn't know what the Eras Tour was or who Taylor Swift was, I did listen to a lot of her hits before but never really focused on who they were sung by.

I started seeing some YouTube shorts about the Eras Tour when I decided that I wanted to become a swiftie so I started investigating who Taylor was and things about her. When I knew enough about Taytay, the next step was to listen to enough of her music so I could actually become a real swiftie. I listened to all of 1989 (tv) when it came out and really enjoyed it, And on a long car ride I listened to all of Reputation and liked it SO SO SO much. Now I'm close to finishing all of Speak now (tv), Lover and midnights. I'm planning on finishing Red (tv) next and so on until I finish with all the albums and get to all the songs without albums (the complete collection). I cannot explain how much I love Taylor and her music, SHE'S JUST AMAZINGGGG. I started a Pinterest account about her and an editing account on YouTube (@Style.swiftie13).

Even though I usually try to stop or hide the things I get bullied for at school and other places, I recently started getting bullied after people at my new school found out I was a swiftie, I was just not gonna take it so I fight back every time anyone hates on me, swifties or Taylor. Taylor Swift just had a good effect on me and changed me for the better. I really wanna go to the Eras Tour but it's not coming to where I live. My favorite album is definitely Reputation! I can't wait for Taylor's version. I can proudly declare being a swiftie and how Taylor Swift is a huge part of my life and personality." -Roha (YouTube@Style.swiftie13)

"When I was 8, my sister introduced me to Taylor Swift and I instantly fell in love with her. My first song was 'You belong with me'. Then onwards, I became a diehard swiftie. Even now, whenever my sister and I go anywhere by road, we always blast Taylor Swift songs on the radio. I remember, when 'midnights' was out, I was on cloud nine. My favorite era is 'speak now' or 'reputations'. My all time fav song is 'You belong with me' cuz it was my first song and I have soooo many beautiful memories associated with it. My 11th bday theme was 'midnights' cuz it came on the 21st of October which is just 3 days after my birthday. Unfortunately, I can't go to the Eras tour but thanks to the Eras tour movie, I could enjoy it in the full experience like the concert. Her songs are just the best. I love Taylor Swift and her melodious voice." -Saanvi D., age 11

***

"I have been a swiftie for 8 years! My very first favorite songs were "Shake it off (T.V.)" and "Bad Blood (T.V.)". I have never been to one of your concerts, but it's a dream of mine. I went to your Eras Tour movie, and I have the cups. Sadly, they were sold out of the popcorn buckets, but I did make lots of bracelets! My friends think it's crazy that I know the words to almost all of your 243 songs! I chose your song " I don't wanna live forever" for my first figure skating routine! Have a great birthday!" -Maddie, age 11

***

"Let's fast forward to 2014 when 1989 OV (original version) came out. I was at my cousin's house and I was 8 months old! Any way they were playing shake it off and I stood up and started dancing to it!

Let's fast forward back to 2019 when Lover came out and I'm heading to church camp and I notice and say to my dad,"OMG Taylor came out with a new album!" And so the first thing I do is listen to ME! And You Need To Calm Down!

Now let's fast forward to 2022. Midnights has just been released and me and my dad are listening to it and I'm thinking," Holy Crap! This is amazing!"

Now it's 2023 and 1989 TV has come out! So I listen to Is It Over Now? And I start breaking out in tears and I'm so excited!

That is why I became the swiftie I am today!" - Miriam

***

"I'll always remember first seeing the Eras Tour movie. I hadn't been able to get tickets for the real thing, plus my autism wouldn't have been able to handle it. I was so excited, I wore my folklore cardigan, painted my nails with the eras manicure, drew stars around my scars (and wrote "do u like dem" next to it), and even wrote "no its becky" on my collarbone. The only way I can describe how I felt watching that movie, is that you saw me. You understood me. You cared. Words can't describe how much respect I have for you. To be able to deal with so much shit and still be the most incredible and kind woman this town has ever seen is honestly so remarkable.

I've lived with anorexia for over a year, and when you played 'you're on your own kid' as a surprise song in the movie, I can't describe how much that meant to me. I often struggle to put my emotions or experience into words, but that song does it for me.

I also remember dancing to your songs with my mum in the car, or shamelessly in my bedroom at 3am to cheer me up when I felt I had nothing else, and thinking how happy 15 year old Tay who moved to Nashville to pursue her dream would be to know her music was making people this happy.

If you're reading this, I'd like you to know how incredible you are. I know you probably hear that a lot, but it's true. From the bottom of my heart, I really mean it.

Thank you for everything you've done for us, thank you for everything you stand for, and thank you for being such a ray of sunshine (or midnight rain, we don't mind!)." -Pep

***

"I was three years old when I heard shake it off and I LOVED IT. It was my favorite song and it was also my sisters favorite song and when I turned five and started growing up I listened to more of Taylor's music and I became OBSESSED and now I'm still obsessed with her music and every time I go out with friends and they play one of her songs they don't know the words but I do and now I just love Taylor Swift so so much!" -Eliana C.

***

"I have never been to a concert of Taylor's, but I would love to someday. But Taylor has helped me so much throughout my life, going through different breakups, or even just inspiring me to go out of my comfort zone to start singing for others and entering competitions. I am now so trained because of her I do covers with super high notes, and I just won the US Reflections Competition county and state level! I started listening to her since I was little, so I just grew up with her and that's how I became a swiftie. My favorite albums are Reputation and 1989. If I could say anything to Taylor it would be thank you so much for being so honest and really being a good person who just loves writing, singing, and meeting fans, not just for the money. She has made a huge impact on so many people's lives including mine. Thank you, Taylor, for everything you have done!" -Zoe

***

"I was around 4 years old when 1989 came out in 2014, and it changed my life. I've always loved to show emotion and the way that the songs in that album made me feel was great. My sister was very sick and in the hospital in 2015 and that album helped me through so much. Taylor also sent shirts and bracelets to the hospital because she wasn't able to come and visit and I got some, which made me very happy. I still wear the shirt to this day. Through all the things I've been through, Taylor's music has gone through it with me. I have gotten into my All-State Honor Choir twice, and I also play guitar and perform frequently. Taylor, if you see this, I am incredibly grateful for what you have done for me and I want to be a famous singer and do the same thing for other people that you have done for me and so many other swifties. I truly am thankful for everything that you have done for me." -Sadie

***

"The only reason I'm a swiftie is because of my best friend Hannah she has been a swiftie since we were in kindergarten but I was at her house one day having a sleepover and she started playing Taylor Swift. And I said this an amazing singer and I asked who was this she was looking at me like I was crazy and she said you don't know who Taylor Swift is! And like that who it is so when I got home I just sat on the couch and started playing your music my mom was you know who Taylor Swift and I said yes and she was shocked! So that is how I became a Swiftie! And I have been a swiftie ever since which was 5 years ago! I wish I could have attended the Eras Tour! We love you Taylor Swift!" -Palmer

***

"the first taylor song i fell in love with was highway don't care. i'm from the south, so we always listened to country in the car, and i remember this being one of the first songs i knew.

then in kindergarten it was bring your device to school day and i brought this old ipod that had been my moms. all i could really do with it was play solitaire and listen to music. a lot of the songs i'd grown up listening to were on it but i gravitated towards the taylor songs. i still remember which songs were on it: should've said no, picture to burn, our song, white horse, and love story. these were the first Taylor Swift songs i sang all the way through. this was how i fell in love with you.

now im older. i know every one of your songs. my friends and i take buzzfeed quizzes about you instead of doing our schoolwork. i went to your april 29 concert and you were amazing. your film was awesome as well. i did 89 of your 1989tv google puzzles. it's incredible how you bring people together. my birthday was september 30 and i got a speak now vinyl and im obsessed with it and with you.

you've taught me so much. your music has helped me through so many bad times. truthfully i think i would be a different person without your influence on my life.

"ain't no use defending words that you will never say" from cold as you is something that i carry with me and that song changed the way i think about my silence.

tied together with a smile has also changed me. i've always been incredibly insecure but your music is really helping me love myself more.

white horse was my favorite of your songs for a while. the line "i didn't know to be in love you had to fight to have the upper hand" resonated so deeply with me at the time as i had just been through my first breakup. thank you for helping me through it.

the best day reminds me to be grateful for my family. its rough sometimes because im the oldest of four and my mom is harsh sometimes, but every time your song comes on i cry thinking about how much i love them.

back to december taught me to apologize. im stubborn as shit, taylor, and i hate being wrong. but it's incredibly inspiring to me that you found the strength to apologize so publicly and so sincerely. same goes for innocent. it's unbelievable that you wrote something so sweet and beautiful about someone that caused you so much hurt. both of these songs make me a better person. it is insane that you have the power to change someone so much, and i'm forever grateful.

speak now taught me to be brave. i'll only live once, but you are alive in all the millions of people whose lives you've changed. please don't ever forget that.

i've never felt a love like the one you sing about in timeless, but i hope i will someday. this is one of my favorite songs in the world and definitely my favorite on speak now. it's such a beautiful concept.

i forgot that you existed taught me that closure isn't forgiveness, it's indifference. i hold so many grudges against people who have hurt me who i don't think i'll ever forgive, but this song gives me hope. i don't have to forgive. i just have to forget.

tolerate it didn't give me some grand epiphany, but somehow i still gained a world of knowledge from it. i think it's just awareness. i've become more aware of when im wanted and when im tolerated, and in turn i know who is important.

it's time to go helped me get over a bad friendship. i was writing an apology text to this girl while listening to your music and when this song came on something clicked inside me. i deleted the text. it really was time to go. how did you know?

the outside, stay beautiful, iomwiwy, forever and always, jump then fall, ciwtr, superstar, tosotd, twaf, that's when, dear john, never grow up, last kiss, long live, ours, superman, foolish one, itwam, the last time, holy ground, sad beautiful tragic, begin again, tmik, cbbh, ronan, nothing new, forever winter, run, all too well 10min, iwyw, hygtg, new romantics, slut!, is it over now, komh, dwoht, dress, ithk, dbatc, sygb, afterglow, daylight, my tears ricochet, timt, invisible string, mad woman, peace, hoax, gold rush, tis the damn season, happiness, coney island, ivy, cowboy like me, long story short, rwylm, vigilante shit, the great war, bttws, high infidelity, would've could've should've, dear reader, and hits different are all my other favs. i could have written a whole paragraph about any of these. (and believe me when i said i had to take so many off this list just to save space)

i know it sounds like im just rambling by now.

but i promise im not. i mean every word of this. you changed my life, and i hope this tiny gesture changes yours in some miniscule way. thank you for everything and forever. i love you." -Kacy

***

"Dear Taylor Swift,

I have been a swiftie since I was 4. My mom would always play your music in the car and I would quietly sing along because I was too shy to sing in front of my mom or anyone. But, then my mom started listening to country and I got annoyed by that pretty quickly. I still love country music, especially yours. Then when I was 10 I started listening to more of your music. I would dance and sing on my trampoline. I liked the albums red, fearless, 1989, and lover. Then one day my dad demolished my trampoline. I was very sad about that. Then I got a new trampoline but this one didn't have the same vibe. so I took matters into my own hands and took a pair of my brother's headphones, plugged them in and listened to your music and fell more in love with it. Now I got my mom to listen to your music again and, we both sing your music in the car on grocery store runs, or whenever. I also love all your albums now. I really like speak now, 1989, lover, debut my favorite song has to be All too well (10 minutes). I can finally sing the whole song.

I love your music but you know what's also amazing? Your show. So I also saw your movie with my friend who's a new swiftie and loves your music and I sang your songs and wasn't shy for once. Love you Taylor I hope one day I can see you and your concert in person. You made me more confident. Love you Taylor." -Brooklyn M.

"I was in fourth grade and my friend was singing Mr.Perfectly Fine during lunch. I decided I liked the tune so I went home and started listening to her songs. I started out with just fearless, but I listened to all her albums one by one, and now Taylor is the most important thing in the world to me." -Sylvie

***

"I started listening to Taylor when I was 3 or 4. I heard her on the radio and my mom started playing her more and more. Then when 1989 came out I was addicted. Shake it off and Out of the Woods were my favorite songs. I'd play them non stop. When I was 6 I stopped listening as much and kinda just stopped listening to music over all. Then around 6 months ago I decided to just play one of her songs and I couldn't stop. Her music has gotten me through so much and I'm so grateful. The stories in her lyrics just hit different (Pun intended) Hopefully one day I'll get to meet her! Thank you so much Taylor!" -Mya T.

***

"One day in 2015 I was driving in the car and a song came on. My mom turned it up and started singing it and I wasn't paying all that much attention to the song. But when I got in the shower that night I couldn't think of what music to turn on. I thought and thought for a few minutes when I remembered that song that had really good lyrics... what was it called? Our Song, that's it! I turned it on repeat and learned the lyrics within three listens. Anyway, that was the only Taylor Swift song I knew for 8 years. Until my friend told me I just had to listen to more of her music. I pushed the suggestion aside for two weeks until I was bored and put Midnights on. When the album was over, I craved more of her music, so I turned on Debut. Then another album. And another. By the time I'd finished her discography, I started it over again. I considered myself a Swiftie, and I still do. And Taylor Swift has helped me so much and her songs are the most relatable pieces of literature ever. And to wrap up my Swiftie journey here's a few of my favorite things and why:

Album-reputation (the vibes are perfect and the overall message is awesome)

Song-I Did Something Bad (it's just the perfect song and the bridge is amazing)

Era-Midnights/1989 Taylor's Version (they both make me so happy that she's happy)

Tour-repuation Tour/Eras Tour (omg the production level is TOP TIER)

Bridge-champagne problems (do I have to explain? YOUR MIDAS TOUCH ON THE CHEVY DOOR-)

Anyways, I love you, Taylor!" -Vannie

***

"I became a swiftie because when my best friend, Carolina, who lives very far away came to visit over the summer and we started listening to Taylor Swift! At the time, we loved the songs 22, Cruel Summer and Karma!

We were singing T.S. Songs practically the entire time she was here. Wherever we went, we were always singing those songs! We are now huuuuuge swifties and just recently found out we are going to the ERAS TOUR!!!

We still have a long time and have only known for about a week but we are so excited and have already made over 10 friendship bracelets each! We are hoping we get the 22 hat because that is our all time favorite song! My favorite albums are 1989, Speak now,

Midnights and Lover! Our motto that we go by is " Being a Swiftie is not a phase, It's a lifestyle!" -Laura, age 11

***

"Me and my best friend Laura love you so much. When I visited her in July 2022, we got obsessed with the songs Cruel Summer, 22, and Karma.

Now we're the biggest Swifties ever. We were so sad that we couldn't get 2024 ERA TOUR tickets for the USA.But we convinced are parents and now we're going to the Indianapolis concert. We couldn't be more grateful and excited.We both love you so much and hope you have a GREAT bday.

Here's our motto: being a swiftie isn't a phase, it's a lifestyle." -Carolina age 12

***

"Taylor, I want to thank my cousin, who I am going to keep anonymous, for becoming a swiftie. When we started High school together he would always sing your song "Karma" and I absolutley fell in love. So I went to check out the rest of your "Midnights" album and I was in LOVE. So I listened to the rest of your albums and now its all I listen to. I listen to your songs when I'm happy, sad, mad, whatever i'm feeling, you always have a song to fit the mood. You will never understand how much your music has forever changed my life and I want to thank you so much for that." - Aislin

***

"When I was 4, my dad introduced me to Taylor. I became a HUGE fan. When I was 5-7, I shared a nanny with one of my friends who liked Taylor. We used to go on YouTube and think of dances to all her Lover songs. (Lover had just come out) Then, I still listened to her and when I was 10, she announced the Eras Tour. I really wanted to go, but we couldn't get tickets. Then, 2 weeks before the concert, we got last minute tickets and I was so excited. It was the best night of my life. Then I went as her for Halloween, and now I'm practically speaking Taylor Swift lyrics." -anonymous

***

"When I was little (around 4 or 5), I LOVED listening to all of 1989. Dancing around to "Shake it Off". We bought the CD and I listened to all of 1989 every day. I loved Taylor and only listened to 1989 and Lover for the most part. The past few years, however, I have become a hardcore swiftie!! I know every Tay Tay song, lyric, and music video by heart.

Taylor truly is bigger than the whole sky. She means the world to me!! She has helped me and millions of people around the world through so much and I will be grateful for that forever and always!!

Taylor, I cannot tell you how grateful I am for you and your music. You have helped me and so many other people across the world get through so many tough times. I can listen to your music, and it makes me so happy and gives me something to relate to! I love how kind, funny, and caring you are!! You truly care for everyone and are the most genuine person!! You have the most amazing voice and such a big heart!! You really are bigger than the whole sky! Long live Tay Tay!" - Brynn

***

"As a kid, I used to love listening to Bad Blood. I'd always watch the music video on repeat and think "Wow, she's so cool. I want to be like her." One day, I just stopped. A couple of years later, my friend and I made a Spotify playlist together. She added the song, "The Lakes". Once I listened to it, I fell in love. I started exploring more of her music. When I did, I realized what I missed out on. Then she released Midnights and I realized that she does not make any bad songs. Her music helped me get through tough times. She gave me hope that one day everything would get better. I realized I wasn't alone. I love you Taylor, thank you for everything." -anonymous

***

"I became a swiftie when I was 3 years old. I would beg my dad to play Taylor Swift in the car. The first album of hers I ever owned was Speak Now. She got me through middle school and now almost all of high school. She inspired me to write songs and find my love for music. My 2 most precious memories of Taylor are when I bought the 1989 album on it's release date with my own money. I made my entire family, even my cousins, listen to that CD 3 times in a row. My second is the Eras Tour. It was my first time seeing her in concert and I was so happy. I still consider that the best night of my life." -Mariah S.

***

"I started out as an indie gamer where I had a couple friends who were swifties. I wondered what was the deal with Taylor at first by listening to Lover as it was their favourite album and I immediately started loving her music. This was how I started joining the swiftie community. When I was younger, I heard the song 'Never Grow Up' played from my mom's phone. It helped me sleep and it was so nostalgic as I listened to it years later, especially the re-record of the song in Speak Now (Taylor's Version). This is a very memorable song and I hope more people will give it more recognition someday.

I really love Taylor so much as her music is so damn beautiful and amazing. The lyrics in her songs are really wise, especially in the albums folklore and evermore. I even learnt some new words just by listening to her music. The language techniques in the lyrics are really genius of her. Taylor Swift would really be fit to be an English Teacher as she said in her 73 Questions interview by Vogue.Taylor' music really means a set of stories to me. A Taylor Swift album is like a book and the songs are like the chapters of the book if it is placed in the right order. The lyrics are like the text written in the chapter. When some music videos of these songs were released, I've always visualised what kind of music videos songs like "Getaway Car" or "betty" could get. This is like visualising the story when reading a book. Overall, Taylor is like a musical author or writer.

Whenever I feel down or angry, I listen to a calm and/or sad song to move out of my downstate. It somehow works for me as Taylor's sad songs are quite powerful. Her happy songs have helped motivate me into doing things I'm unable to do. Taylor has songs of every mood possible like if you have nothing "Better Than Revenge" or if you feel like the story's "Anti-Hero". Taylor is the music industry.My favourite song by Taylor is 'happiness'. It's such an immaculate and soft song and really hits different from other songs about moving on from a breakup. It honestly sounds like the time Taylor went into hiding in 2017 when nobody physically saw her for a year due to overexposure. It was happiness without anyone's input. The song really represents that which gives a strong reason why it's my favourite song. It's very hopeful and resilient and I wish more people will realise that.

The best part of being a swiftie is getting to hear remixes and mashups of Taylor's songs. It was so good listening to "if this song was on another album" mashups and even the phenomenal Complete Eras Megamix which was unfortunately taken down on YouTube. This shows how much Swifties appreciate the music of Taylor and how they mix her music.

If I could be able to tell Taylor something, I would first say that her music is the best and that Lover is my favourite pop album." -DP

***

"I became a swiftie from my friend just when Midnights came out. I had just listened to anti hero on the radio for the first time and absolutely loved it. Later, I got Eras Tour tickets, where I had the best night of my life. Ever since then I have adored her." -Ava

***

"I became a swiftie while watching YouTube when the look what you made me do pop up in my for you. Since then I have become a swiftie." -Felix

***

"I first heard Taylor at a party, shake it off was playing. I started listening to 1989 and I loved it. Through Reputation and Lover, I was a fan but not a swiftie. Then, when folklore came out I realised I love her music. Folklore will always be my favourite album. Its so beautiful and poetic. I've been a die hard swiftie ever since." -Emily

***

"A few years ago I saw a few p.o.v s on YouTube and the background music was blank space... I thought it was a nice song but at that time I didn't know the name of the song but my sis told me about it a few days later and since then I started listening to her songs and now I am a huge swiftie." -Aina

***

"Well it started off when I heard about reputation from Taylor! I didn't know at the time who Taylor was because I was little. I asked my dad for some platform with music to download and he said yes! Well when I opened the app I saw you can search with voice. I, of course, did. I listened to it and loved it!!I later listened to some other of her albums and saw so many things about her!And that's how I became a swiftie." - Mila

***

"I was really close to my older neighbor. She was practically a sister to me and she would babysit me all the time. And this girl was a huge swiftie. She had Taylor Swift and Fearless on cd and when Speak Now came out her mom drove her, my older brother, and me to five different stores looking for it and I was a baby at the time. I grew up listening to Taylor. She was always playing so I began to be obsessed but when I went to school I got made fun of for being a swiftie so I stopped listening. But one day I was on our family iPad when a video was recommended to me. It was the Look What You Made Me Do music video. I watched and was petrified. I refused to listen to the rest of the album cause it was "scary" to eight year old me. After years of being bullied for liking Taylor and not listening to any of her songs I decided to finally get back into her music last summer. I listened to every song from every album, even the ones I missed out on listening to. And soon I was obsessed again. I bought vinyls, cds, and went to the movie three times. Now I don't get bullied because I'm not afraid to be myself. Thank you so much Taylor and Happy Birthday!" -Gianna

***

"I became a swiftie last summer, this is how it went. So it was after my cousin went to the Eras Tour we have a tradition that we go up north for a week and stay in a cabin. My cousin had told me all about you like your songs, and merchandise. And now I can't stop listening to you. I went to see the Eras Tour movie. You were amazings!" -Loa

***

"I became a swiftie when I was 6 years old. My mom would play love story and you belong with me all the time. I also listened to some songs from 1989 but wasn't that big of a swiftie until I was 11 years old. You are so motivational and I love you so much. I can't even describe what you did to me. I was unable to get tickets to your concert. But I went to the movie and SCREAMED MY HEART OUT the whole theater was staring at me and my friends. I love you so much and thanks for all you've done." -anonymous

***

"Hey, I'm Sarah and I live in Slovenia. I've been a Swiftie since the 1989 era. The first few songs I've ever heard were love story or you belong with me. I really liked Taylor in her country years, but when 1989 came out, I was SOLD. I've decided to spend the rest of my life as an ultimate Swiftie. As I already said, I live in Slovenia. And if you don't know yet, Slovenia is a small country. We don't have a stadium big enough to hold 73.000 people for Taylor's Eras tour. So I don't know if I'll ever actually see her live. So it would mean the world to me if I made it into the book. I rly hope Taylor sees this and if she does, I wanna thank the channel @alltooswift (on youtube) for giving me the opportunity to type these words to Taylor. I also have a YouTubechannel called @TaySwift13- So Tay Tay if you're reading this, I just want you to know that you are the best thing that has ever happened to me, you inspire me so much, not just your music, but YOU as a person. I really hope I can see you live someday. Being a Swiftie isn't just liking your music, it's a lifestyle. So thank you for that." -Sarah, Slovenia (YouTube@TaySwift13)

***

"I first became interested in Taylor after attending a summer camp where they played her song "You Belong With Me" and I fell in love with it. I'm sure I drove the counselors crazy requesting that song be played over and over again. After that summer camp I decided to take a deep dive into the fearless era... and then speak now, and then Red, so on and so forth. I was in love. Taylors music is more than just notes and a melody to me. It has gotten me through loss, heartbreak, and pain. It has in a way, healed me. My all time favorite Taylor Swift song is "Style", but my current most relatable song is "Marjorie." I recently lost communication with someone very important to me in my life and even though "Marjorie" is a song about death and grieving over a lost loved one, I feel that this person is practically dead to me and I'm grieving that loss. My favorite thing about being a Swiftie is the community. I love how the people are so uplifting and it's like one big family. Finally, I leave you with a message for Taylor.

Dear Taylor,

First off I love, love, LOVE you and I will be attending your Indianapolis show on November 3rd, 2024. I'll be seated in the 549th section and I would probably die if I got the "22" hat, and so with that being said...come and find me Taylor!" -Ava, age 15.

***

"I became a Swiftie on May 7th, 2019. It started out as a normal day, and I had just come home from school. Being in 5th grade, a lot was changing for me. I had been bullied that whole school year, and I started to wonder if I had any worth left. Just then, as I went to my bedroom and turned my radio on, I heard Taylor's song "Change" for the first time. I listened carefully to every lyric. After it was over, I had to know who it was by. I looked it up, and there was Taylor's name. Weeks after that, I had listened to the entire Fearless, Speak Now, Red and Debut albums. After getting to know Taylor a bit better, I decided to get to know the fandom. I found several different fan channels on Youtube, but the one that stood out the most was Lauren Lipman. From her, I learned everything I needed to know to be a Swiftie, but I wasn't a proper one yet. You see, I was only at the edge of the rabbit hole. That all changed when the Lover album came out. When I heard "Daylight" for the first time, I was pushed down the rabbit hole, and I've been falling ever since. Now I'm in my Freshman year of high school, and I'm faced with several of the same challenges, but I now know that I can always turn to Taylor's lyrics, and the Swifties for guidance." -Keira J.

***

"When I was a little girl, I always heard lots of Taylor's hits like shake it off and blank space, I always thought they were so fun and cool but never got round to trying to discover more of her songs. When I was 10, I discovered lots of her albums and quickly and swiftly became a huge fan. I listened to her music everyday, her songs took over all my playlists. My parents thought that it was a phase but they quickly discovered that it wasn't.

For years and years since then, I've been listening to her music everyday, my favourite song changing ALL the time depending on my mood. Taylor Swift is now such an important part of my life and her songs have helped me get through so much. My favourite albums are Speak now and Folklore, I am obsessed!" -Tamar

***

"I became a Swiftie in 2014 when I was 4. I loved sitting on the couch watching music videos but my favourite was always when Shake It Off came on. I would get up and scream and sing and dance my heart out to this amazing song that I loved so much. It was always my favourite and as I grew up I held the song dear to my heart.

Love Story is my song. The night I went to the debutant ball with my family to watch my brother and when the music came on they invited families to come and dance. When love story came on me and my dad got up and danced our hearts out and it felt absolutely magical that night with the disco lights shining pink and blue over us. That's just one of the many experiences i have had with Taylor that make me who i am. Thank you Taylor for all you have done for me. Also, shoutout to my friend Matlida, who's also a swiftie like me!" -Millie E.

***

"I became a Swiftie in late 2022 (although I already knew some of her songs pretty well) through Midnights and it was honestly the best discovery I ever had in music. This summer I failed to get tickets for the Eras Tour in France (my country) but I went to the Eras Tour movie in my local movie theater on October 14 with my girlfriend. I kissed her for the first time during Lover, and it turned out we had both planned to do it during that song which was so surprising and wholesome. This was truly one of the best nights of my life and I would do it again a thousand times if I could."
-Bleuenn

***

"What convinced me to be a swiftie is my awesome step siblings that were swifties and then I got hooked on to it!! The first song I ever heard by her was either blank space or you belong with me.

I love Taylor bc her music is awesome and she's an amazing person overall. Taylor and her music helped me because I was in a very dark place like depression and whenever I started listening to Taylor it made me feel way better and now I'm in a safer place and I love Taylor for that.

My favorite song is sparks fly from speak now because I just love jamming to it and I know all the lyrics and it's such a good song!! Best part about being a swiftie is the amazing community and there is always something new and everyone is sooo nice!

If I could tell Taylor something it would be that I literally LOVE her and I wanna thank her for making my life wayyy better and for everything she does." -Ava

***

"'I'm a huge swiftie! I first heard shake it off on

the sing movie and i immediately searched you up and you have been my favorite artist ever since. Sadly I've never been to one of your shows but I dream of going one day. I have a full document of my favorite songs but some of them are All Too Well 10 min version, Gorgeous, Ready For It and Illicit Affairs. My favorite album is reputation. I hope to see you live one day. I love you so much! I have been to the movie 5 times and have countless friendship bracelets. I have also made and printed posters and have all of your album covers taped to my wall. I love you!!!!!" -Zoryana

***

"Last year I discovered Taylor with the song enchanted and ever since I have been the biggest swiftie ever. I absolutely love her country eras and my favorite era is speak now . I can't go to the Eras Tour but it would literally be my absolute dream to go. I love her so much I can't even imagine in my wildest dreams meeting her." -Steph

***

"I became a swiftie when I was 3 years old. It was when 1989 came out and I absolutely loved it. I would sing it in the car with my mum everywhere. Since then, I've been obsessed with Tay. My favorite song is the last great american dynasty, because I just love the bridge. btw i'm a huge rep stan!" -Liliana

***

"Since 1989 (not tv) I had known her music, but only the popular ones like Shake It Off or Blank Space. But my horseback riding stable does a trip to Belgium every year during the summer. All my friends were swifties (this was right after midnights came out) and reintroduced me to Taylor Swift. When I was younger, I memorized a lot of popular Taylor Swift songs, without knowing that Taylor Swift was the writer. So, when I amazed all my friends by singing each word to each song in the car to 1989, they were so surprised. And that's when I fell in love with you, and your music. I have become a diehard swiftie ever since then and have been to the movie and the Eras tour with my friends who reintroduced me to Taylor Swift. Taylor, you made me find the joy in my life that I've been needing. Thank you, even though I'll probably never get to meet you, we all love you. Happy birthday my queen!!" -Emerson

***

"I vividly recall a particular day during those early school years when our teacher gave us the opportunity to choose songs to play during lunchtime. Excitedly, my friends and I gathered around a computer, scrolling through Spotify, trying to find the perfect song to share with our classmates. Little did I know that this seemingly ordinary day would lead to a life-changing discovery.

As we clicked on each song, my ears were met with various melodies and rhythms, but none of them quite captured my heart like a song called "Love Story." From the moment the first notes played, I was immediately captivated. The melody was so addicting, and the rhythm perfectly complemented it. However, what truly moved me were the lyrics, which told a tale reminiscent of Shakespeare's Romeo and Juliet, coincidentally, a topic we were studying in class at the time.

In that exact moment, I became a swiftie. From that day forward, your music became an integral part of my life. Every day and every night, before drifting off to sleep, I would listen to your songs. They became the soundtrack to my dreams, filling my heart with joy, inspiration, and a sense of connection. Your artistry and ability to capture emotions through your lyrics and melodies have touched me in ways that are truly indescribable.

Your music has been a constant companion throughout the years, accompanying me through various milestones, celebrations, and even difficult times. Your songs have given me solace, uplifted my spirits, and reminded me of the power of music to heal and unite.

Thank you, Taylor Swift, for being an extraordinary artist, for sharing your talent with the world, and for being a beacon of light and strength. May your birthday be filled with love, joy, and the knowledge that you have made an incredible impact on the lives of so many." -Elisa C., Hong Kong

***

"Dear Taylor,

I can't remember when I first heard your music, but I know that I can't imagine life without it. I've listened to your music on repeat, and I think I fall more in love with it each time. You put so much time and effort into your music andI truly love and appreciate every aspect of it.

As someone that has struggled with mental health, your music has been the 'invisible string' for me. I have been told countless times by family and friends that I talk about your music too much, but it might just be impossible for me to stop. I don't think I will ever be able to explain how grateful I am for your music, as it means too much to put into words. I am so incredibly grateful for the swiftie fandom, and love the sense of community and belonging found here.

Having a safe space in which I can share my excitement or nerves over something, and receive support and encouragement from people across the world is amazing! I love being able to discuss the latest surprise songs, or speculate about which outfit will be worn for each era.

I found out the best news today, that I will be going to watch the Era's Tour with my best friend and my mum! I'm so incredibly thrilled that I will be able to watch this concert in-person and share the excitement with everyone around me.
I don't think I could ever explain just how much you and your music means to me, but I am filled with awe for you every day." -Olivia

***

"I remember when you became a singer and no one really knew who you were, and now you're the top singer! I can't express how proud I am of you! I've been to the Eras Tour and the Movie! I'm such a big fan and I know you will move mountains. Wait, you already have! I can't believe you've started from a little 16 year old who didn't know anything and now are a huge artist who everyone knows! I'm just so proud of you and can't believe you've made it so far so fast! Most people just like your music (maybe not even) but your personality is the best personality anyone can have. I wish I could meet you in person but I know that probably will never happen. I just hope this one stands out to you from all of these. I love you sooo very much!" -Claire

***

"It was October 21st, 2022. My school was alive with the buzz of Taylor Swift's influence. My classmates were talking about Taylor, and how she had dropped a new album that day. My best friend, let's call her F, was an enormous swiftie, and she had been recommending Taylor to me for years. I had always turned her recommendations down, because I thought it was "quirky" and "different" to dislike her and her music. However, that day on October 21st, 2022, everything changed.

I sat down at my computer, opening up the Spotify webpage. I went to Taylor's Spotify profile, and I played Lavender Haze for the first time. This was the very first occurrence I had ever willingly sat down and listened to Taylor, and I loved it. The production, the lyrics, the visuals, everything was perfect. Taylor became one of my biggest inspirations.

I can always talk to my friends about Taylor, and how much we clown about theories. I went to the Era's Tour Movie with F and we had the time of our lives! We were singing and dancing, and I don't know any other force of music that could bring people together like that other than the one and only Taylor Swift.

Taylor had been an anchor for me. Any time I felt like I was floating off to sea, the anchor tethered me down to reality and kept me grounded. When I moved to a new school, I had no friends. I used Taylor's music as a comforting tool for me. I had her music on repeat, and it was almost like I had someone there with me, telling me it was all going to be okay.

I have moved so far from my mindset of being "quirky" and "different". I have been inspired by Taylor to become a songwriter, and she has been such an amazing inspiration as well. Compared to that sunny October day over one year ago, I am both better and kinder than I used to be.

Thank you so much, Taylor." -Marco (@meliodys on youtube)

***

"Hi, I'm Ava! I'm a really big fan of you and your music. I wanted to tell you some things about how your music has impacted me in many ways!! If you don't have the time to read this, of course it's alright!

My story begins at 4 years old, sitting in my aunt's car. I started finding my passion for singing at the time..my love for music was somewhat starting! Now, my dad visits his family a lot, in Los Angeles! Driving from restaurants, the song that would play in the car all the time was the first song I've ever heard from you, maybe the only song I've ever heard so far because my aunt wouldn't stop playing it. I can understand why now!"Long Live the walls we crashed through". That phrase will forever be in my heart.

Over the next 3 years, I listened to a lot of your hits, specifically Blank Space. Man, I don't know what kind of energy that song brought out of my tiny six year old self, but it was so great that I almost broke my dad's heater. But I also watched your Reputation Concert on Netflix! The next couple years up until I was about 9 were a bit hard. At school, I started experiencing people making comments about how confident in myself I was, or what I would wear, how I would act, you name it. Over the pandemic, hormones set in, and puberty hit... gross. I started feeling really insecure about myself, and my self esteem was NOT doing good. But I remember, Folklore and Evermore really helped my mood and helped me calm myself. I also discovered your Miss Americana documentary! I really appreciated, and still do appreciate how real you are to your fans and people in general. Some celebrities aren't like that, but you definitely are!!

When I was starting sixth grade, your Midnights album came out. My gosh I was so excited for the actual tour and album! Those things were pretty much the only things on my list for Christmas. This was also the time I could finally start a small fan channel for you...because I finally gained the confidence to. You have created the kindest, greatest, most beautiful fan base anyone can ever have. The community...it's just..unreal!! I love them all so much. The day of the public sale for your Eras Tour had come...but I couldn't participate because of school. When I found out they were all sold out....I broke down. I don't think I could stop crying for three nights straight because of the fear that I would never get to see the person who has impacted my life so much, saved my esteem, and most importantly inspired me to chase my dreams.

Christmas Day, I had just finished unboxing my gifts. I got my first vinyl of you!! It was the evermore one! I played it for the first time on my first record player, and sat there in silence listening to Champagne Problems. My dad spoke. "So you have your ego, save your own money, and continue doing good in school for this. Mom and I are very proud of you.". I was very confused. "For?" I responded. That moment they pointed at the vinyl player. My heart dropped. I bursted out screaming and crying...I was actually gonna experience your amazing talent!!! See my Idol! I will never forget that moment. Ever since that day I tried to emotionally prepare myself, but I don't think that worked. July 29th, the timer started on the stage and

I was already screaming, crying, and jumping all over the place. From the moment you came out to the end of Enchanted...it was just unreal for me...screaming and dancing plus extra singing like no one was watching. The moment I saw the Koi Fish Guitar I couldn't breathe. When you played the first chord to Long Live... I don't think I've ever cried so much for something. Thank you for making that happen Taylor, I can't thank you enough for adding Long Live to the set list. From listening to it in the car, to watching it on a screen, to finally experiencing it...the memories all flashed in my head. The rest of the concert, trading bracelets, singing, and losing my voice was a blast. That moment was also when I got to show my best friend Sara who you truly are!! She's never listened to any music...and she's 17!! I was really glad you were at her first concert, and she could really live her life without lots of restrictions for a night! I would do it all again, I could never get sick of it. Now, "I'm doing better than I ever was". Dressing up as a Smurf in honor of 1989 TV, Watching your movie at 9:30pm on Oct. 13th, and growing up with your music...I would do it all again. I hope you continue doing what you're doing Taylor, you've helped me with confidence and become who I am today. You've taught me how to not be hard on myself in sports, music, songwriting, and so much more. If you ever feel down or need a break...please take care of yourself. If you ever feel sad...just know you're not alone, we all got your back!! Without a doubt, forever your legacy will "Long Live"!" -Ava

**

"I was born in 2010 and at that time I guess Taylor was getting more and more popular in the whole world I think I first heard of her when Shake It Off came out I don't remember the date or the exact moment but I know that I loved it from the beginning on so I guess my parents just downloaded the album red and 1989 and from that point on we were streaming the songs over and over again.

And by the way I also loved Rihannas and Calvin Harris' song This Is What You Came For and now I know that Taylor wrote it. I think I was just meant to become a swiftie. And my birthdate is actually 1.2.10 and that equals 13 I guess that's another sign. And when I was younger, like eight or nine, I always told my friends I wanted to be 13 because you're a teenager then and everything's better and I think it's funny looking back to those days. Actually, I also loved the number 13 because of how it's pronounced. I don't know why So I think that's why 13 and Taylor Swift are so important to me. Die hard Swifie: 2014-forever and always." -Siesie

***

"I have been a swiftie since I was 6 years old (I'm now 13) and her music means everything to me. We all love her dedication to her fans and her music and we wish her all the best for anything she wants." -Jasmine

***

"I think I became a swiftie around July 2022. I know that's not that long ago but I was entering a new chapter of my life at the time, and had a lot of challenges ahead of me so I think her music came to me at the perfect time.

I was at the Reputation tour when I was younger but I honestly don't remember much of it because I didn't know that many songs at the time which really annoys me!!! I'm so lucky I was able to attend nonetheless.

I have this really distinct memory of hearing I Knew you Were Trouble when I was maybe 4 or 5 in a play center for some reason, so I think that must've been the 1st Taylor Swift song I ever heard.

If I had one message to tell Taylor? Probably that her fans want nothing but the best for her. She could stop making music right now and disappear for the rest of her life and that would be enough for us. I am forever grateful for everything she's done to change lives around the world. If somehow you're reading this Taylor, thank you." -S

***

"I have been a little swiftie since the 1989 era. I was also born with spina bifida which has caused some obstacles in my life but I would like to thank Taylor and her music for truly getting me through hard times and motivating me to keep going. Her and her music makes me feel like I can conquer anything and that I am not alone.

I'm not sure what the first song was I heard but I have a core memory of getting the 1989 cd for Christmas from my aunt who introduced me to her. My whole family has always been so supportive of my love for Taylor and I can proudly say I have also converted them into swifties! I remember from then on blasting the music in the car just singing my little heart out. For the next couple of years my aunt gifted me more Taylor cds such as Red and reputation. Because I was only 6 years old I could not fully comprehend all of the lyrics and fully appreciate them like I do now although I have not even gone through a break up yet!

Fast forward to the last day of 2018, I distinctly

remember getting home from a ball drop thing that my town does and I remember my mom mentioning that she was coming out with a reputation stadium tour film. I was so excited I still got to experience the concert even though the thought of going to the actual tour was kind of out of the picture because I was still young and she was not touring anywhere nearby. Soon after she announced Lover and this was the era I became a diehard swiftie. I loved how powerful I felt after listening to "The Man" and the lyrics in "Death by a Thousand Cuts". This was the era I received Lover Fest tickets for my 12th birthday. I was elated! When it eventually got canceled, I was obviously devastated but from quarantine we got my favorite album ever: folklore. I remember my dad was looking on social media and he told me that Taylor would surprise drop an album at midnight. I love this album because I can relate to the feelings and the lyrics she displays in the album. So basically ever since then I have been a hardcore swiftie! I cannot thank Taylor enough for what she has done for me and the whole world. I love that her music has brought together such a tight-knit loving community from all different backgrounds. I am grateful to have grown up in a world with Taylor Swift in it or the world (Taylor's Version)." -Campbell H.

***

"I have been listening to Taylor since I first heard YBWM and Love Story on the radio as a kid. When my cousin danced to Mean at her recital I was so happy. The Red singles were my favorite. But when 1989 came out, as I preferred pop music, I graduated from fan to swiftie status. Wonderland was my favorite song and I wrote a poem about my best friend and I based on Wildest

Dreams in middle school. As time went on, I loved her music more and more, especially when folklore and evermore came out, and I discovered I love this genre the most. Since the release of Midnights, I've caught up with everything in the Taylor Swift Cinematic Universe. She has been the one artist who inspired and stuck with me throughout my whole life and always will!" - Madeline

***

"It was summer and I was going through transitioning gender wise and I was having a tough time figuring out who I was myself. But then when I was over at my friend's house and all of a sudden I heard the shake it off bridge, let me just tell you, it was a sick beat. From that point on, my life was Taylor, I was always telling myself "Next time she goes on tour, I'M GOING" when she came to Minneapolis I went through the great war and got seats for the tour, it was the best time of my life. Taylor helped me through a difficult time and I will forever be thankful for that." -Sullivan C.

***

"I used to not listen to music, but my friend said it helped her focus while she was working, so I decided to try it. Spotify made a playlist for me and it included some of your songs. I loved the songs, I didn't really get into it though, but spotify kept adding more of your songs to my playlist. As I continued listening I realized how good your songs were, and started learning more of your songs. I realized music could change my mood from sad to happy in just a minute or two. Your songs specifically did this. About five months after I realized you were such an amazing singer and songwriter, you announced Eras Tour dates in Toronto, and I have some family there so i decided to try to get two tickets to that show but no luck): A few months later, The Eras Tour movie came out and so did 1989 tv. (Is it over now? Hits different.) I saw the movie with five of my friends and the experience was unreal. About two weeks ago you announced dates in Vancouver, but I didn't get tickets yet (I still have hope for the avion sale!) Your holiday collection dropped today, and I'm asking for the seagull ornament for Christmas this year! Happy 34th birthday!" -Kay

***

"I was about 3 when I heard my first Taylor swift song (shake it off) me and my mom were in the car driving to my gymnastics class when it came on and I started dancing my heart out! We got home and immediately she turned it on for me and by the next two days I had the whole song memorized. Since I was like a 3 yr old, I wasn't technically a swiftie but when Reputation came out, my aunt somehow got tickets for Dallas N1 and I had the time of my life. I had so much fun and I was so grateful!

I can't really remember when I stopped listening to Taylor but I'm assuming it was around fifth grade because I had this whole phase of just yeah you get lol, but when midnights came out I was obsessed because I had made a friend her name is Stella and she introduced Taylor to me again and one day in the car with my grandma, mom, brother, and grandpa, we were all waiting for my dads store to open up so we could go to this big event and my grandma said "hey evie you know she's doing a concert I think she's coming to Houston" Taylor was the only thing on my mind for 6 months. I spent those 6 months memorizing every single song which was a struggle since I hadn't listened to her in so long, but when April 21st 2023 came around I was so excited and had the best concert experience of my life!! Trading bracelets, singing, dancing, everything!" -Evie, Texas

***

"Being a Swiftie is 94% of my happiness. When I listen to Taylor it just fills me with so much joy and emotion and I always feel better than I did before. I started to become a swiftie just this May (2023). It happened that after the Eras Tour had started I started hearing about her more. I would start to listen to her music and explore some of her songs and albums I hadn't heard of before. My friend also began being interested in Taylor, so that encouraged me to listen to Taylor more. By June she was 89% of the music I listened to and now she's 99% of the music I listen to. Taylor is just so awesome!

There are 2 songs where I will always remember where I first listened to them. The first one is Hits Different (it really hits different to me!) I was in the car with my best friend (the one who is is a swiftie) . We were going to the mall when she's like "there's this new song by Taylor I want to listen to." I'm like "Sure, let's hear it." It was HIts Different and for some reason that sticks in my mind. The second is New Romantics, it's me and my friend's special song. We were just sitting on her bedroom floor and it came on and we were like "Damn, this is a good song!" Now we have choreography for it!

Taylor, if you ever see this just know you bring so much joy and happiness into my world." -Poppy V.

***

"I was in a very dark spot last year. I wanted to

give up so many times. Life felt so overwhelming.

But then something happened one magical night. I rediscovered Taylor Swift. I fell in love with Love Story. Whenever I listened to it, I felt like life was 100% worth living. I listened to Love Story day and night; at school, at home, at the park... Wherever I went. I got better; my grades got better, my social life got better, and I realized that I wasn't depressed anymore. Soon, I was the opposite of depressed. Then I listened to 1989, then reputation, then Lover, Midnights, Red, Speak Now, the other songs of Fearless, evermore, folklore, and Taylor's first album. And I can't express how much I adore the Lover album. Every day now, I feel like I'm living in a world that's all baby pink and blue.

Now I remember all the time that when I was so little, my dad would turn on the Shake It Off music video on the TV and we danced like there was nothing wrong with the world. As if nothing could ever go wrong.

I don't know why, but I feel like Taylor's my best friend. I've never met her, I've never seen her in real life... But I watched her documentary, Miss Americana. I listened to her NYU graduation speech. It feels like she is the best, the purest person I know. At least, it feels like I know her. I don't know if I'll ever meet her, or if I'll ever have the opportunity to talk to her. Maybe someday. But for now, I'll keep listening to the music that makes it all worth it." -Lahar

***

"Hi Taylor, I really want to wish you a happy happy birthday and I love you so much. I've been listening to your music for as long as I can remember. I had your red CD and you still listen to it whenever I can. Your music helps me get through hard times and good.

died and this was very devastating. Your music really helped me get through these hard times. I appreciate you and your music very much, my favorite album has to be 1989 or folklore. I wish you a very very happy birthday as I said in the beginning and also I am trying to go to your US tour to the concert in Miami and hopefully see you there. I wanted to also know how I became a swiftie! How I became a swiftie was simple, you are an amazing woman with an amazing talent, never change! Love you so much!" -Emma G.

***

"When I was around 5 years old my mom was listening to sio (shake it off) and I heard. I loved the song and looked up on YouTube kids for Taylor swift and found fearless 1989 speak now Taylor swift and so many songs I loved I would listen to them every single day after she released Lover I started to not listen very often I grew apart, but then right after evermore started to blow up I listened it was amazing how fast I started to "swiftie-ify" now I listen EVERY SINGLE DAY and will never stop.

I love Taylor!!!!! Thank you Taylor swift for all you have done for my life and I would have NEVER made it without you!! Taylor if you end up seeing this HIIIIII!!!! Ahhhhhh you know I exist!! Okay! Thanks, bye!!" -A. Embry

***

"When I first fell in love with Taylor I didn't really know that she was famous. It was in 2012 when her album Red came out. But the only song I knew from it was "We are never getting back together". I was in LOVE!!! It was my favourite song and whenever we got in the car I had to listen to it. After that I didn't know who she was and didn't realize how much I needed her music. Then the night before Midnights came out, I'm sitting with my friend and she was so excited because Midnights was coming out that night. I was very confused because I had forgotten all about her! So when it comes out I listen to it and of course it's AMAZING!

Then one day I'm in the car with my mom listening to "Anti-hero", then she wants me to listen to Folklore. She explains to me that there are three songs that are connected. And after that I fell in love! I started to listen to every album of hers. Then before you know it "Speak Now" Taylor's Version comes out. I listen to it, skipping a couple of songs that I don't know but then I decide to make a rule for myself, and I'm not allowed to skip any songs. Then "Mean" comes on and I'm like, "hey, I know this song". Then it started another memory of listening to her music as a young child. So now I'm making a playlist of all her songs.

So now it's Swiftober and "1989" Taylor's Version is coming out, and I'm like I need to make a new playlist with her albums in order. So I make a new playlist and I start adding her albums but I can't finish it because "1989" Taylor's Version isn't out yet. So I wait and I'm so happy when it finally comes out! Then I finish my playlist of my happy place.

Then on November 4th my mom takes me to see The Eras tour movie!! Of course it's a surprise so I don't look like a swiftie (it doesn't help that sadly i don't have any merch other than stuff I make). But it was awesome!! I loved it sooo much and I think "Karma" was a perfect ending song! So now I pray that someday I will go to one of her concerts. I sadly didn't get the code for her Vancouver concert, but I know that someday I will go to one of her concerts.

Anyway, I love you Taylor and I hope you get treated right!

HAPPY BIRTHDAY I love you!!" -Isla

***

"I heard that her album Midnights came out and I started asking people if it was good and that Christmas I got a lot of Lego sets so I decided to start listening to her while I did the Lego sets and now I have two posters of her on my wall a calendar two CDs a lot of artwork I have done two shirts I'm begging my parents for Eras Tour tickets I seen the movie once and I'm going to see it again this weekend and I'm I've already made two of my friends swifties by showing them your music and telling them about you I made 40 friendship bracelets hoping that one day I could trade them at your concert and I think you are the most beautiful amazing person ever- hope you have a good day!" -Raelynn

***

"When I was around 4/5, I got a new portable pink cd player for my birthday and I wanted a new cd to listen to. My grandma took me to the store to pick one out and out of all the albums, I picked Red by Taylor Swift. I had never heard a Taylor Swift song but the album was new and had a pretty cover so I chose it. Every day I was at my grandparents house after that, I was carrying around my little cd player and headphones listening to Red on repeat learning all the songs and lyrics. I kinda forgot about Taylor until a few years ago when she started to resurface, and I decided to listen to her more. It went from a few songs on my playlist by her to now knowing almost all of her discography. About a year and a half ago I really started to get into her music. During COVID, I was extremely lonely and lost a ton of friends not being able to see them. I was at such a low point and listening to Taylor always got me in a good mood and lifted my spirits up. I started to make new friends, including my best friend who always talks about the latest with Taylor or the songs we're obsessed with. Last year when she released Midnights, I was so excited because I truly felt like a real Swiftie preparing for the release. Midnights was on repeat for MONTHS and I felt like I had found my music. Music that makes me laugh, makes me cry, makes me smile, but most importantly makes me feel genuinely happy.

I was able to attend The Eras Tour (the best night of my life) and I had the most magical time. As soon as the countdown clock hit 0:00, it all felt real. I was in the same building as my idol, about to see her perform live. I immediately started crying and feeling so grateful. I spent all night screaming every single word as loud as I could, and when she sang my favorite song of all time live, Lover, the moment felt truly surreal and created memories I'll never forget. Taylor, if you actually see this, thank you. Thank you for teaching me that you are what you love, for showing me that nobody can change anything about me, and that life is too short to stay unhappy. I cannot express how much you mean to me, and the millions of Swifties you've inspired." -Ryann

***

"One day when I was like 8 or 9 years old, my dad took me to Target and bought me the 1989 cd. After that I listened to it all the time and learned all the songs, but I wasn't a swiiftie yet. A few years went by where I didn't really listen to Taylor's music. About a year ago, when Midnights dropped, I started listening to her music again. Now, I've been to the Eras Tour movie and I listen to Taylor Swift every day!" -Rebekah

***

"I became a swiftie the first time I listened to her music. It was during the Speak Now era. I first heard Enchanted and it just sounded so beautiful. I also just thought her lyrics were so relatable and they always got me through hard times. And Taylor is so sweet and kind because of how much she cares for everyone and everything. Her songs always get me through hard times and just watching videos of her makes me so happy when she is happy. I went to Seattle night 2 and I lost my voice for probably a week. Taylor, you are my favorite person in the entire world and I love you!!!!!" -Katherine

***

"I love Taylor Swift. I have been a fan for almost 2 years, but I have known and loved her as a person for almost all my life. I love to use her music to theorize on the people and things the songs are about, make connections, and overall listen to her because I like her music and songs. I love how she treats her fans, and it is my dream to meet her. I love her songwriting, too. I think she puts extremely unique and interesting lyrics, making amazing songs. I overall love her as a person, and think she is such an amazing influence, celebrity, and person." -Ashwin M.

***

"I love Taylor so much. She is an amazing woman. A few words that I think describe her are smart, independent, beautiful, and hardworking . Her songs are amazing. Taylor, I am a 11 year old fan. I don't think I'm able to go to your Toronto concerts, or any other ones, but I hope one day I will get to see you. I hope you see this. I have been a swiftie for 9 years, and I love your songs!" -Ava

***

"I always kind of grew up a fan, around people who like Taylor, around her music in the car, I was born in the beginning of her career. I have a ton of cousins that love Taylor. When I was little, my cousin told us that he was dating Taylor. He did so much to make us believe him. I still have a pink cowgirl hat that he told me he got from a tour that he gave to her when I was 4 (obviously it was fake, but I wore it to the Eras Tour as a fun little memory). I went to the Rep Tour with my mom and got lucky enough to go front row in the 100 level. I don't really remember it, but I remember it was super fun. She has been at the top of my spotify wrapped forever. I was in the top 2% of listeners last year, and I got lucky enough to go to the Eras Tour in the 500 level (the best night of my life even though I was far away from Taylor). I have been a diehard Swiftie for about 4 years now. She is my favorite person, and my best friend and big sister I have never met. She has gotten me through so much and I don't know where I would be without her. My dream is to either meet her or go front row to a show! Happy Birthday Taylor, I love you to the moon and to saturn!!" -Antonia A. (@nialuvsts on pinterest)

***

"For most of my life I wasn't really allowed to listen to you, but as soon as my family allowed me to listen to you/I got old enough to make my own decisions about the music I listened to, I haven't stopped listening to you.

I now have a great friend because of a pin on Pinterest about you and the comment section of said pin. Your music has brought me out of some of my darkest times in my life. And it has brought me so much joy. I love you so much Taylor, never let the haters make you feel less than what you truly are." -Emily S.

***

"Dear Taylor,

When crowds of thousands of people scream they love you, it's so much more than those words. Each and every person wants to let you know so many things. You give me joy like no one else. You're there for me in times good and bad. Relating with your lyrics teaches me something about myself. Everyone who knows you is so incredibly lucky to have you. We are so grateful for how much work you put in for us. And most of all- if you're ever going through a hard time, take your time, we don't expect you to bounce back, just like that." -Sinead

***

"I have always been a Taylor Swift fan but not super big like SWIFTIE until like a few weeks ago. So I was Just sitting in Science class and I have this BFF, Larissa and she is a HUGE SWIFTIE And was like "watch the eras tour movie" so i did and have been a fan ever since." -EllaMarie

***

"Hi Taylor, I don't know if you're actually reading this but I have loved you since I was about 5 years old. At school my "friends" are kinda mean to me, but I have no one else to go to. Your music has helped me through this, and one of the songs that helps me a lot is Your On Your Own Kid, thank you. Say hi to the kitties for me!. -

anonymous
***

"Dear Taylor,

I have always loved your music growing up listening to shake it off, bad blood, lwymmd,etc. but I reply became a swiftie during the lover era listening to the song ME!. I discovered so many other of your songs and followed the path from folklore to evermore to now midnights. Your music inspires me daily and have become my at home therapy.

My top three albums are Folklore, Midnights, 1989. And my top three songs are My tears ricochet, would've could've should've, and tolerate it.

I love you so much Taylor and hope you continue to make music, you're doing great." -Livia
***

"When I was a little kid my mum put on blank space in the car and I immediately fell in love with the lyrics and beat I loved it so much every single day I would ask to play the pretty girls who is a great singer and my mum would play Taylor swift I am now still a swiftie and appreciate Taylor's talent and dedication to us and her music and she has made such an impact on society as a whole and so smart that she made her eras tour into a movie so I and everyone can watch it especially if you couldn't get tickets like me." -Eden
***

"I always liked Taylor Swift, but I wasn't a swiftie until 2023. I became a swiftie after Speak Now Taylor's Version came out, and I think I became a swiftie because I appreciated her hard work at the Eras Tour. I think I became a swiftie after listening to 1989 because 1989 has a lot of big hits like 'Shake It Off' and 'Bad Blood', and

I grew up listening to 1989. When I was going through some hard times, I would always blast 'Shake It Off' in my room. Speak Now Taylor's Version really encouraged me to delve deeper in Taylor's music, and that's how I became a swiftie. We love you Taylor Swift!!!!!!!!" - Sragvee

***

"I became a swiftie in July of this year, it was when I decided to check out her songs and see them and that's when I really loved them and I decided to listen to more of her songs. And now I am a swiftie and I love Taylor so much! I think her writing style is absolutely beautiful and gorgeous. I hope Taylor sees this and realizes how much we love and appreciate her." -Fayrouz

***

"I became a swiftie a while after the Rep era, I first heard from the rep album "Don't Blame Me" then I listened to the whole album + Shake It off Was my childhood song so I became a fan. After listening to more songs of Taylor's I became a huge fan of Taylor/ Mother. Now, I have 2 swiftie friends. I made them swifties and I went to The Eras Tour Movie with them. My biggest dream is to go to The Eras Tour Next Year on my Birthday.She's my idol and I love her. She made my life better." -Selena

***

"I was very little when "1989" originally came out. I adored "Blank Space" and "Wildest Dream"s and listen to it every day when I was small. When I was in elementary school in 2019 our class got shuffled and I didn't have any classes with my then best friend. So, I started talking to other kids and she stopped hanging out with me. I remember this one day, when I went to play with her during PT (a period where everyone plays on the ground) she told me that we shouldn't be friends anymore because I was hanging out with other kids. I remember coming home and tearing up all the cards she gave me and telling my alexa to play "Bad Blood". This is very funny to think about now, but this was the first time that Taylor's music help me get over a personal thing. Back when 2021 ended I watched her documentary "Miss American" and I fell in love with her music. I was so impressed with everything Taylor had done. In that moment I started listening to all her albums, making fanart, watching swiftie youtubers (mainly "Swiftie Forever") and bingeing her music videos. I would listen to "Lover" and "1989" and feel nostalgia. I remembered falling in love with "Lover" when it came out. Then, the school year started again after covid and it was really hard for me. My grades got low and I felt really bad about myself but Taylor's music always helped me. We have 2 terms every year and I failed 2 exams in the 1st term. When 1st term ended and the 2nd began "Midnights" came out and "YOYOK" ("You're on your own kid") made me feel like everything was going to be okay. So for the 2nd term I worked really hard and at the end of the year I got As on all my subjects. The next year started and I still have amazing grades. I was even the top in my class for the first exam. Every time I felt like life was horrible to me I would listen to Taylor's music and it Helped. Every. Single. Time. She made and still makes me feel that everything is going to be okay. I'm still in middle school so my grades don't matter that much and now I'm in a better place." -Blair

"My story of how I became a Swiftie started a few months ago when I was scrolling through YouTube Shorts, and found this "Swiftie Test". I didn't know all the songs on the Swiftie Test, so I decided to learn more Taylor Swift songs to be a Swiftie. I started listening to her music more and realised HER MUSIC IS AMAZING! However, when I finally became a Swiftie, Taylor Swift tickets were already sold out :(But a few months later after that, I found out that more tickets were being sold, so I waited at my phone for hours, hoping to get a ticket (spoiler alert: I didn't get any tickets) But to this day, I can still name every album in order (Debut, Fearless, Speak Now, Red, 1989, reputation, Lover, folklore, evermore, and Midnights), and I am a huge Swiftie! Even though I haven't been around from the start, and I don't know every lyric to every song, it's supporting her that makes you a Swiftie, which is a message to every fan out there!" -Trish

***

"I was in the 11th grade when my friend recommended that I listen to Love Story but instead of that I accidentally listened to Blank Space. That was the first song of Taylor I had ever listened to and since then I just kept exploring more and more about her and became a Swiftie. It's been a year and I've never had a day since then where I didn't listen to her." -Sia

***

"Hi Taylor if you are reading this I really just love your music so much and you are my idol. I love how you have so many different types of songs so if i want to listen to your country I can but I can also listen to pop! I became a swiftie in 6th grade. You really helped me and my friend through 6th grade and since then I have loved your music. I went to your movie and it was just amazing I loved all of the songs. I will always support you and your music and I love how you made a movie so if some people could not make it to a concert (me) we could still see your movie which was much cheaper but still an option to see you. I love you and your music and I hope I will get to see you one day! Love you so much!" - Jocelyn

***

"Hi Taylor, it all started 3 years ago when I met my best friend and she told me all about you cause she's a swiftie too and since then I have been a fan of all your songs and 'you belong with me' and 'paper rings' are one of my favourites. I want to come to one of your tours but I am too young (teenager) and I live too far but I hope I will see you in the future and just remember that all the swifties love you." -Kavya K., India

***

"I became a Swiftie when one day I was at my friend's house and she was listening to love story. I asked her who sang that song and she told me Taylor Swift! I looked into her music and I LOVED it! Then, one of my dance teachers asked me if I wanted her tickets to see her Eras Tour Movie because she couldn't make it. I accepted right away and when I went it was magical!! I love you Taylor and you are such an inspiration!!" - Sophia

***

"Hi Taylor! I have been a fan since RED! I remember when "We are never getting back together" came on the radio for the first time and I asked my mom who this was and she said it was you and long story short I listened to it on repeat until 1989 was released! I have so much respect for you and how you are showing young artists everywhere that there is no limit or rules that says you can't change your music style or be 1 in the world (congrats!) or let a man take advantage of you and your songs. I seriously cried when I couldn't go to the Eras Tour because it was 8 hrs away but I did see the movie and dressed up (even if we were the only people who did) and made bracelets! My favorite album has to be folklore. I just love it so much even if other people hate it, it really is a masterpiece. It's my wildest dream to meet you someday! I LOVE YOU SO MUCH!!!!!!!!!!!!!!" - Kirra M.

***

"I have loved Taylor for years, but she is just such an inspiration. When I was younger, I created a dance to shake it off and performed in front of all my family. Honestly, I think it slayed. Taylor has been through it yet she still performs. We all love you very much Taylor!" -Lou

***

"You are such an inspiration to me and you are also my favourite artist. Your music is so relatable and I love all of your songs (my favourite album is reputation). I have seen your eras tour film and I think you are amazing in your work and I am so excited to see what music you will release next. I hope you have an amazing birthday with your friends and family (don't forget the cats!!!). Thank you." -Charlotte M., England

***

"The first time I ever heard of Taylor Swift was when I was six years old. "Shake It Off"and "Blank Space" were blasting from every speaker in 2014, and

I loved it. My friends and I would sing "Shake It Off" together, and I have a lot of good memories of that time. My older cousins even went to the 1989 tour! Taylor Swift was always around me, playing on the radio, or being mentioned in circles of people. However, I didn't really listen to her for many years.

When I was eleven, I made a playlist of all the songs I loved. And, predictably, "Shake It Off", "Blank Space", and "Style" were added. So was "Look What You Made Me Do."I never branched off from these songs, until a Swiftie friend changed that.

I had a friend who loved Taylor Swift. She would constantly be humming or singing her songs, especially "Our Song." I liked "Our Song." Its catchy lyrics and melody. That sparked a renewed interest in Taylor.

I started with Fearless- an album that appealed to me, though I don't remember why. It was phenomenal- and I moved on to Speak Now. Then jumped back to Debut. Then the rest of Taylor's discography.

Around the time I started listening to Taylor, Red (Taylor's Version) had just come out. I didn't know what Taylor's Version meant yet, and I wasn't a Swiftie, so I didn't stay up for the release or listen right away.

But after a few weeks, Taylor was all I listened to. When Midnights came out, I made cupcakes and stayed up to listen. It was one of the best experiences of my life.

I started collecting her CD's and her merchandise, and even started making friends through shared interests in her music.

During this time, I had been struggling at a school with situations involving peers and teachers, along with other situations outside of school. Taylor's music may be the only reason I'm still here. That may be dramatic, but I believe it to be true.

Fast forward to now, and the Era's Tour movie has taken the world by storm. I have seen it four times, and each time has been fun, and healing.

1989 Taylor's Version has just been released, and staying up for that was even more fun than Midnights! Currently, All Too Well (Ten Minute Version) and Champagne Problems are my favorite songs, but I have so many more.

Taylor, if you ever read this, thank you for everything. For all the memories. For the songs to cry in the car to. For "Fifteen" on my fifteenth birthday. For the dance parties alone in my bedroom. For the friends. Most of all, I want to thank you for understanding me in the times when no one else can. Thank you!" -Sophia R.

***

"Dear Taylor,

You have saved my life in so many ways, you are my mender of broken things when it comes to anything, I listen to you when I'm sad, happy, angry, scared or any other emotion in this world. I love you to the moon and to Saturn and all I pray is that one day I will see you in person. Unfortunately I couldn't go to the Eras Tour but I watched the movie and it was the most magical night to see all the swifties dancing and singing. Where you have come in life is so crazy and I'm so so happy for you. Back then when you started music and now, I'm sure the younger you would be so proud. You deserve everything this world has to offer. Happy birth-Tay to the best woman that ever lived and my saviour in this world." -Sarrinah

***

"I have loved Taylor since I was four. My aunt

would let me listen to Bad Blood in her car, so my parents got me "1989" on my iPod. I listened to it on repeat and it was my whole life.

When "reputation" came out me and my mom listened to it constantly, little did I know that she had scored two tickets to the stadium tour for us. It was my first concert ever. When "Lover" came out I played "Death by a Thousand Cuts" so much on my best friend Alexa that it became her most-played song of the year. When "folklore" came out my little sister and I would sing "hoax" together. (We have never gone through anything to relate to that deep lol)

My favorite album is "Speak Now" but my favorite era is "reputation". My favorite songs are: Long Live, Timeless, Better than Revenge, Our Song, Dancing with Our Hands Tied, Is it over now?, Suburban Legends, betty, coney island, and Karma." -Addi, age 13

***

"My mom has always been a Taylor Swift fan and she has always been really sick. She has a condition called Crohn's disease. When I was little I could barely comprehend it. It started getting worse and eventually she had to get another surgery done. The surgery went ok but she had to go back to the hospital the day after she came home because she was bleeding a lot. When the dr. look further into it she ended up having cancer.

We would always listen to the Lover album. I've been trying to get Eras Tour tickets for so long now. We are not going to be going most likely. We are still on the waiting list though.

It's been a really hard time for me and I've been struggling with depression and anxiety for a long time. I'm doing a lot better now and the only reason is Taylor

Swift. She helped me through more things than I can count and got me and my mom out of those rough patches. Not a lot of people like Taylor Swift in my family. They all say I need to get a life outside of Taylor Swift. I will never listen to them and I will always write songs. I know how to play guitar and sing.

I have been homeschooled since Covid first hit. It was really hard for me and I have no friends outside of my family anymore. It has been the hardest years of my life seeing my mom in distress and depressed. You should just know how many pills she has on her table. It is devastating how this happened to her. She deserves everything but cancer. I hope that this paragraph finds people that need help and tells them that there still is hope. There's so many people you have not met yet, and people that are waiting to meet you. Hope is not lost and Taylor Swift helped me find the hope I needed. Please don't give up. You are worth it, you are awesome, you are beautiful, and more. Thank you for everything." - Rozzie, age 11

***

"I'm a teenager and I've recently been struggling mentally with school. Before school starts at 8:40 I just listen to Taylor Swift with my headphones as it instantly helps and reassures me for the day. After school I just turn on Taylor's music as I often come home stressed from school. I love her because she has always been a part of my childhood, I always remember shake it off playing when I was like 5 or 6, and now to hear Taylor's version makes me look back at who I was at that age. Thank you Taylor." -Emily

***

"At first, I listened to Debut/Taylor Swift. I was

thinking, hm, this sounds a lot like me! So that album was how it first started. I was listening to fearless, speak now, red, 1989, etc. And I was just like "oh my gosh, this girl I'm listening to, is an amazing singer, and songwriter." I could not believe how amazing she was. When reputation came out, I was soooo excited!! And I was trying to get tickets. But unfortunately, I couldn't. But that's totally okay! I wouldn't let that stop me. I listened to her all the time, and when lover, folklore and evermore came out, I went on a huge Amazon shopping spree! I got shirts, posters, bags, and so much more. And then midnights came around. And also the one and only The Eras Tour. I was so excited and I got tickets! I was so excited to go and it was the best concert, and experience I've ever seen. I love you Taylor Swift!" -Bella

***

"One of my friends told me to add a Taylor Swift song to my playlist as I had little to none on there. I almost forgot how amazing her music was before that. When I was younger my mum had a 1989 cd in the car so that also influenced me. I guess I kept hearing her songs and loving them so I looked around for more. I want to thank this friend every day for pushing me to become a swiftie. I have no idea where I would be today without Taylor. Her music has really influenced my life for the better. It's more than just about the music now. I really do feel inspired by her and I think she's awesome! I love, love, love her and her music. I just recently watched the eras tour movie and I had an absolute blast! If you're reading this I don't know what else to say other than thank you, Taylor, I always feel so much better when I listen to your music!" -Holly

***

"It was a school day near summer break and we were allowed to have headphones and phones. I was really mad because this teacher I hate so much was teaching my class the whole day. So I just decided to try listening to Taylor. Once I put her music on I felt magical. I couldn't stop listening to Tay's music. Taylor seriously heals everything. She puts so much into her songs it's so relatable sometimes I even feel like some songs are written about me. Oh god I love Taylor and Her music so much. And for those who don't listen to Taylor try i swear it's better than revenge and you'll finally feel clean." -Nina

***

"I became a swiftie when I was younger when 1989 was on the radio. It feels so surreal that I've grown up on the original version, and now i can listen to the new version that she owns!!!

Taylors Swift's music always helps me when I don't feel like myself, or when I feel down. She's basically been my therapist forever. She's such an amazing friend to me because of her music. It always puts me in a good mood when I need it most.

She has a song for every mood that I'm in. I love her and her music so much and I really appreciate everything she's done." -Marissa

***

"So it all basically started when I was in 6th grade and my parents did not allow me to have my phone after 8pm. So I would take my mom's old phone and watch YouTube there. And the more I scrolled the more speeches by celebrities popped up. And so of course Taylor popped up a lot. So I just thought she was cool but nothing more. Around 2 months later I heard one of her songs. (I can't remember it, it was so long ago, don't blame me) And I was just like oh that's Taylor. Many years later, I randomly decided to listen to the latest song of random celebs that came through my mind. And I listened to Lavender Haze for Taylor. Later I just started obsessing over her and here I am now!" -Elise (@HopEsmEnola13)

***

"I've been a fan of Taylor all my life but I really started LOVING her in late 2022. I became a major swiftie when my mom would play Back to December in the car and that song will always have a special place in my heart. Taylor is pretty much my whole life. I have posters all over my room. While I've never seen her live I did go to the Eras tour movie and it was my Wonderland. My favorite songs by her change every week but right now it is probably tolerate it or You are in love. My favorite album is Speak now. I just love Taylor so much!" -Kaybrea

***

"I started listening to Taylor for as long as I can remember. I truly appreciate Taylor for the artist, poet, performer, singer she is but the thing I truly respect is how amazing of a person she is. She is the literal sweetest person on earth as well as the funniest. My favorite album is for sure reputation, because before that era taylor was a much loved, light hearted artist until she disappeared for a time period. Then she came out with reputation and I loved seeing that side of her that showed how strong of a woman she is. Her music is the most cathartic thing that has ever walked this planet. Every sentence is so amazing. She is my literal therapist. I attended Gillette stadium night 3 in Foxborough, Massachusetts and it was the most extraordinary night of my life. Taylor is such a professional in all that she does. Whenever I listen to her music I am in my own wonderland. Also not to mention her cat's are AMAZING. I can't put it into words how big of an impact she has had on my life and I hope she has the best birthday ever!" -Kayla

***

"Hi Taylor! I'm a huge swiftie! I love all of your songs so much even if I only became a swiftie a year ago. My friend got me into your songs and since then I have just been in love with you and everything you do! I haven't been to your concerts but I'm going to your movie and I can't wait! I hope that I can someday go to the Eras Tour. I know most of your songs and my favorite is Miss Americana and the Heartbreak Prince or Blank Space there so good it's hard to choose! I hope you have an amazing day and I love you Taylor!" -Karalynn

***

"I became a swiftie not too long ago honestly. I have always listened to your top hits but never really got into your songs until about a year ago. I always shared an AirPod with my friend and she started putting on your more underground albums like folklore and evermore and I was like hey I'm vibing, so then I started listening more and more and now the only thing I listen to is this one playlist that's every single song you ever composed and it's such a bop. Especially when Dear John comes on and I scream that bridge.

Overall I am currently in my evermore and rep stage bc like champagne problems is a literal masterpiece I feel like you def wrote that and others with like a quill some ink and an old piece of paper like you are a philosopher and rep doesn't even need to be explained like New Year's Day I screamed when you played that on your tour I wish I was there anyway. Ugh I would do anything to go but my family isn't the most rich people ever so it's not gonna happen unless we win the lottery or something but if I did go I would be screaming to every single song." -Gabrielle (Brie) P.

***

"I became a fan when I was 2, I can remember my mom blasting your song "mean" in the car and me screaming the lyrics. I just really love you and your music of course!! But I really hope you have an amazing birthday. We love you so so sooo much Taylor!!! Happy birthday!! I am also going to your concert in Toronto and I can't wait to see you!!" -Marrin A.

***

"I'm a HUGE swiftie but I wasn't always. When I was around 3 I would scream the lyrics to I knew you were trouble and around 8 years old on a long road trip I would listen to some of her classics like our song, Love Story, and You belong with me.

Now at 9 I got introduced to other artists like Olivia Rodrigo, Shakira, and I listen to a lot of others except for Taylor Swift. But when I was older I got surprised with Eras Tour tickets and I was BOUND DETERMINED to get all of her songs down. What upsets me most is I didn't sing anything from Folklore and didn't completely know all the lyrics. A few months later I went to the Taylor Swift Eras movie and I knew every song word for word. Taylor has Made my Life better than it was!" -Callie

***

"I have been listening to Taylor Swift and dancing

and singing since I was 4 years old. And going back and watching videos of me singing and dancing to Taylor Swift is what I like to call my childhood. I support and love Taylor and all the work she does. I have cried, laughed and danced through every song she has put out, I even recommended long live as a song for my graduation. And if I had to describe Taylor in 3 words I would use Kind, Amazing, and Talented the list only goes on from there.

Taylor Swift has helped get through some really hard stuff through my life and where I am today, whether it's crying to come back...be here because of a close family friend moving away or singing illicit affairs in the shower. I would ruin myself a million little times to meet her and see her live.

I sit there and wonder sometimes what it would be like to meet Taylor swift or maybe she read something I put in a book or I made a funny Tik Tok and she saw it. But whenever I do I freeze at the thought of Taylor Swift knowing who I am even though I don't think she knows.

I became a swiftie 4 years ago when reputation came out and I would only watch the reputation stadium tour nothing else was acceptable. I respect Taylor's decisions and when listening to her music don't think about what boyfriend it's about but what messed up friend it's about for me. I have made 106 bracelets for the eras tour but would make 13,000 more to get a glimpse of her walking by or in her car. And when I think of Taylor I think of how much joy she has brought to people and how much joy she has brought to me I will refuse of anyone listening to the stolen version of fearless, speak now, red, or 1989, I have gone as far as to rip the phone out of someone's hand to make it Taylor's version.

And whenever someone hate hate hate hates on Taylor I always stick up for Taylor and I can't even remember the days when I wasn't a swiftie." -Andie

***

"Taylor, there aren't enough words in the world to describe how much I love you. Your smile and your beautifully majestic voice brings a light to my days. You were there when it was really hard. Your songs give me a comfort that nothing else really does because they're always there. I have the most vivid memories of being six years old and screaming Shake It Off and dancing forever. Around the time that Midnights had come out, I started listening to you, every single day. Maroon was my favorite song. It was the song that made me a true fan. Maroon convinced me to start listening to all the albums, in much greater depth than I had ever before (since I was younger before). Soon enough I knew and loved almost every single song from every single album. I listened every day, on repeat, until I knew every song. I became immediately obsessed with you. When I found folklore (which is my favorite album ever), I instantly fell in love. The poetry and the wonderful words; the sad themes of some of them, that I could relate to so well. You are kind, lovely, thoughtful, and a great inspiration. I couldn't begin to explain how much I look up to you. Becoming a Swiftie is one of the best things that ever happened to me. Your songs pulled me out of darkness and really made me happy again. Taylor, I really don't know if you'll get to see this, but I love you. So, so, so much." -Emma W.

***

"I became a swiftie whenever I first listened to "We Are Never Ever Getting Back Together". I thought it was an amazing song and it was super catchy, so I started listening to her other music and thought to myself "Oh.My.Goodness." The only people who don't like Taylor, are the people who never took the time to listen. If I didn't have her, I would be an absolute emotional wreck. I get up at 5am everyday, and the first thing I do is put in my earplugs and turn on Taylor Swift. I can't remember the last time I went a day without listening to her music. It is so spectacular and so much more than what it looks like on the outside. I didn't get the privilege to see the Eras Tour, but I saw the movie and I broke down into tears in the middle of it, because I thought about how lucky the world is to have a beautiful thing like music, sung by a beautiful artist named Taylor Swift." -Devri

***

"Dear Taylor,

I am 12 years old, and I have been a fan since I was 4 years old. I've been to your reputation tour and your Eras Tour in Seattle. Although it seems crazy to love someone you've never met as much as I do, I do. You've helped me through so much and I love you like crazy. There's not a single one of your songs that I don't have memorized." -Anya, age 12

***

"Dear Taylor,

Words cannot express how thankful I am for you. My name is Emilie and I love your music! I'm in 5th grade and I am super happy that you are reading this. As a kid, I have always loved Shake It Off and Look What You Made Me Do. I have just re-entered my Swiftie Era!

If you could please respond back, it would be greatly appreciated and maybe we can be pen pals! I have dreamed of meeting you in person even though I never went to your concerts. My friends also love you and one of them is even writing a book about you!" -Emilie H.

***

"One day I was just walking in the park and I saw this giant billboard with a big sign saying "TAYLOR SWIFT'S REPUTATION TOUR" and I immediately ran home to look her up I found out that she was a songwriter so I started listening to her songs and they were SO amazing. Ever since then I have been a massive Swiftie and loved every minute of it. Taylor has made me happy when down or made me cry when I needed a good cry. She is an inspiration for me and for many others all around the globe. Thank you Taylor for not giving up in the hard times and to show me to keep on going." -anonymous

***

"On November 10, 2017, I was eating lunch at the lunch court and my best friend came running up to me saying, "Taylor Alison Swift released reputation!!" The next day after school, I went to his house and he showed me her music videos... I FELL IN LOVE WITH THE STORY OF US! I began to listen to Taylor Swift every single day. Now, 11 is my lucky number due to becoming a Swiftie on November 11!" -Emma

***

"Actually it was a depressing day where I was going through many things and I'm so much into music so I started listening to Taylor Swift. She is the best singer because her songs heal me and she is the best for no reason. Her music is like therapy to me and I always have a dream to meet her in real life. I hope I could ever meet her in real life. I have been a swiftie since 2019 and she made me happy with her music." -Aayushi

***

"The first song I ever listened to was shake it off. I was obsessed with it. I didn't really listen to music much in til July. When I found you belong with me. I would play it over and over again. I didn't really understand who Taylor Swift was at that time. But in August I started to listen to her all the time. And now I love Taylor Swift so much. I can't wait for the rest of her rerecords to come out!" -Iris

***

"Dear Taylor,

You've always been a huge part of my life, even without me realizing. When I was younger I'd hear love story, you belong with me, we are never ever getting back together, style, blank space, shake it off and many more. These songs were the soundtrack to my childhood. When I was younger I never knew who sang different songs and was never focused on music that much until middle school, when one of my friends got me obsessed with a boyband. This is when my whole life started filling up with music. I stayed realizing how much music helped with my anxiety and how music was always there when I felt the most alone. I had always liked your music but never even particularly knew it was yours. I heard your songs here and there, knew the lyrics to many, but never even realized how much I loved your music.

This was until one day I was scrolling on instagram and saw my friend add to their story the announcement of your new album: Midnights. This was the day everything changed, on August 28, 2022. I didn't know this would change everything for me, but fate is a funny thing and that invisible string of the universe always seems to guide you the right way. When I saw this announcement, I was overjoyed because it brought back so many childhood memories of your music. I decided I was going to binge listen to all your music and learn more about you, so that I could enjoy the album release and relive the simpler times. But it turned into way more than that. I listened to your albums in order, and the first time a song really hit me was when I was listening to white horse. This was when I first realized there was much more to your music than blank space and shake it off and catchy pop, but there was confessional, sad, honest, GORGEOUS music. What really made me realize how well you convey emotion through your songwriting was when I was listening to you are in love. I didn't even think that you wrote songs like that, and it instantly became one of my favorite songs of all time. I enjoyed learning about you music, and by the time Midnights was released I was already a huge fan of yours. Midnights was on another level. I remember not even being allowed to stay up to listen to Midnights, so I woke up and listened to it getting ready for school. It was absolutely INSANE. Your On Your Own Kid hit so hard, labyrinth and Mastermind were instant favorites, Karma was so fun, Midnight Rain shocked me with the voice at the beginning I thought my phone was glitching, Vigilante was shocking (another favorite) and don't even get me started on three am tracks and hits different. I became so obsessed with this album, and my friends started to get annoyed of how much I talked about it and you. At this point, your music has taken over my life.

That's when you announced it: THE ERAS TOUR! Never in a million years did I think I would ever be able to go. I was too scared to ask my parents to pay for tickets, and I felt bad and didn't want them to spend their money on that. I got a code because I signed up anyways, but didn't even try to tickets because I knew I'd be unable to go. After watching thousands of people fight in the Great War, I was super devastated. I would miss out on my first chance to go to one of your shows as an official Swiftie. That's when the universe worked in my favor once more. It seems to always happen when I need it the most. I get an email from Ticketmaster on a random day "you have an opportunity to buy two eras tour tickets". Taking this as a sign, I took my chances and asked my parents. I ran into my kitchen where my mom was, and rambled to her about how I had a chance to see you in concert. She said that I had to ask my dad if he could pay for the tickets and drive me up to Tampa since I live about three hours away. My dad says yes, but I choose the lowest price range and didn't think there would be any tickets available. That's when I leave school one day and open my phone to a text from my dad: "we got the tickets" I start freaking out yelling out to my friends that I was going to see you. I was SO excited. It was months of planning, getting an outfit, doing an Eras themed birthday party, my friends helping me make bracelets, making sure I knew all the lyrics, and watching all of your tours ever on any platform I could find them in, until the day came. I went to Tampa Night 3 (4/15/23) and it was the most surreal thing I've ever experienced. Singing (who am I kidding I was screaming them) lyrics with you was so fun and so healing at the same time. The Eras Tour allowed me to hear my old, and my new, favorite songs. I will forever be grateful for having the opportunity to experience the biggest tour ever. I can't believe The Eras Tour will end one day, but I can't wait to see what you come up with next.

Ever since I went to Eras, I've lived a lot through you. You got me through lots, including losing most of my friends, and lots of middle school drama. I went through my first re-record as a fan, which also happened to be the re-record of my favorite album Speak Now, and most recently got to go through 1989 Taylor's Version, the album most prominent in my childhood. Your music is now getting me through freshman year, which is not at all how I'd imagined. My friends are good but they all seem to get annoyed when I talk about music and same goes for anyone I meet, they always judge me, which hurts because they don't know how much you've truly gotten me through. I've also been trying to learn guitar for years but recently I've been taking live classes with Nena Shelby (you should check out her YouTube!) and it's the first time I've actually learned many of your songs and I want to get into writing music too!! I hope one day I actually have the courage to sing in front of others, and I will do it looking up to you. You have given us fans so much, and of course, we all wish you the happiest birthday. We've seen you through good and bad, and you seem to be at one of your happiest times right now, which makes me overjoyed!!! I love being a silly fan girl, meeting other fans, wearing merch places and hoping a fan will come talk to me, saying I love what someone is wearing anytime i see them wearing merch, trying to out Easter eggs together, TAYTOBER, Swiftmas, New Year's Day, hoping to one day to go NYC for the first time and live the dream. Words cannot describe how much I have to thank you, and I have so much more I could say to you, but this is getting super long. I truly hope I can get to meet you one day, until then, you will keep being my greatest inspiration. Thank you Taylor for making us so happy! We are so proud of you. Never stop being as kind as you are." -Alice (@aliceramosdutra on instagram)

***

"When I was around 12 yr old, I used to get bullied in school with the other kids and tried to fit in with the "Cool Kids". At that year Tay Tay was having her Rep fall. Then she came right back up. And I learned that they can't tell me what I can do. I can do what I want to do. Her songs make me emotional and I love her. Now I am 18 yr old and still listen to Taylor Swift." -Leo

***

"When 1 was like a 10 years old , I watched a video on YouTube, the video was ybwm's video clip with barbies. And then I watched the original, then the other songs.

And now 1 am a huge fan. And not just me, now all people around me know Taylor's songs very well. And in my country (Türkiye) there is an exam which is so important. And my dad promised me, if I will be successful in that, he's gonna take me to the Eras Tour, so I study really (literally) hard, and we love u Tay, happy birthday!" -Zeynep

***

"I have been a swiftie since I was in yr 1 and went to her rep tour with my nanna. It was a magical experience and I loved her ever since. She is so amazing and her music is priceless. I own one of her t-shirts and hope to grow my collection. Taylor is just such an amazing human. I mean bonus for her staff and paying for fans' flights. I went to her Eras Tour movie and everyone was jumping at the front and it was so fun (I even got some bracelets). I'm so happy to be a swiftie." - Lola, age 13, Australia

***

"When I was around four, my family would always listen to wildest dreams in the car but it was only when I was around six that me and my dad listened to other songs like blank space and bad blood on youtube. I started to really like her music and started to ask my dad to play it more often (as I didn't have a phone). When I was ten, I got my first phone and I played Taylor's music non-stop. I started exploring all of her different albums and quite quickly became almost obsessed with her songs. I would play them whenever I could and I never really stopped." -Lilly

***

"I was never a big tech girlie.. in fact I started browsing YouTube properly in 2020 during lockdown. I vaguely heard her songs in videos but never paid attention. But this year I read the love hypothesis in March and was hooked to it. I searched for one of those book playlists on YouTube and found a good (slowed +reverb)one. One of the songs was 'wildest dreams' and at 3 am listening to it with the feels of the book..I fell in love. I was obsessed with that song for days. Then I searched for the song and came to know it was from Taylor. Slowly but steadily I started an adventure into her musical world and I was amazed by her storytelling skills and the lyrical geniuses. I learned all about her and her music in the past few months....... Now I am proud to claim that I am a swiftie.

She has taught me a lot and is an inspiration I look up to and also my favorite comfort person. I love her, her music, this fandom and everything. I remember during June and July I was having a hard time and she released speak now TV and now I am over that she released 1989 TV as if she is also celebrating my strengt .

I love you Taylor...one of the greatest gifts to humanity in today's world. Thank u so much from everyone all over this world. Hope you break the limits of the sky everyday and continue touching lives. Your music is the best thing that has been 'ours'." - anonymous

***

"Happy Birthday Taylor,

I've been with you since Love Story released. I loved the song so much and became friends with two other girls who loved the whole album too. We were convinced we were going to start a band inspired by you. Although that never happened, I'm still with you. I love every era you've been through and can't wait to experience many more with you!" -Jess H.

***

"I was like 8 years old when I became a Swiftie I was listening songs then Taylor's song played I had no idea which song is playing, then I saw that it was Taylor Swift and the song was lover I was amazed by the song so I played her album I thought all the songs will be nice and I was right all the songs were nice actually they were the best. Then I started listening to them and then

I became a Swiftie. Now I am 12 years old." -Mehar, India

**

"I've always liked Taylor since I was seven and I always used to vibe to shake it off, bad blood, blank space and all her well known songs back then. Ever since I listened to the song wildest dreams I was attached! I started listening to more of Taylor's songs and quickly got to know her songs really well. Later on I became the biggest Swiftie I never imagined myself to be and found out that one of my best friends was a Swiftie and has created one of the most unforgettable memories with her, all because of Taylor! My friend and I later on watched The Eras Tour movie and had one of the best times of our life! We got to yell and sing all the song lyrics at the top of our lungs with other Swifties, even though they were complete strangers It felt like we were all really good friends! Taylor Swift has brought so many Friendships together andI really hope that someday I might get the chance to meet Taylor in real life!! Every time I'm feeling sad or aren't having a good day, I just open Spotify and play all my favourite songs from her! Its like a happy pill!! I can't imagine my life without Taylor Swift and her songs! Taylor Swift has impacted my life so greatly and I will always be thankful for that! I LOVE YOU TAYLOR and wish you all the best!!!" -Emma L.

**

"I became a swiftie when everyone was hating on Taylor's music and I was like...who is this Taylor girl? So, I started listening to her and now I know all of her songs and all the words to them and most of my playlists are Taylor Swift." -Addy

**

"I heard my first Taylor Swift song when I was two. It was love story. By the time Red came out my new favorite was we are never ever ever getting back together. Growing up I loved all the music Taylor came out with, at least the singles. When I got my phone and was able to listen to my own music and dive deep into albums was when I really became a swiftie. I'm still in the process of getting eras tour tickets though, because I have been waitlisted for every single presale. I still have hope though. Thank you for making music." -Lucia B.

***

"I was in 1st grade and I remembered my mom playing Taylor on the radio and it was love story and me and my mom started to dance together and now everyday we listen to all her songs she made. By the way, I'm in 9th grade now and I'm still listening to her!" -Leylah

***

"I have been a swiftie since I was 2. I was either singing my heart out to ME! Or listening to her calm music when I was sad. She has always made amazing music for whatever mood you are in. She is an absolute icon and cares so much for her fans. She is my favorite artist of all time and she is incredible!" -Colleen

***

"First of all Happy Birthday to you, Taylor! I wish you all the best, I hope you are always happy and healthy with your family and friends!

When my two best friends broke up with me I had to spend a lot of time by myself. You can say that it is a very delicate issue. If they say music is therapy then ,honestly, Taylor Swift is my therapist. I listen to your music and I see a piece of me in it. How

I sometimes feel like an old cardigan under someone's bed, how all of my bridges burn and the pages turn ,and I'm on my own again, how everybody moved on but I'm right where you left me. A lot of my friend's say 'Taylor Swift is your favourite singer?' ,and they laugh. They make fun of your fans but they will never understand. You are way more than the blondie with the red lips and those lips are more than the guys you have kissed.

Because you are fearless, you are not afraid to speak now, stand up amongst the croods. You took as through your folklore but it won't be forever and always like evermore. You gave as the key to stay beautiful, be gorgeous, be the man. You showed us your midnights and taught that karma is real. You told us that love can be black and white, burning red, but eventually golden. You showed us that love isn't always about having a lover and that your reputation is valuable ,but it has to be broken for your life to unfold. Saying goodbye is death by a thousand cuts, but when you finally do then is when you find peace. When haters hate you just shake it off. You could build a castle out of all the awards they throw at you. And thanks to you I'm finally out of the woods! So yes you are more than the guys you 've kissed. You are a gift that I will never ever forget! So I wish you all the best!" -Andrea

***

"I was in PE one day (around may-june i think) and my best friend, who's a Swiftie, asked if she could teach me a Taylor Swift song and I said okay. She taught me GORGEOUS, which is still one of my favourite songs after listening to her whole discography a million times on repeat. It means so much to me.

Anyway, then I asked what album it was from so

she said reputation and told me to watch the reputation film on netflix (i've seen it 3 times already and i am NOWHERE NEAR sick of it - there's always some new surprise that i didn't notice before) so I watched it and then listened to the reputation and 1989 album. After a while I knew most of the songs and couldn't wait for Taylor's Version of them (STILL WAITING FOR REP TV). So now, we are both swifties and were SO excited when Taylor said she would add two new dates for London and my friend got a presale code but we didn't get tickets." -Tamar

***

"I became a swiftie just over time. At around 5 years old, I started hearing shake it off, you belong with me, and bad blood on the radio, and my older sisters played taylor on speakers a lot. I fell in love with the bad blood music video, and I always listened to her popular songs. When I was about 8 I just slowly lost interest and began to forget about her. i knew her songs but i didn't think her music was good since i had listened to the same songs too much, and i didn't know she had more. Now I'm 13, I heard about the Eras Tour and started seeing videos on YouTubeabout swifties and taylor's music in about July of 2023. I hadn't really given her a second thought for years until then. I started off with just This is Why We Can't Have Nice Things, since I had seen it on a YouTubeshorts trend, and my obsession slowly grew. Now, in November 2023, I'm almost 14 and I'm nonstop listening to Taylor swift. I'm basically a new swiftie but my love for her music is more than just the amount of time i've been a fan." -Eva S.

***

"My story on how I became a Swiftie is pretty

basic but I love Taylor's music. It started around when 1989 came out and it was all over the radio. I would always hear Bad Blood, Blank Space, and Shake it off (of course) and I love those songs. Eventually the 1989 hype fell out and didn't listen to much Taylor Swift then. Then when Evermore came out I heard it on the radio and loved it, but then it wasn't on the radio anymore. I started working out with my mom so I made a workout playlist and she said "I thought you would have had more of Taylor Swift's music." And I thought I should add more of her music, so I did and now it has spiraled into me being a big Swiftie. I think it is kind of fitting that I first heard of Taylor Swift when 1989 came out and I became a Swiftie in between Speak Now Taylor's Version and 1989 Taylor's version." -Piper

***

"Growing up I was never interested In specific artists and generally just listened to the trending music. When quarantine came along, I decided to start listening to Taylor's music. I remember it all started with Mr Perfectly fine and Message in a bottle. I started realizing how impactful her music is to everybody in this world, and just like that I started listening to more of her music. I also had a lot of swifties in my life who encouraged me to start listening to her music. I watched the documentary and listened to every song from Debut-Midnights. Ever since then I've been absolutely obsessed with her music and I am so glad to have somebody as influential as her. I have tons of merch, been to the eras tour, and the movie multiple times. That is why I love Taylor swift and can't wait for her to hopefully receive this present!" -Talya

***

"Although it was kind of late, I became a swiftie during the Midnights era. Me and my cousin were making up a dance for a Thanksgiving party and we were stretching while listening to the new album. After that, a bunch of videos about you came up on my for you page and that's when I started to get into it. My friend and I have been wanting to go to the Eras Tour ever since it started and we just couldn't get tickets. So when you announced that it was coming to theaters I immediately got tickets and have already gone twice. I hope you have an amazing birthday and I love you so so so so so so much Taylor!" -anonymous

***

"I became a swiftie in the Reputation Era, after I went to the Reputation tour. I was a casual fan in the 1989 era, but something about that night changed me. Ever since then I've had a deep love for anything Taylor Swift related. I went to the Eras Tour in Arlington, TX, and had the best night of my life. Thanks Taylor for all you've done. You've changed my life for the better!" -@Taylor_Tuesday

***

"Dear Taylor,

Remember when you were 16? 17 years ago! How the time flies! You started making music 17 years ago! Can you believe that?! You have grown into such a beautiful, strong woman! You are incredible! You are an independent queen!! You are amazing!

Now onto a you and me note. I hope you're doing amazing and doing well! I hope you are living your best life, remember you only have one life so live it! I hope your cats are doing great! Have a great year!!" -Isabelle (Izzy) Z.

"The first Taylor swift song I every heard was anti hero, I started dancing to her songs with my friend, and I made a playlist! I love her songs and me and my friends love her too! I love how she has a great relationship with her parents." -Rose

"I have been a Swiftie for almost a year now and I've had so many fun experiences listening to her and learning more of her songs. When I watched "Sing" and heard "Shake it off" that was immediately my fave song in the movie and I still think it's amazing now!!! I am in love with her music I wanted to go to the Eras tour so bad when I first heard it was coming out. I went to the movie with my friends on October 22, 2023 and it was seriously one of the best things EVER! I have made SOO MANY BRACELETS and traded with so many people! My favorite album is Speak Now and I can't wait for her to release more music!!!" -Sammie Z.

"The very first Taylor Swift song I heard and absolutely loved was Willow. Since then, her music has greatly impacted my life. I listen to songs from every album, and it feels almost as if there's a song for everything I'm feeling. Her music just makes me so happy. My friends and I went to the tour movie and during every single song in every single album I thought, "I think this might be my favorite." I have continued to discover more of her songs and I really love her." -Jinx

"I am 16 and I started listening when Red came out. I used to go around saying 22 was my favorite number because of my favorite song. I used to watch the WANEGBT music video everyday before school. When 1989 came out I bought the cd and listened to it every time my family go into our car. I have been a fan since and I have made so many friends through the fandom!! On twitter I met an amazing group of friends and our swiftie group chat is called "Yes Whale!" I would like to thank you for always being there for me. Every bad day, every fight with someone I loved, every new crush and much more your music has been there. I had the chance to see you in Philly, night 3 of the Eras Tour! It was the best day of my life and hearing you perform my 2 favorite songs (Hey Stephen and The Best Day) That night was so enchanting. I really do hope to meet you one day because you are my biggest inspiration ever! Every birthday wish, every time I shake my Lover snow globe, every eyelash and many more wishes have all been to meet you!! One of the most important lessons that your music has taught me is that people will get their karma because maybe I got mine but they will all get theirs. I love you to the moon and to Saturn!" -Molly D. (@tsoncorneliast on twitter)

***

"It all started when I was little and grew up hearing sparks fly, 22, and wonderland and I loved them all so I decided to make bracelets and decorate my room with her stuff and I finally went to the eras tour last year in may! It was the best night of my life. I cried a lot, but it was worth it!" -anonymous

***

"I used to be very skeptical of her music because I wasn't very impressed by the songs that everyone else would play. Then me and my mom watched her documentary. Suddenly she became a real person to me that actually had a lot in common with me. I loved that she stood up for women's rights and lgbtq+ rights. I then started listening to her songs. I discovered my neighbor was a swiftie when midnights came out and he started giving me advice and explaining the backgrounds of each song. Eventually I was able to form my own opinions on my favorite albums and songs, and now I have multiple Taylor Swift shirts and vinyls as well as a Taylor Swift tote bag because I believe in taylor as a person and what she represents as well as her music. I went to see the eras tour movie, and would eventually hope to see her in concert. But for now, I'm happy to support her in any way I can." -A.E.E

***

"This is how I became a Swiftie!!! I was about 6 or 5 when I became one. I don't really remember when I started liking Taylor, it just kinda happened. Me and my 2 sisters were young and obsessed with your album "Red". I remember watching the music vids over and over and screaming your songs. Songs that I remember listening to are. Red, WANEGBT, everything has changed, IKYWT and 22. My parents surprised me and sisters tickets to the Red Tour in New Jersey. I remember being soooo excited. And I remember screaming red and wearing classic red lipstick. Ever since that I've been a HUGE fan of you!!!! and I don't not regret it. And I'm still a Red girly!!! Also when you released Red (Taylor's version). I felt like I was reliving my child hood hahah. Thank you so much for bringing me joy Taylor!!! I love you so much!!!!" -Clara J.

***

"When I was about 2-3 years old, Shake it Off just

was released and I started dancing to it lots whenever it turned on. It was very popular and I would always dance to it and I loved it. Whenever my mom was playing music I would ask her to play Shake it Off.

I slowly began to listen to Taylor every now and then and whenever her music turned on, it calmed me down and I instantly became happy. Her music would cheer me up whenever I was having a bad day. I began to learn the lyrics to a bunch of her songs and I would always sing them in the halls at school, in the shower, during dinner, and lots of other points during my day. Her music always cheered me up and she was my favourite artist. I love listening to her music. I would ask my mom if she could take me to the Taylor Swift concert for a while, and that moment happened after asking for so long. I get to go to her concert next year and I look forward to it every single day, it's like a holiday to me. Taylor Swift is my comfort person and her music is amazing, she is so talented and I'm extremely proud of her. Her songs are amazing and she just blows my mind how amazing her music is.

Whenever I'm stressed out or I'm frustrated, I will listen or sing her songs and it always makes me calmer and focused. Taylor is incredibly talented and her music is awesome. She is truly the best singer ever. WE LOVE YOU TAYLOR!

I hope my story can inspire others to never be ashamed of yourself for who or what you like. Everybody is their own person and that's what makes them unique. You should never change yourself for someone else and always follow your heart. Do what makes you happy!" -anonymous

**

"I think I should start the story off with I WAS NAMED AFTER TAYLOR SWIFT!!! (Just with a twist of the end).

When my mom was younger, she was In LOVE with Taylor's music, and even named me after her! My mom really loved her country albums but she lost interest when Taylor went pop, leaving me to continue the legacy years later. I first started listening to Taylor's music about a year ago when my cousin told me that she was going to the Eras Tour. Of course I had listened to her when I was younger, and I knew that I was named after her, I heard her songs on the radio, but I had never REALLY listened to her.

I started playing some of her songs, the first one being,"Love Story" and then suddenly I knew all the lyrics! Day after day I listened to her more popular songs like,"Anti-hero", "Lavender Haze", "Midnight Rain" and my at the time favorite off of Midnights, "Bejeweled" My love for Taylor grew and grew until I knew every song off of every album! I bought lots of merch, named my cat after "August", and even got my mother back into her, (She's obsessed with "The Man") For my birthday, my mom bought me tickets to The Eras Tour and it was THE BEST NIGHT OF MY LIFE!! Right now, one of my favorites is, "Long Live" I LOVE this song because the lyrics really speak to me and my mom, especially the lyrics," If you have children someday, when they point to the pictures, please tell them my name! Tell them how the crowds went wild! Tell them how I hope they shine!" Anyway, LIVE LAUGH LOVE TAYLOR SWIFT!!!" -Tayla

***

"Taylor,

You are such an iconic part of my childhood. I remember jamming out to your songs with my sister and family together on car rides belting the words. Me and my sister would watch your music videos on repeat and I still do. We went to your eras tour and it made us love you and your music even more. We stayed up so listen to your 1989 album release together and we loved it. Me and my friends love your music and I am so happy that you are who you are!" -Avery W.

***

"I became an infinite Taylor Swift fan sort of recently, the start of 2023 in around March. Ever since I was little music has been apart of who I am. Singing is one of my greatest passions in life that I only fully figured that out once Taylor Swift was a part of my life. I have always been searching for a music artist that has songs that I can jam out to, be sad to, be elated to, and overall find myself in. Through my whole life I've only found a few songs that I love, I didn't love the artist though. Those songs either stayed with me for a while or a little bit, but at some point I didn't like any of them anymore. At last I found a music artist that completely grasps the music industry. Heck she doesn't know it, she is it, she has reinvented it. Taylor Swift has honestly always been in my life I've just never realized it. In my childhood years, the present time when I'm a teen, and she will stay with me through the rest of my life.

How, you might ask, that she'll be my favorite through the rest of my life? It's not a topic that's a gut feeling or a thought. It's a concept I know is real, because this is the most real I've ever felt about music. Through thick and thin, she's there for me. Through the light and dark, she's there for me. Though happiness and sadness, she's there for me. As she may not literally be standing next to me or sitting by me, I found myself in Taylor's music. Every song has a different meaning for me that helps me get through the most viral things in my life. It's not just me that feels this way the whole world has a different part of themselves in each music piece. That's why she's so awesome! Anyone can love Taylor! Personally speaking, I go through more than anyone knows I've never been able to genuinely overcome some obstacles. With her I can listen to one little song that helps me overcome even a big obstacle. Just the other day I was having some anxiety with homework. Ya know what all I needed to tell myself was "Ok Chloe, 'You need to Calm Down'". Tiny to huge situations make the most for me. As I have been studying Taylor Swifts music for nearly a year now tell me, how is it that not one of her songs has ever gotten old, when with other music artists I like a small selection and those songs get old fast? This is my words coming from the heart. You are the Music Industry! Keep being you, keep inspiring, keep loving, keep being Taylor Swift!" -Chloe M.

***

"ive been a swiftie since i was a kid. she inspired me a lot to sing and i still listen to her today. i went to the eras tour movie with my mom and my best friend and after, my mom had told me that she thinks she's a swiftie and it was such a heartwarming thing to hear. taylor has kept me alive for so many years and she deserves the best birthday." -@localaveragehuman

***

"Becoming a Swiftie was an awesome experience for me, and it all started with my best friend, Harper.

I had always been a fan of Taylor Swift's music, but never had the chance to attend any of her concerts due to financial constraints. However, thanks to Harper's invitation, I got the opportunity to attend the Eras Tour movie and witness Taylor's great performance on the big screen. It was an unforgettable experience that left me in awe of her talent and showmanship. To top it all off, we even dressed up for Halloween as Taylor's iconic eras - I went as the Red Era, while my friend dressed up as the Speak Now Era. It was a fun and memorable night that strengthened our bond as best friends and fellow Swifties." -Anna P.

***

"Ever since I became a swifte, my life has changed. I can't remember exactly when I became a swiftie, but I know that it was around the time Taylor was doing her eras tour. I knew a little bit about her, and I listened to her music sometimes.

But I soon saw her eras tour concert pop up on my for you page, and that's where I got hooked into the magical world of Taylor and us swifties. I have read up on everything about Taylor, because I wanted to understand her more. And when I heard about her Miss Americana documentary, I knew I had to watch it. Now I know what Taylor's been through, and I feel great sympathy for her. Taylor's music helped me so much when I was struggling, because I could relate to what she sang in her songs. What lyrics she put in her songs made me realize that I'm not alone, and I greatly appreciate that. She's such a fighter, and I'm so proud to call myself a swiftie. Taylor has influenced us and the world in many ways, she cares so much about each and every single one of us, and I know for a fact that she's making the world a better place for everyone. I'm so glad I could share the ways that Taylor helped me, and everyone, in this world. Thank you so much for reading this, and have an amazing rest of your time reading everyone else's perspectives and thoughts on Taylor." - Luna

***

"Ok so I've been listening to Taylor Swift since well forever. when i was 8 or 9 i got my first ipod which was used for music, not knowing anything other than common songs and musicals, i listened to what almost every swiftie listened to at that age, 1989. i remember listening to all her tracks and watching the bad blood music video over and over until some people at school said she was "out of style" and such an American singer.

i kinda stoped listening to her because i was a pretty delicate person back then. but a couple of months ago my best friend whom i've known forever expressed her love about taylor which gave me the boost to become a swiftie again. i still could remember the songs all too well almost like i was 8 again. she helped me through a break up and as much as i wanted to go back to december because that's when i was really innocent and felt loved, last summer (2023) i learned to love myself through her music. i stopped hurting myself, became healthy, and forgot they all existed. it felt better than revenge because this was the real ME. i hung out with my friends who actually value me and my friend who made me love taylor again, i think might be the one but im too scared to admit it. she gave me peace after all the stuff that'd happen. taylor and my best friend have healed me. made me clean and happy. yeah you can call me basic for liking Taylor Swift but this, what i said, is why im confident and feel that little spark that flew away come back." -anonymous

***

"The first Taylor Swift song I ever heard was Red. I remember dancing and singing along to it in my parents bathroom. Red and 1989 were my childhood albums but since I was so young I never got to go to any tours. A few months after midnights came out Taylor announced the eras tour. My dad waited in presale for hours to help get me tickets while I was at school but we had no luck at any shows. I was devastated and knew even if I tried to save up I wouldn't be able to afford resale tickets. I prayed every night I would be able to go and one magical day my parents surprised me with two lower bowl tickets to the eras tour and that wonderful night Taylor announced the rerecording of my favorite album at my show! Thank you so much Taylor for all you do. You have helped me through so much with my anxiety and depression and I love you so much. Thank you for changing my life." -Lucy

***

"Hi Taylor,

I'm a huge fan. I listen to your music 24/7. I've listened to you since I was like a kid and my childhood song is obviously one of your songs, you belong with me, I've never stopped listening to you, but lately I've just been obsessed with you and your music.

Your songs have gotten me through so much, heart aches, boy drama, love, and sad times. I always find one of your songs for each of my moods and I love that you have such a different variety of songs it's incredible.

Since this summer when I met my friend Becca,

197

who has been listening to you since she was 3 and has never stopped listening to you, we were some huge swifties. We've both made a ton of friends because of you, because we all love you and appreciate your art. I met Becca when we were both in singing camp and all we were listening to was your songs. I remember blasting all too well (10 minute version) and screaming to it. Becca was always a fan but ever since your album Midnights came out she's been obsessing over your music. She's even going to your eras tour concert in Toronto. We love you so so so much!!" -Sophia & Becca

***

"I became a swiftie in the lover era. I fell in love with all of the songs in lover and started listening to other albums such as Taylor Swift, Fearless,Speak Now, and more. I had a great time at the eras tour movie I had so much fun trading bracelets I got a 1989 one, 1 2 3 let's go b*ch and more. First ever song I heard that you made was Speak Now. Your music helped me so much when I was going through rough times such as Covid, family passing, illness and more. My favorite album is Reputation I never really knew why something about it just gravitated me towards me." -Ava, New Jersey

***

"I remember watching the Teardrops on My Guitar music video on CMT after I was told about it. I was hooked. I remembered Our song and all the rest. When Fearless came out I bought the cd and read every lyric so I knew every song. Tell Me Why is so amazing and in my opinion underrated. I decoded all the messages in every CD. My dad took me to the Speak Now tour and I love it so much. It was stunning and blew me away. It even impressed my dad. I will always be a swiftie even though I missed out on Eras tour tickets. Hoping my luck is better next time." -Natalie

***

"I have been an offical swiftie for about 2 and a half years. I heard your songs over the radio, (blank space, style, shake it off, bad blood (which my mom still has a video of me dancing to it), never getting back together, love story, you belong with me) and if I knew you wrote it I loved it.

Then when I started having to the freedom to listen to my own music, I found your other albums. You helped me get throw a really hard time in my life when I has struggling with eating disorders, self harm, depression, and other issues due to the abuse I faced after I lost my grandmother.

Now I listen to you nonstop and I dream of meeting you. I may not have been a switie from the start, but I will stay one forever (even when I get made fun of). Thank you for everything!

PS:

I plan on being a writer, and Kaila Lynn's my pen name. Maybe one day I'll be as amazing as you!" -Kaila Lynn

***

"Hi Taylor- I have been a swiftie all my life and 2 years ago my father chose his girlfriend over me and listening to your songs helped a lot. I can not get tickets to the eras tour as they are too expensive . I just wanted you to know that you can do anything!! My name is Isabel-Alice and I love you so much." -Isabel-Alice

***

"I was actually born near when Fearless came out but luckily I was still able to listen to Fearless even after I was in middle school well mostly her song you belong with me because the radio in my area adored the song and so do I, it was one of my favorite songs and I also fell in love with speak now! I remember watching her mv's and acting as if I was in them in my room. I wasnt actually a big swiftie though since I was young and I just enjoyed trends more which obviously will die as time goes on. And one day one trend popped up it was the song enchanted and it gave me flashbacks, but I didnt became a swiftie there I became a swiftie when I found out that speak now was getting rerecorded which led me to a whole rabbit hole about Taylor and I just felt so much nostalgia. I continued to listen to her songs and slowly became a swiftie, though I have a lot of things to learn because many things happened to Taylor while I was a kid and I was to young to understand or to care for it. But yeah now Taylor is my safe place, someone I feel like a friend from childhood who I need to catch up to after years of us being away." -Meta

***

"I became a big swiftie in 2017 during reputation and lover and she has changed my life. I was so little and my mom took a video. I look back now, realizing that was the best desion of my life . My siblings make fun of me cause I cried so hard when I saw the Eras tour movie cause that was the closest thing I would get to the tour (take this as sign to come to India!) anyways I love you so much, continue what you love doing!" -Rhesa Marie, India

***

"I'm from Pakistan. I'm a medical student here.

I became a swiftie when I heard Anti-hero from her newly released album (at that time) Midnights and

I started lovin' her as much as I could. Her advices, her interviews, her songs always help me cope with my depression and suicidal thoughts. Sometimes I fight with some of my friends for hating her but idc it is enough for me that she's such a big star shining bright. I just want to meet her someday. Be friends with her. I know it's not possible but I can wish. I have so much to say but that's it for now! I love you and I always will Taylor... U are my strength." -anonymous

***

"When Reputation was released it was playing on the radio. My sister and I thought the "cuz she's dead!" line in LWYMMD was funny, and we started asking my dad to play more Taylor Swift songs. That's when it all started. 6 years later I still love her music and don't know what I would do without it. Thank you so much Taylor." -anonymous

***

"Happy Birthday Taylor! I still remember the moment all too well, when I decided I would listen to your music and support you through your music industry. My friend who is the biggest swiftie ever, would listen to your music in the car, and I was never really involved. Until, I realized what your music really meant, and the quality of them. When it comes to the ideas, the artistry, and the tones behind them, every album and song has a big meaning. I now listen to your music every time I get. On the bus, in my room, in the car. Being a dancer, your music genres give me ideas and an extra boost of artistry. You have really taught me to speak up, be fearless, break your reputation sometimes, and that love can be burning red. Thank you for everything you do." -Claudia

***

"I have been a swiftie as long as I can remember. My mom had me pretty young and was born in October of 1989, a few months before you. She grew up with your music and listened to the original versions as they came out as a teenager and she is what really brought me to your music. I was listening to the original versions of Fearless as a baby, I was born November 13, 2008. 2 days after Fearless came out.

In 2014 when I was 5-6 me and my grandmom watched the premier of Shake It Off on good morning america where I danced in the living room. My earliest memories of music at all are all related to your music, whether it was playing in the car on the way to school, or when my mom used to sing me Never Grow Up as a lullaby when I was in elementary school.

When I was 9 in 2017, the original version of Reputation came out I remember my mom waking me up for school and her screaming "TAYLOR SWIFT RELEASED A NEW SONG" and we watched the Look What You Made Me Do lyric video on her phone. It was shocking and completely jaw dropping for my little brain. Some of my most rememberable memories are on the way to elementary school listening to reputation. My cousins are also major swiftie's and I remember a long car ride where we listened to the whole album front to back, screaming the lyrics into the late hours of the night.

I went to the reputation stadium tour at arrowhead stadium in 2017 and it was one of the greatest performances I've seen. I saw it with my best friend at the time Katie and her mom made us custom Taylor Swift t-shirts. It was a long concert and I was

202

really tired towards the end and my mom noticed I refused to sit down and she asked why and I responded "I don't want to disappoint Taylor!"

The surprise song was The Story Of Us, becoming one of my favorite songs for the rest of my life because of the memories of that live performance.

Folklore & Evermore were and are some of my biggest inspirations and guiding lights. After 2020 things were extremely tough at home. My mom was very unhealthy emotionally and took it out on me a lot. I was getting in trouble at school a lot because I hated being at home so much. I was in a custody battle with my mom and my dad, and I never knew who to believe. I didn't really get into folklore & evermore until 2021 when I was in 7th grade and things were the worst than ever. Those albums inspired me to start writing songs myself.

In 2022 I was taken advantage by a boyfriend and he broke my heart into a million pieces. I had stopped listening to your music for a bit but fell immediately back into the music as it all felt like it was about me specifically. Any emotion I was feeling there was a song I could scream. I listened to Red (Taylor's Version) on repeat for months. I listened to Midnights on the many nights I couldn't sleep and was haunted my my own life and mistakes. I started writing my own songs and playing guitar and I am still currently working on an album. I dream of being half the songwriter as you and you inspires me every day.

Family things got tougher and school and all the stress it brings got rougher, but I reminded myself that I always had you, and I will always have you. I genuinely don't know where I would be without your music as a support system, as a friend when nobody else would talk to me at school.

No matter how hard things get I can take comfort in the music. She's always gonna release music and it's always going to be amazing.

Taylor I hope you're reading this and know you are my biggest inspiration. You have been a friend and a therapist and even a mother when nobody else could be. I want to be like you and make my own music. Things are shitty but it's going to be alright and I know that now.

I run a Taylor Swift club at my school and I am raising by 1 year old brother to be a swiftie as well. I hope to continue the generational legacy. I love you to the moon and to saturn Taylor and I will always have your back." -Lapis, age 15 (@lapisthelovely on YouTube& tumblr)

*

"For most of my life I was not really into music and did not have a favourite singer but I liked some songs. But a couple years ago I started listening to music more (really viral songs) and I enjoyed it so I was looking for more artists to listen to. That's when I realized that a some of the songs I already knew were by Taylor Swift. I started listening to here more and I discovered that I knew a lot of her songs so I listened to a playlist with all her songs and learned more and I realized I love here music so every since I have been listening to her music (and loving it) following more stuff about her and watching A LOT of swiftie videos. I am so grateful that this happened to me because now here music brings me so much joy!" -Sara

*

"When I was nine my mom was going to take me to a Katy Perry concert. Since I was nine I kept confusing Taylor with Katy Perry so I kept asking "omg when are we going to Taylor Swift". And my mom soon noticed that I definitely liked Taylor more than I wanted to see Katy Perry. She started playing me more Taylor Swift and it became my personality. Everyone started knowing me for being the girl who was obsessed with Taylor Swift. As I grew up I started spreading the love with my friends and soon they started loving Taylor too! Taylor helped my friends and me get through our hardest times with her music. Wishing her the best birthday ever!!" -anonymous

***

"I am a swiftie to the core, although I didn't start till about a year ago when my friend said that she was a swiftie and then I was like okay I'll be one too. Which I know might sound odd to just become a swiftie but it's been two years since then and it truly is the best decision I could have made. I stated by listening and memorizing all of red then after midnights came out and I learned all of midnights and from there on I just started listening to everything on shuffle till you could name any song and I would know it. I used Pinterest as a way for me to know what was going on in Taylor's life. Taylor really is so important ti me especially since I have had a rough childhood since I have a really awful father. Listening to Taylor knowing how much she loves her fans gave me a sense that I'm not alone and someone cares. My dream was to go ti the eras tour but since my mom is a single mom I figured there was no way, however in my birthday my grandpa surprised me with tickets and the happiness I felt to see Taylor in real life almost made me faint. There I met tons of swiftie friends and am now part of a community and I wouldn't be anywhere else. I just want to say Taylor I love you and hope to one day really meet you." -Olivia

***

"I was born around 2010, so I grew up hearing shake it off and other popular songs on the radio, and definitely knew the name Taylor Swift. I didn't really start listening to her until the pandemic, though, when my mom and I listened to Folklore every day at lunch. That's when I started listening to more of her music, but I didn't truly become a swiftie until Red TV came out and I listened to the vault track "Nothing New" which really stuck with me due to the relatable lyrics and amazing vocals. I couldn't afford the Eras Tour but went to the movie and lost my voice from screaming the lyrics! My favorite album is Reputation or 1989 TV." - Zadie

***

"Taylor literally saved me. My grandfather had just died from Covid around the time Lover came out. I remember crying in my room when Taylor came on the radio and I stopped crying and started dancing and I didn't even know the song. Listening to Taylor helped me so much and I got through it. As of now almost 4 years later I am a huge fan of Taylor and my favorite album is Lover and Midnights! Happy Birthday Taylor!" -Reese

***

"What convinced you to become a swiftie?
I remember 2020's end, I listened to the Evermore album and some of her country eras songs and I realised that yeah, this is my sign to become a swiftie. I believe

her debut album songs really attracted me. Being a young teenager who is an avid daydreamer, those songs spoke to me.

<u>What was the first Taylor Swift song you ever heard?</u>

I was 13! (Yeahhh!) And in eighth standard, and my best friend suggested me to listen to blank space. She thought that I would love it as it might seem a teensy bit relatable to me. Plus the song is such a masterpiece. And then, every single day for the rest of my school year, I screamed that song in my school ground with her! Some of the best moments of my life!!

<u>Why do you love Taylor?</u>

I love Taylor because why not? She is an epitome of kindness, the personification of joy, the leader of humanity, the sass queen, the mastermind and yeah, the music industry! She takes care of the people around her, she's aware of her surroundings and speaks up against injustice. She has never let anybody get to her. She has this elegance, a grace with which she handles criticism. She treats her fans like her friends and is one of the most cute people on this Earth!!

<u>What does her music mean to you?</u>

Her music is like free therapy for me. At a point of my life where I was so low that I would spend hours sobbing in my room or just merely existing, when I stopped smiling, started hiding my problems from my parents, her songs helped me get through that phase. Not only melancholy, her songs have the capability to capture each and every emotion a human being could ever feel. No matter whether you're feeling like an antihero, or feeling like the most powerful woman in this world, she has a song for EVERY situation.

How has Taylor or her music helped you?

I guess I answered some of it earlier. But apart from helping me cope through the different phases of life, her songs are an inspiration. As I'm a budding songwriter, I listen to her songs and often try to decipher the meanings behind the lyrics. "What she must be feeling while she wrote them?" "Is it possible to write something this sad while feeling perfectly okay?" "Can I ever write something like this?" "Can I portray the same charisma in the words that I engrave on a white emotionless sheet?" These are things which often go through my mind while listening to her music. If we talk about Taylor, her personality has helped me to come back stronger than a 90s trend. She made me realise that it's not okay to be okay with the bad things that people say about you or the image that people make of you because of something that happened in the past; you have to speak up. Even before I got to know about Taylor, her journey and her career, I stood up for myself and for others. But I believe Taylor has taught me how to do it in a graceful manner. And yeah, I'm still making progress on that!

What is the best part of being a swiftie?

The best part of being a swiftie is the indirect interaction that we can have with Taylor through those Easter eggs and puzzles that she leaves for us to tackle! It's a thrilling experience, watching her music videos and be like - "oh! Isn't this scene referring to Wonderland?" I'm being very serious when I say that I have actually become more observant in real life due to the Easter eggs.

Another thing that I really adore about being a swiftie is the fandom. We aren't just a fandom, we're this huge family spread all over the world who connects with each other through social media, fan pages and what not! Never have I ever felt like I'm messaging a stranger while replying on community posts on YouTube (I'm sorry I don't have any other social media app except YouTube!) Everybody's so cordial, so respectful and just amazing!

If you could tell Taylor something, what would it be?

I love you Taylor! 1989 TV was amazing! I really loved the song "Say Don't Go"!!

It's my dream to meet you one day and also go to one of your concerts. Being from India, the chances that you'll perform here are really very less but I hope someday you will come here! Or maybe I could attend it in some other country!

My friends have nicknamed me "Swiftie!"! Whenever they find something related to you on any social media site, they send it to me, knowing I will have a fangirl moment!

I have dreamt of becoming a singer since I was around 8 years old. If fate agrees, and I do become a singer, it would mean the world to me if I could collaborate with you! I would love to share my songs with you so you can analyse them and help me find my shortcomings.

Thank you for everything Taylor!" -Azkiya, India

***

"I've been a swiftie since Midnights, I became a swiftie by hearing some of taylor's songs in edits or videos or whatever and being like "these are actually really good", then i started to listen to her music more and then I became a swiftie! My favourite albums Speak

Now, Fearless, 1989 and reputation! My favourite song right now is probably "is it over now?". I haven't been to a tour of Taylor's, but I love taylor so much because her music has helped me get through some things. I've watched the eras tour film and it was the best concert film I have ever seen! I love taylor for who she is because she's so talented, funny and so, so, so generous and kind. TAYLOR YOU ARE SO AMAZING AND SUPER TALENTED AND I WOULD LOVE TO MEET YOU!!! You/ Your music are SOOO much to me!!!" -Evie

***

"Hi! My name is Michaela, I'm 12 years old and I live in Israel. It's hard to explain what you mean to me. Your music has helped me through hard times, and is doing so right now. There's a war in my country, and not much things to smile for. Your music has been the exception. Your lyrics touch my heart. You inspire me so much, as a powerful woman, as someone who decided to follow their dreams no matter what people said, as a person who went through hard things in life and decided to make art out of it. Thank you for sharing your gifts with the world. Even though you don't know me, I still feel like you love me together with all the swifties. I Love You So Much! HAPPY BIRTHDAY!" - Michaela, age 12, Israel

***

"I became a Swiftie right as Covid 19 rolled around. My mom loved the album Folklore, so I began playing songs on the piano. Since then, I have listened to her music religiously, and fell in love with it! Taylor's music has truly brought so much joy into my life. When I struggle with Anxiety, Taylor's music has shined a light to my path and helped me through so many things.

I know I can speak for all the Swifties when I says this, we are all so thankful that you are in our lives, and you have brought so much happiness to us all! Taylor, we love you so much and Happy Birthday!" -Annabel

***

"I became a swiftie when I was 7 years old. I was listening to your new music from 1989 and I fell in love. My mom ended up buying tickets to your concert and it was the best night ever. 10 years later, I am still a huge swiftie. I listen to your music non stop! I love as how I grow older I can relate to your songs. The ones I especially relate to and love is You're on Your Own Kid, Now That We Don't Talk, Picture to Burn, London Boy, Is It Over Now, Cruel Summer, and Anti-Hero. Thank you for everything you have done for me!" -Natalee K.

***

"I first listened to Taylor when I was at a birthday party (I'm a relatively new swiftie) and my cousin was a swiftie at the the time (still is) so she introduced me to Taylor! She said her new album midnights was coming soon so I listened to it when It came out and I loved it! I listened to the rest of her discography and it didn't disappoint! My only thing that I wish I could do was go to her eras tour or even watch the movie. I live in Puerto Rico. A small island in the carribean and Taylor will most likely not come here. Anyways sorry for rambling!! I love you Taylor so much!" -Ian

***

"I guess I can say I really became a Swiftie around January 2023. That's when listening to music changed from something I did occasionally to something I did all the time and really connected and related to.

Of course, I always knew who Taylor was. But

instead of a real person, with feelings and ambitions, I viewed her as just another one of "the celebrities," which consisted of a very broad group including people like Kim K. and Brad Pitt. I heard her songs on the radio, and they were pretty cool, but I didn't think about them too much at all, really. I always took a liking to "Style," though, and it's my favorite song ever. Anyway, yeah. She was never really a part of my life until recently. Some people don't like how Taylor became super popular because that meant a surge of new Swifties joining the fandom. But I think it's a good thing because otherwise I never would've discovered what music could really be.

I can't exactly pinpoint when I became a Swiftie, just that it happened. I remember making this playlist with about five or six of her songs, which I now call OG's because those were the first of her songs I really listened to. This consisted of songs like "Forever And Always (Taylor's Version)" and "Paper Rings," and of course, I can't forget about MA&THP. I loved (and still do love) that one. But yeah. Just songs you first start listening to as a new Swiftie. This was all happening a little after she released Midnights, and it was probably largely due to the fact that my sister wouldn't stop talking about it. She's not much of a Swiftie anymore, as she doesn't get emotional connections to stuff like music and movies like I do. But that subconsciously affected me, and I kept discovering new songs of Taylor's that I really liked, including "Getaway Car" and "willow" and "cardigan." Eventually, I was like, why not make a playlist with all of her songs? And that was really the jump off the deep end for me. I started a Pinterest board for Taylor, really educated myself on her songs and associated lyrics, and started closely following the Eras Tour (as well as watching the Rep tour a couple of times. It's so good!).

This happened around the first half of 2023, and by summer, I was head over heels in love with her. I mean, not in love, in love. I just mean with her personality, and Swifties, and her music, and all the feelings that come with. She started to become a really big part of my life. Whenever I need a good cry, I still turn to "The Last Time (Taylor's Version)," and when this guy I liked turned out to be a jerk, I admit to changing the lyrics of ATWTMWTVFTV to fit my situation! I mean, now I literally know and use acronyms like ATWTMVTVFTVSGAVRALPS!

And I know she's mega-popular and can't possibly personally know every single Swiftie, but I think the reason we like her so much is because it sure feels like she does. She always does something special on a day I'm feeling down, like a merch drop, or a new Eras outfit. Some people may think it's silly to derive joy from these seemingly "meaningless" things, but I feel like you should, because spending more time happy than not is an excellent goal, and Taylor's helped me achieve that more than anything. So, in conclusion, I can't pinpoint when I became a Swiftie, not exactly, but I can certainly tell you why, and I think that's so much more important. Tay, if you're reading this, I hope it makes you happy. I hope your days are spent smiling and laughing and being enjoyed. Thank you, for everything." -Dorothea

***

"Dear Taylor, happy birthday!!!!! You inspire me in every single way!!! I became a swiftie about a year ago. I have learned so much from you. I learned how to value the important people in my life and ignore the people who are rude to me. I learned how to feel like I matter and that I'm amazing. I appreciate you so so so much and would love to meet you someday. I haven't had the opportunity to go to your tours but hopefully I will someday. I'm also a December baby (December 22) it's the best month ever!!! I love you so much Taylor and I hope you have an amazing birthday!!" -Eliana C., age 13

***

"I never realized I was a swiftie until I looked back and even when I was young, I still used to pick a song from my mom's playlist and it always happened to be a Taylor Swift song. Later on, I got deeper into her music, discovering all sorts of songs that made me laugh, cry, and smile. It's crazy how a song by Taylor can completely alter your mood. I went to the movie last month and I almost cried, it was amazing. I want to go to the Eras Tour, but can't get tickets. Love you Taylor!" -@SwiftieNation4You on YouTube

***

"It all started when I was a toddler, spending the summers swimming, listening to my mom's and aunt's Spotify radio. Of course, it was (and still is) all of the pop hits, like Katy, Lady Gaga, and... Taylor. I think the only songs I knew were You Belong With Me, I Knew You Were Trouble, Look What You Made Me Do, We Are Never Getting Back Together, Bad Blood, Blank Space, and Me.

I was obsessed... but as the years went on I got tired of the same ten or so songs, and wasn't a fan of Folklore and ESPECIALLY Evermore due to how young I was, and started to only listen to music on YouTube because of how much I hated using Spotify. The main thing that caused this to end was... my dad, a proud hater of any music love related, and pop. Even in hindsight I'm still surprised.

In hopes it would get me and my sister to quit spending every hour of free time we got, he bought our entire family a membership to Apple Music. This made my life 1000 times easier when it came to looking up and playing music, but you can't completely change what music you're into overnight. So, I kept listening to whatever was trending, just on an actual streaming app instead of YouTube. This all changed when I saw an animatic to Right There Where You Left Me, and it became my favorite song in less than a week.

I thought, "One point for Taylor huh? Still doesn't change the fact she's only a singer for kids.", it was such a lie, believed by almost every girl in my class as lots had a story similar to mine (sadly a good portion of the girls haven't yet become a swiftie). Then, Miraculous: Tales of Ladybug and Cat Noir plays a really big part.

I was scrolling through the usual MLB Gacha Reaction videos when I saw an MLB AMV to the song Paper Rings. I clicked on it thinking, "This is an editor I like, and it'd be nice to learn a new song". Just like what had happened with RTWYLM, but this time I had come to the conclusion that, Taylor wasn't that bad, but I wasn't a full blown swiftie.

Next, The Eras Tour happened. The previous year or so my love for Taylor had steadily increased, and one of my favorite artists being everywhere I looked only added more fuel to the wildfire that was my soon-to-be-swiftie heart. I made the executive decision to not yet call myself a swifte, just because of a few niche things.

And then, I realized that you don't need to be able to name the lyrics to every single song Taylor has, or ever will write. That's pretty much where I am now!" -Olive

***

"When I was five years old I was driving with my mom and Taylor Swift's song, "Mean" was on the radio. I asked her what song it was and she said "Mean, by Taylor Swift" that was the moment something clicked in my head and I was in love. About a year later I was taking the same drive with my family and my Dad gave me an IPod to download music. This poor iPod's storage was filled to the brim with "reputation," "1989" and the rest of her albums before them. Years later, I am still a die-hard Swiftie and I just saw The Eras Tour Movie and am in love. Thank you, Taylor, for being a huge part of my life." -Charleigh T.

***

"So a few months ago I was at my lowest I couldn't taken it anymore and me and my sister went over to my aunt's house every Thursday and she would put on all to well - tmv - and it really wasn't that important because it was just a song you know and I had already heard a few songs from Taylor but that song especially anyways my sister told me I gotta learn the lyrics so we could sing along so everyday i would listen to atwtmv just so i could learn the lyrics and when i started actually listening the lyrics meant so much to me and then something happened in my life that was exactly like the song so i feel really connected with that song especially but i do love all her songs." -Tabitha

***

"Hey Taylor, I LOVE your music and I would love to meet you but I live pretty far away from where you are. I watched your movie and it was amazing. I've been a swiftie since I was 3 years old when I was singing You Need To Calm Down, and when I was in primary I was so happy that I memorised all of the lyrics of Look What You Made Me Do. My favourite song by you is definitely Say Don't Go (Taylor's Version)(From the Vault) and Haunted. I hope one day I will meet you and I hope you loved this message. I hope one day I'll also be on Taylor Nation as well." -Rachel Q.

***

"At the end of 2022 I started listening to Taylor Swifts' music..... and then just got obsessed.

I find school hard, not the subjects but making friends. After I moved states back in 2021, I have never really found any good friends, they all seem nice and well at the time but after a little while they always find a way to get rid of me. But after I started listening to Taylor, I never really felt like it was as hard. Each day I come into school listening to Taylor's music and I know that at the end of the day if someone says something that upsets me, I can always come back and Lisen to Taylors music.

After that I got really obsessed. I tried to get Era's tour tickets, but I live in Australia and They sold out so fast. Now I'm a massive swiftie and would do anything to tell Taylor just how much she means to me. So, Taylor if you're reading this, THANK YOU so much! I Love you so much and I know that I would not be this happy as I am now if not for you!

I look up to you so much and think that you are an amazing human. I hope you have an amazing birthday and just know that you are loved by so many people.

I hope that one day you and I will meet. that is and will

always be my biggest wish!" -Tarryn S., age 13

***

"I became a Swiftie not too long ago, about mid 2020. Before that, I knew only one or two of Taylor's songs, and now I literally know them all. I love Taylor so so much, and it's not just because of her crazy amazing songs and voice. It's because she is kind, funny, honest, confident, fearless and true to herself and others. My parents think I'm too obsessed, my friends think I'm crazy, but they don't understand that I do genuinely look up to Taylor. I do. Taylor influences my daily life so much, and I'm so thankful for that.

When I'm sad or helpless, I plug in my headphones and let it all disappears. Taylor, you influence so many lives, more than you'll ever know. I will, sadly, probably never get the chance to meet Taylor or go to the Eras Tour, which is my biggest dream ever, just because of where I Iive. But I will never, never stop hosting the mini concerts with my broomstick as a microphone and the couch as the stage. For your 34th birthday, I wish you all the best, and the only gift I can give to you is letting you know how much I admire and look up to you. No one else will ever mean the same as you mean to me." -Matar

***

"I became a swiftie because my sister listens to Taylor all the time! So I just have to listen to Taylor and now I think Taylor's songs are really amazing. So if you are not a swiftie you should try listening to Taylor Swift!" -Luke

***

"Hi! My (YouTube) name is Swiftie Affairs! I first became a swiftie in 2014 when 1989 was released. I feel like every little girl had the same experience lol! My mom was actually the one who introduced me to her, she loved the album and played it all the time which got me into it! Unfortunately, around 2022 i started losing interest in Taylor for unknown reasons. Thankfully, my mom and sister was still big fans of her still and we went to the Eras Tour on April 15th, 2023! There i remembered how much i loved her and became a swiftie again!

Taylor has helped me in many ways with my mental health. Her songs like Anti-Hero, The Archer, and dorothea have all showed me that i'm not alone, and other swifties who relate to those songs are supporting me too. If i could tell Taylor anything, it would be "thank you for saving my life" because she really did. Back in 2022 and the beginning of this year my mental health was really bad and I was on the verge of committing. I felt depressed and like no one wanted anything to do with me, so I shut everyone out. Music was the only thing keeping me alive. The first song I listened to after i saw her in concert was this is me trying, because i remembered the song and not knowing what it meant, but I related to the lyrics perfectly. So, you can come after me saying i'm "basic" for almost worshipping Taylor but I have a reason.

My current favorite song changes literally every hour, but right now I would say "Slut!" I don't know why but it feels nostalgic in a way and it's literally the best vault track to exist. Lastly, my top 3 albums are all a tie in between the ore sisters and Midnights. They are all my aesthetic at the same time and the songs are on top.

In conclusion, Taylor, if you see this, I love you SO MUCH! I can't wait to see you on October 18th 2024 in

Miami!!!!" -@girlinred_stan5.fanacc on YouTube

***

"Ciao! My name is Alice, I'm from Italy and I'm here to tell you, Taylor, how I became a Swiftie. So, my brother, like three years ago, was obsessed with your song 'welcome to new york" he heard in a movie and I was curious about this Taylor Swift, like 'who Is she? I'm sure I heard from her, but...' so I started listening to some of your song and I started liking you, then loving you and now I litterally live for you! This is now I became a Swiftie!

And Taylor, if you're reading this, it means that the work of the amazing person who had this idea was worth It, because it bought all our love to you!" -Ali, age 12, Italy

***

"When i was younger i was kind of a swiftie but i didn't call myself that bc i never heard it but she was my fave artist. this was around the time of 1989 and rep and my favorite songs were shake it off and bad blood etc bc my gym teacher always played them in class! i kinda didn't really listen to her for a while until i was in 6th grade and my ela teacher who was a huge swiftie (she has Taylor Swift literary device posters in her room and stuff) kinda reintroduced me to her. after that i got hooked on her music and this summer i listened to more than i ever have in a summer! i rly wanna go to the eras tour or some concert of hers and i'd give everything to go but for now i saw the movie and gif all the merch they had at the movie ILY TAYLOR HAVE THE BEST BIRTHDAY!!!!" -taylorswiftieeeee13 on YouTube

***

"When I was a baby my mom would always sing

to me never grow up by Taylor swift I grew up loving her music and became a big fan around the age of 6 i am now 14 I never have gone to her concert but want to so badly though her movie was great! My favorite album is folklore and she is such an amazing person!" -Livi Q.

***

"I became a swiftie recently but I listened to Taylor's songs for a while. I fell in love with her songs in 2016 and jammed to her hits a lot. I even memorized Shake It Off when I was 7! Around April-May of this year I became a swiftie. I really got to know Taylor and listen to her songs! My favorite album is Speak Now and my favorite songs are Dear John, How You Get The Girl and London Boy. I absolutely love Taylor Swift and I dream on going to her Eras Tour!!" -Alicia

***

"Dear Taylor,

You have been in my life for so long. I thing I watched the shake it off video 10000 TIMES! I have been your fan for years but became a MEGA SWIFTIE when Midnights came out! For my birthday my dad got me tickets to see you on Night 3 in Philadelphia. I literally cried! Thank you so much for being in my life and happy birthday!" -Ophelia

***

"I have been a swiftie for quite some time now and this is how it started. I've been listening to Taylor for almost as long as I can remember, and one day I just decided to binge her discography nonstop. I instantly fell in love with every lyric she wrote. She is an incredibly talented songwriter and vocalist. She is not only an unbelievable singer, but also just an awesome person. I've watched video after video of her singing in the rain at the eras tour, smiling and laughing through it all. She includes such fine detail in every line in every song that a lot of other talented artists don't do as much. She is so compassionate about every song, every word, every fan, and so much more. I love Taylor so, so, so, SO much and I really hope that I can see her in concert one day." - C.Q.F

***

"So when I was little me and my aunt always listened to shake it of on the radio and we danced to it like it was some dance show. But when I grew older I never did it with her again. When I was 14 I heard music a lot (on Spotify) so I also listened to random playlists and one time I heard shake it off. I immediately starten dancing around and then I started listening to her and after 2 years I was an official swiftie. My only wish is to once meet taylor or see her on a concert. Thanks taylor for being there for me when no one else was even if its "just" with songs." -Cara, Germany

***

"I first heard Taylor's song "Look What You Made Me Do" on the radio and my little sister fell in love with it. She quickly memorized the song and danced to it all the time. After hearing the song I played more of her songs and now I'm in love with her. Now I'm a real SWIFTIE and listen to her beautiful songs every day. THANK YOU SO MUCH TAYTAY HOPE YOU HAVE AN AWSOME TIME! Also, yoou have such an amazing impact on my life and so many others." -Ava, Georgia

***

"I became a swiftie throughout the summer of 2023. I love this fandom so much! I wanna start off by saying that I love how you always gives us Easter eggs that we get to make theories about. I listen to your music all the time and my favorite album is reputation so far. My family has financial issues so I don't have that much merch but I do have a folklore cardigan, a pin that says "proud swiftie", 11 friendship bracelets and 3 stickers. I hope to get more merch in the future.

I want you to know that you have millions from all around the world that loves you so much and you deserve all the success that you have! If I haven't had found you I wouldn't have friends from around the globe and a girlfriend so thank you so much for everything that you have done for us! You're a mastermind don't forget that! I love you Taylor." -Jolin N., Sweden

***

"Let me just start off by saying Happy Birthday! Thank you for being there when I really needed it. I've always been bullied for being a "Swiftie" but I never let that bring me down... In fact, I was able to introduce you and your music to my friends! Believe me, I've cried to your songs, smiled to your songs, danced to your songs, even lost my voice from screaming! You're an amazing, powerful, loving, generous person! I don't know what to say but thank you.. Thanks for showing me what love is. If you ever see this I just want you to know that I love you." -Brooke

***

"I'm 13 years old and it's been a tough couple years for me. I've had to learn that not as many people care as I think do. But when I listen to Taylor it can just make my whole day with just one song. You've got a song for every emotion and every situation that you didn't even know existed until you feel them. And when you do your words paint the picture just right. I can't believe how many times I've just nodded my head along to one of your songs because it gets my feelings just right. My favorite lyric is "love you to the moon and to Saturn" from seven. It just reminds me to go easy on myself and other people. I know you don't even remotely know that I exist but you and your music is the one thing I know I can always turn to whenever I need to. Your lyrics are truly amazing, I don't know how you come up with these things. Each and every song is a masterpiece, a short story filled with the most beautiful life and emotion. Thank you from the bottom of my heart for being the wonderful inspiration you are." -Evy

***

"The first song of Taylor that I heard was Love Story in 2008. I didn't have much access to the internet.. I mean I was 8 at that time so obviously my parents wouldn't let me use the computer at home.. but my friend's mom owned a cybercafe and she would let us use the computer for free.. So one day my friend played the music video of Love Story on youtube and the song was just got stuck in my head and we'd listen to it over and over again along with all of her other songs..

15 years later not much has changed.. Love Story is still my favorite song but now it's my mom's favorite as well and she is also swiftie just like me!" -Daisy, India

***

"I only recently discovered Taylor, about when Midnights came out. I did not listen to much music and I came across the album and fell in love. Her lyrics were so relatable and I felt like she was speaking to me. I kinda knew who Taylor was before hand from obvious songs like shake it off, but this was when I really realized how talented she was. I found more and more of her music, and I loved every album. She really helped me feel more confident and her songs are so uplifting. I know now so many songs, and was so disappointed that I couldn't go to the tour, but was able to go to the movie. In all, she really gave me a love for music, and I love everything she does." -August

***

"I remember being 9 or 10 years old, listening to music on the family Alexa. This one song came on and it just captivated me. I danced like a mad woman, arms flailing and heart racing to "Shake it Off". After the song finished, I was tired and my hair was a mess, but I was happy. I wouldn't say that was the exact moment I became a Taylor Swift fan. She'd always been in the background of my life, I was aware of her and I thought some of her stuff was pretty good. I really started to become a fan around sixth grade, listening to Taylor's music and watching her music videos. Some songs that will always be special to me are "You Belong with Me" and "Mean". I remember listening to "Mean" and thinking about my fake friends who made me feel like I didn't belong. I sang along; "Someday I'll be living in a big old city and all you're ever gonna be is mean." It gave me hope, made me feel like I was the bigger person, the stronger one. And of course I dramatically sang and danced along to "You Belong with Me" in my room thinking about this one boy I really liked. My love for Taylor and her music continued to grow from there.

Something that's really special about her songs is that you can pick your own meaning for them. While I was excitedly waiting for the arrival of Speak Now (Taylor's Version), I listened to "Innocent", not knowing who she wrote it about. I interpreted it as Taylor singing directly to me, telling me something I needed to hear; "You're young and you're going to make mistakes. You can't expect to be perfect. I know you're growing up and it's hard, but 'your string of lights is still bright to me'". That made me feel safe.

I love how Taylor always cares for others, especially her fans. In addition to being an incredible, talented mastermind, she's also a sweet, funny, down-to-earth person. She's very brave and puts herself out there, something she's been doing from a young age.

So dear Taylor Swift, if you're reading this I want to thank you for making my life brighter and inspiring me. I love you to the moon and Saturn! Happy birthday! P.S: Now would be a really good time to bring back the secret sessions. We're ready for it." -Simona

***

"It all began on my birthday. I was really bored and waiting for my friends to come, so I switched the TV on to look for something to watch. I was scrolling through Netflix's bountiful selection until I came across a movie titled "Taylor Swift Reputation Stadium Tour". My first thought was "Wait, isn't Taylor Swift that girl who sings Call Me Maybe?" (I know, my knowledge of music was very bad back then). And then I realized that she was the person who sang two songs that my dad would listen to; You Need To Calm Down and the last great American dynasty. So I thought to give the movie a try because I loved listening to You Need To Calm Down with my dad.

I clicked play, and when Taylor came on to the stage and said "Are you ready for it?", I became instantly hooked. And then... the strangest thing happened, I started dancing to the music. It was just so catchy and I loved it. Eventually, my friends came over and I had to pause the movie, but after that day, my life was forever changed.

I started to listen to reputation a lot after that. I would listen to it in the car, on the treadmill, in my room, literally everywhere. At first, I thought it was a dark and emo and scary album but I began to really get the feel of reputation. Reputation is really just a love letter written in black ink.

After listening to reputation a lot, I decided to look for other albums in Taylor's discography. My next pick was Lover because it had You Need To Calm Down in it. I started listening and it was like the opposite of reputation. Reputation was more synth and black aesthetic, but Lover was more bubblegum pop and pink aesthetic. Surprisingly though, I loved it. But the song that instantly caught my attention was Cruel Summer, just everything about it was perfect. And I blasted it the whole summer.

From Lover, I branched out to other albums, even reaching to Debut and folklore. But it wasn't until 2022, when I started listening to evermore.

Before that, I had always hated evermore, it seemed so boring to me. But there was this point in my life where I was going through lots of emotional problems and evermore just really resonated to me.

Crying to champagne problems in the middle of the night.

Dancing to willow before school.

Humming ivy during the day.

Evermore started to really become my favorite album.

The thing about evermore is that it feels like you can listen to it anytime. When I'm happy, I listen to evermore, when I'm sad, I listen to evermore, when I'm mad, I listen to evermore.

Words cannot explain how much I love and adore this album. Thank you so much Taylor for creating this because it really helped me through some of the hardest parts of my life. My favourite song from my favourite album evermore, is happiness. There's just something's about it that is just so powerful in every way. It's a bittersweet song and I just really got attached to it the more I listened to it.

Some of my happiest memories are built around Taylor. Counting down to Red TV with my best friend. Listening to Midnights after I come back from school. Screaming along with All Too Well (the ten minute version of course).

Thank you Taylor so much for bringing so much joy into my life. We Swifties are so grateful for everything you do and your music resonates with so many of us around the world! Have an amazing birthday!" -anonymous

***

"I have always loved taylor since I was 7, but when I turned 13 I became a die hard swiftie. I became a swiftie during midnights. anti-hero started playing on the radio and i thought it was the coolest song. so i started listening to midnights, which led to lover, reputation, 1989, etc. then when i heard about the Eras Tour, that's when i officially decided that this is my life from now on!" -Grace F.

***

"I was a swiftie since a little girl. I was always

listening to shake it off or look what you made me do but just a year or two ago I became a real Swiftie and started listening to her every day she made me happy and in a good mood. My sister and my mama are also a Swiftie, my mom got to go to the Era's tour with her friends for her birthday and her friend's daughter went to Era's Tour and got the 22 hat! Almost all my friends are Swifties. For Halloween I was Taylor Swift, and I hope I can go to the Era's tour sometime. I went to the movie it was a blast, I got the bucket and the cup and I just want you to say you are amazing Taylor." -H.S, age 10.

***

"Around a few months ago I felt sad because there was no one else that liked my favorite thing at school (which was weather). There are a group of swifties in my class and my objective was to fit in so I became a swiftie. Now I felt like I was fitting in finally. I have this thing where I get an obsession and just stick to it. That's exactly what happened and is still happening.

I have been to The Eras Tour movie because tickets to the actual tour are obviously expensive and it was good. As of right now, I have 3 TS vinyls, SNTV, Red (stolen version, and 1989 TV. One more thing, Thank you for all of this Taylor and all the Swifties out there." - @Sharkbytee on YouTube

***

"Hey my name is Shahrzad. I started becoming a swiftie in 2014 when taylor released 1989. I remember driving in the car on my way home from dinner and hearing Wildest Dreams on the radio. I made my mom do 5 laps around the neighborhood to hear it. Then when the song ended my mom switched to another radio station and guess what was playing again... Wildest Dreams! I absolutely loved how she sounded and little 4 year old me was mindblown by her singing. I would listen to the album on repeat 24/7 and go to class telling all my friends about her. Then a couple months later for my birthday my mom gave me the 1989 album with a cd player to play them in. I still remember being so excited about the polaroids and thinking taylor sent it to me specifically.

My 14th birthday just passed and my mom bought me 1989 (taylors version) and i was soo happy. ever since 2014 have i been a fan. i was so happy going to the eras tour and being able to relive all of the old eras. I went night 3 at gillette and was section 13 seat 13 row 13 and wad 13 years old, 13 years ago u first performed at gillette and it was your 13th time performing at gillette and I got 13 written on my shirt. (you could say i was lucky.)

Every 4th of july we would go down to the watch in rhode island to watch the fireworks and every year i would sit right infront of your house and wish u would come outside and give us a concert (yes i know i was delulu) Happy birthday taylor i cant wait to continue this journey with you." -Shahrzad

***

"I remember the first song I ever heard was Lwymmd (Look what you make me do)in kindergarten. I don't know if I was out of my mind or just an idiot but I was dumb enough to listen to it at least 1 million times and not become a fan. Like why? The second song I heard (that was not shake it off) was blank space. I heard it on some shorts in 2021 and I still didn't care. It was only until January of this year that I heard a song. I really liked it and did research. I saw that most of the songs I've heard and liked were from Taylor. I started listening and in no time I fell in love. I didn't listen to her in albums but instead in songs. Whenever I heard a song that sounded like her, I would listen to it. I started to learn about her life and saw all the things Dr. Taylor Alison Swift has achieved. The progress that I have made in these 10 months is incredible. I finished 1989, Reputation, Lover, and Midnights! I also finished folklore in a very minor way because I watched Folklore: the long pond studio sessions. I've started watching Miss Americana and it has touched me. I just turned 11 on November 14 and Taylor swift is such an idol for me. She has gone through so much. Sometimes, when someone says they don't like Taylor swift I ignore what they say. I will never ever leave Taylor's side. I will keep listening and supporting. In fact, I'm listening to 1989(T.V) right now while writing. She writes such masterpieces. Each one deserves a Grammy and a VMA. I recently watched Taylor swift: the eras tour on the craziest date ever. October 27th! The day that 1989 tv released. I went with my swiftie friend and we both were 1989 obviously. She had a shirt that said Style! So jealous! Anyway, our seats were almost at the top but that didn't matter because we went all the way to the front in the open space and we danced our hearts out. I wish she would have played Maroon, Glitch, Getaway car, End game and a few more in the movie but the songs that were there were absolute masterpieces. My favorite albums are 1989 and Midnights but the transition between Ready for it... and lwymmd was just the best." -Nabhya, age 11, Canada

***

"One of my first memories of Taylor is when in 1st grade, my teacher had us sing a parody to Shake It Off saying that growing up isn't as scary as it seems, and everything will be alright.

I am growing up right now and feel separated from the other kids my age, in my theater classes, at church, school and everywhere. I feel as though I have no one to turn to who can truly understand me. 'You're on your own kid" perfectly encaptures how I feel every day, especially when it speaks about a boy, and the line "I gave my blood, sweat, and tears for this."

I'm the stage manager for a play we're doing at school, and I'm giving it my all. The thing with the stage manager though is that there's no one like me. There's the actors, crew chiefs, and crews, but just one stage manager. I feel as though I have to carry my burden alone, and I am literally giving my blood, sweat, and tears for it. The only thing that is getting me through the stress, the pain, and even the suicidal thoughts of having to keep my grades up, please strict parents, and be a good stage manager is listening to Taylor's music.

I know many of her songs by heart because of days I wanted to cry, I know every step of her career as an inspiration for the days I want to give up, and today I got a standing ovation from the cast members, my first recognition for the months of hard work and tears, and if it weren't for
Enchanted when I see a hot guy,
You're On Your Own Kid when I want to cry,
The Way I Loved You when I feel perfectly fine when I shouldn't,
Bad Blood when I want to punch someone's face,
Long Live to feel loved,

Cardigan when I was to give up,
Death By A Thousand Cuts when I feel heart broken,
and Getaway Car when I want to run away, I wouldn't
have gotten my praise today.

So Happy Birthday Taylor Alison Swift! You will
forever and always be written in the pages of my
teenage dreams, and will always be a role model for me."
-Kathryn C.

***

"I became a Taylor Swift fan when I was young
but really started listening to her in 2019. I love folklore
because it heals me. I once cried and realized that I
had to get back up and invisible string did that. I went
through a hard time in my life and I was hurt. Clean
helped me through it a lot. I think Taylor should do
a rock album!! My favorite songs is Would've Could've
should've , Haunted, and Seven because im from PA!
My first songs I listened to were out of the woods and
getaway car. I love Taylor so much and I feel warmed
that I get to be a part of this!!! I LOVE YOU TAYLOR!!!!" -
anonymous

***

"It all starts from when i was about 3 or 4. I was
riding in my aunts car and she decided to introduce
me to Taylor Swift by playing the song You Belong
With Me. I immediately fell in love with taylor from
the moment i heard her. So everytime I would get in
the car with my aunt, i would ask her to play Taywer
Wift (I couldnt pronounce her name correctly, and I also
couldnt pronounce some letters). So after a few years
my aunts moved away, and I didnt have anyone to ask
to play Taylor Swift anymore. Until one day I was in
the car with my mom and heard a familiar voice coming

from the car, it was the reputation album. My mom has been a huge fan of rock for years, and taylors Reputation album was similar to her interests. I immediately became interested in this new album I was hearing and became in love with the song Ready For It by Taylor! A little after that I finally got a tablet for Christmas/birthday and saw taylor more and more everyday. I fell in love all over again. I started watching music videos, dancing to her songs and copying the dancers, and overall just enjoying my time watching her. My overall favorite from youtube was ME from the lover album though! This went on for a couple of years till i kinda forgot about her and didnt own a tablet anymore. But luckily, it all came back soon enough. Last year, I went through some really hard time with friends and family issues. During that though, i met 2 people, and i couldnt be happier. 1 of those people was a HUGEEE swiftie, while the other wasnt lol. So during my time last year with them, i learned a lot about taylors albums, why its called "Taylors Version" and more. There were even some times where the non taylor friend had some tough moments with taylor albums lol. My taylor obbsessed friend asked her, "whats your favorite Taylor Swift album?" And she replied with "uhm, cruel summer?" We all died laughing and its been a joke till now. Without taylor, im not sure if I would be in this amazing friend group and have made it through the hard times, thank you for everything. Happy birthday queen, let your legacy live on!" -Karsyn

***

"Hi! My name is Avery and I have been a swiftie for 7 years now. It all started in December 2016 when I first started listening and supporting Taylor. I felt really bad for her because of the huge conflict between her and Kanye ,and because it was really disrespectful of him. I listened to every single song of hers that she had released up to that point and fell in LOVE with her red album.

In 2017, when reputation was released, I was ECSTATIC! I was especially eager to get tickets for her rep tour when it was announced. But oh, how my dreams were crushed. My parents absolutely hated everything I did, and I didn't have enough money to go on my own. I cried for days after that.

I knew it was just a minor thing, but it was more than that. They never supported me through my toughest times. I tried so hard for them and did everything I could, and was never rewarded. My grades significantly dropped. But there was one person who stuck with me. And that, ladies and gentlemen, was Miss Taylor Alison Swift, the sweetest and most gorgeous (get it?) human on this Earth, with a heart bigger than the whole sky (I'm really good at this aren't I?)

Her music pushed me to do better, and if she could get through bad things, I could too. It's amazing how a person who has no idea you exist could change your life forever. I've been a diehard swiftie ever since."
-Avery

***

"In the year 2020, evermore and folklore had come out. I had loved Taylor's last album lover but I wouldn't say I was a swiftie. My dad comes up to me and says "have you heard Taylor's new album evermore?!" I replied saying I hadn't listened to it yet. He says "you need to it's incredible!" Now In my head I thought my dad likes Taylor Swift!" but soon enough just after I listened to that album I liked Taylor Swift! We listened to the album 24/7 as we were stuck in all the time. My dad even started listening to Podcasts about her leading what the songs were about. Our favourite sounds from the album were tis the damn season and champagne problems. And this is how I found out not just me but my DAD were both swifties." -Juliette

***

"My name is Sophia. I'm a teenage Swiftie from Toronto and here's how I became a one:

When I was younger, I loved Fearless, Red, and 1989, but around Covid I forgot about her music.

Around when she announced that the Eras Tour would be starting, I thought I'd give her music a second chance since everyone was a huge fan. I picked a random song from Fearless since my favourite song ever used to be You Belong With Me, and I ended up choosing Mr Perfectly Fine. I immediately fell in love with that song and now I'm a huge Swiftie." -Sophia

***

"I have always loved Taylor Swift but when her Midnights album came out i became obsessed! Anti-Hero would always play on the radio in the car and i learned every word! To this day i love her much and think she is an INCREDIBLE human. She had broken so many records and needs to be appreciated on her birthday! i really wish i could go to her Eras Tour concert in Canada but i couldn't get tickets! i was so upset but am still IN LOVE with Taylor! i really really REALLY hope she see's this!" -Frannie S.

***

"Hi Taylor. This is how I became a swiftie: I was 4 years old and in my mom's car listening to "Shake it

Off" and tried singing. I know I mumbled trying to sing but I still sung. Then I did the same thing with "Look What You Made Me Do" and "...Ready For It?". Those were my favorite songs by you. Your music is amazing and truly life changing. It calms me when I freak out. Right now my favorite song right now is " Willow". I love singing and dancing to your songs. Your a natural born leader.Thanks for everything you do!" -Zoey L.

***

"Hey Taylor if this book ever works out I love all your songs since I was a little girl and the first so I learned to sing was shake it off I loved the song and sang it to the public multiple times. Singing your songs has now put me in my own band and inspired me to sing. One of my new favorite songs is cruel summer! I have not been to one of your concerts yet but I hope to go to one soon! That's all for now but I really hope you see this my I am 12 years old and my name is Kayla I love you Taylor!" -Kayla, age 12

***

"I'm a new swiftie, only became one a couple of months ago, but during summer i was in this summer camp. I made a new friend that was... A swiftie! I kinda had listened to a couple of Taylor's songs, so i was familiar with her (i really liked Karma at the time). We started talking about what music we like, and we came to the conclusion that we both listen to Taylors music (even tho at that point in time, i had listened to only a few Taylor Swift songs). She asked me what my favorite song was. I said "Karma or maybe Blank Space" (I still LOVE both of thouse songs). She said "Enchanted". I dindnt know Enchanted at the time, so when I got home I listened to it. AND I LOVED IT.

After camp ended, i kinda forgot about the fact that I liked Enchanted and just kinda put Taylors songs down and started to listen to other music, but still Karma and Blank Space were there, i still listened to them. Fall came. I have to go back to school. I completely didnt listen to songs in September, only when i heard them on the radio. In October I pulled up YT Music and went to listen to some music. There I saw my forgotten songs: random other songs, but more importantly: Karma and Blank Space. Those were the lead songs that got me into being a swiftie. I listened to Karma and was like: hmm, maybe lets check out some other songs.

I slowly started listening to more and more Taylors songs, that i just created another playlist for them. At the start there were like 17 songs. Not that much, but 17 songs from one artist in a playlist with all sorts of different music just was kinda weird. Not a swiftie yet. Then, my fyp on Youtube Shorts started to recomend me a bunch of different videos of Taylor and swiftie and of that. Thats kinda where i became a true swiftie. In about the span of a week, my Taylor Swift Song playlist grew to 50 songs from Taylor. And then, i "declared" myself a swiftie. Now that playlist has almost 100 of my favorite songs from Taylor, but I still want to add more, becouse all of Taylors songs are amazing! And if you're curious, the random song playlist is abandoned, i haven't listened to it since!" -Karina

***

"I'm 14 years old girl in Finland. It was a normal day of my life in 2021. I was normally watching YouTube as I used to do a lot at that time. And then I saw the "You belong with me" music video... and I totally loved it! Then few weeks went by and I saw another music video, which was the "Love story"... and I also loved that. So, I went to my Spotify and put them to my liked song. Then I started to get more and more of Taylor's song to my YouTube page, and I found many of the songs including Shake it off, Blank space and I knew you were trouble. Those were songs I had listened when I was a little kid. But one song hit hardest at that time... Wildest dreams!!! I had loved that when I used to made Musically videos with my childhood bestie.

After that I started to see more and more of songs, new and old ones. And I have loved Taylor's music till this day so so so so much that I can't even imagine life without Taylor's lyrics, melodys and all the meanings behind those lyrics. I became Swiftie about 2 years ago, and haven't seen Taylor live, yet. But I went the Era's tour movie. And funny story... I started to cry before even 1 minute had gone by. I also did bite my lip so I was bleeding like half of the show. I had waited so long for the moment to sing every word and have a special evening at the Finland's first evening, with my mother. And I'm so thankful of the help Taylor's music has given me in anxiety, happiness and all the moments I have had bad blood with someone. So THANK YOU!" - Sanelma, age 14, Finland

**

"Dear Taylor,

I was so blessed to become a swiftie from your song " Enchanted" I have been a swiftie since late 2021. I even got to see your tour at Pittsburgh Night 1!! It had to have been the best night of my life. I even sat in seat #13 i was so happy when i realized!

I started listening to all of the your music after the tour whenever i became a die hard fan. However,

I have been listening to songs from "Speak Now" since early 2019 but like i said i really started listening after the tour! I know every song on the setlist of the eras tour and i even saw the movie!! I also recently got your 1989 and Speak Now Taylors Version cardigans!! I know every song from Speak Now, Red, 1989,and even Debut by heart! I cannot even explain or express how much i love you! I have also watched every live stream of you concert! I have your 1989 (Taylor's Version) vinal and CDs in every color. I have your lover book/Journal. Lastly i have 3 magazines and that "Taylor Swift" book. My favorite song from each album is, "Picture to Burn", "If This was a Movie (Taylor's Version)", "Enchanted(Taylor's Version)" or "Ours(Taylor's Version)", " Red (Taylor's Version)", "I Wish You Would (Taylor's Version)", "Getaway Car", " Miss Americana and The Heartbreak Prince", " The Lakes", " 'tis the damn season", and last but not least, "You're on Your Own Kid". I even have all your albums birthdays in my calendar!! I love you so much Taylor, and happy birthday!" -Naveah G.

***

"Hi Taylor!!!! HAPPY BIRTHDAY!!!!

My name is Grace, I'm a 12 year old Canadian Swiftie and I love you sooo much!!

I have always loved you and your music. Shake it off came out when I was really little and I remember when I was in Primary/Kindergarten, my teacher would play the music video and my classmates and I would dance and dance!! It is a memory I will never forget and that is when I first heard about you!

After that, the older I got the more I would hear your music around. When I was in maybe Grade 2 or

3, Blank Space was always on the radio and it was kind of me and my mom's song. I remember saying "Cause darling I'm a nightmare dressed like a daydream" and giggling with my mom. That song has a special place in my heart.

By the time Midnights came out, I was a fan. I remember being excited for Midnights to come out and right when I woke up I went straight to Spotify to listen to it and was obviously blown away by how amazing it was!!!

I would say I became a swiftie when Speak Now (Taylor's Version) came out. One big memory about that day was listening to Enchanted (Taylor's Version) for the first time. I could hear the difference in your voice and I became obsessed with the song.

Now 1989 (Taylor's Version) means so much more to me than you could probably ever imagine. I had a sleepover with my friends to stay up until 2AM so we could listen to it. We made a poster and got all dressed up. I DMd you on Instagram, not expecting you to see it but just for fun! I literally lost my mind listening to it. I was laying on the floor shocked listening to Clean (Taylor's Version) thinking, "you are finally clean" because now 1989 is yours.

Becoming a swiftie was such an amazing decision. The swiftie community online is so kind and in person when I went to The Eras Tour Movie!

Your music isn't the only reason I love you. You are probably one of the kindest, most amazing people ever. You are also so funny and humble and just so genuinely happy. You also remind me of my mom and my mom is my favourite person in the world so that's a big compliment! And you just remind me of her because you both are so, so kind and caring.

Taylor, there is so much more I want to tell you but I think I'll stop here just for now. You are amazing and your music has helped me cope with so much. Byeee! I love you soo much!!" -Grace, age 12, Canada

***

"Hi Taylor, Happy Birthday!!! It's Uzay, I'm a Swiftie in Portugal and I love you, your songs, and literally everything else. The first Taylor Swift song I ever heard was SHAKE IT OFF and I had a gold rush! Literally every single day I vibed and danced to shake it off, and even though it was my worst decision of all time (you could say that I Did Something Bad) I stopped being your fan for a few years, but the second Midnights was released I realized that being on The Outside of the swifties sucked and I became a hardcore swiftie, I listen to your music 24/7, I have a channel that supports you on YouTube, I've watched the Eras Tour movie and I'm trying to get tickets for the Eras Tour in Lisbon, Portugal, I have 3 dreams, I dream of being a pop singer just like you (don't call me immodest but I do have a good voice), I dream of meeting you and I dream of going to the Eras Tour and getting the 22 hat!!! My favorite album must be Reputation, I mean Call It What You Want but it's a masterpiece of yours. Taylor, I would love to know you, unfortunately this is the closest form of communication I can get to, like this is me trying very hard. Anyways, I hope you like the book, and have a Happy Birthday on your Christmas Tree Farm. Most importantly (ILOVEYOU) US SWIFTIES LOVE YOU!!!!!!!!!" -Uzay, Portugal

***

"Hi Taylor! I'm a huge fan of yours from Texas.

I absolutely love your music and you in general. You're an amazing person and you deserve all of your awards and recognition. I hope that you believe that you are amazing and unstoppable. You really are the man, Taylor. I became a swiftie because I realized how awesome you truly are. I went to the eras tour movie to support you and I was in awe. Whenever I listen to your music, I feel empowered and that I am able to do anything I put my mind to. Your album "Reputation" was my first vinyl record that I purchased. Ask anybody about what was going on in our house and they would say, "Oh, that girl would be playing reputation nonstop!" Your music helped me through my first year of middle school. You pushed me to keep going. Now, you keep going, Taylor! You've got this! Happy birthday!" -Remy, Texas

***

"I listened to my first Taylor Swift song (Look What You Made Me Do) when I was in fifth grade after I saw it in a world record book. I listened to that song so much I memorized the song and even the whole music video. I started listening to some of her other songs then and the year after. But just this year I have started listening to her entire albums and discovering her truly poetic song like exile. I have now realized that Taylor is not just an amazing singer, but she is an amazing songwriter, dancer, and is so generous and kind to her fans. I also like how she hides mysteries and stories in her albums and social media. She is definitely the most talented artist out there, and that is why I am a Swiftie!" -Kiki

***

"Since I was three, I have been listening to "Shake

it off" and "Look What You Made Me Do " and I related to her songs, but I never was a Swiftie...until now. I have been on the year-round swim team for 3 years. I made a Taylor joke to my friend, and they said they were a Swiftie. So, I decided to listen to some of her music and research her life a bit. Well, a "little" research turned into an OBSESSION. I always got little obsessions but this one is HUGE. Some funny falsehoods I thought about Taylor. I thought when people said, "Taylor has the best bridges" I thought they literally meant a bridge and I thought the "Speak Now" studio album was called "Sparks Fly."

In July I saw the day it came out, Speak Now Taylor's Version, I listened to the WHOLE thing, I rated the songs, then I began to listen to all her other songs. Speak Now is still my favorite but I have a more "cultured" view of her songs and life, I have learned about the meanings behind her songs, read books about her, and created art featuring her in it. I am the biggest and truest Swiftie you will ever meet. I adore all her songs. Every time I pass a record store with Taylor in there, I long for it so bad even though I do not have a record player. I made a 13-hour playlist of Taylor. My parents got me a Taylor Swift magazine after my first community theater play. I saw Taylor's movie and rated the outfits, the same day I saw the reputation stadium tour movie. I made videos with my friend about Taylor. I did not realize it was picture day, and I wore a faded junior jewels shirt, but I have no regrets.

I have met a fair share of people who do not like me or are annoyed by me for loving Taylor Swift, but she is an inspirations and helps so many people including me and her values are true, and she is the kindest, sweetest person ever. Swifties inherit these traits. The Swiftie bond is strong, and they are the kindest people you will meet. Just look at this book for instance I saw this post at 7:00 on a Friday night and rushed right to tell my story. because all of this to say, I hope Taylor has the best birthday ever, I love her some much and hope the people who read this smile, because Taylor makes her own way, forages her own path, she found a way to own her stolen music, she is an icon and inspiration. all of us could learn a little from Taylor swift. If you read this Taylor, I love you so much, I want to preform and be just like you in my own way, so if I'm ever famous I just want to say, you started this for me and it is something to look forward to and a JOY to live my life Taylors version!

I hope you have an AWESOME birthday Taylor, be true to yourself, happy 34th birthday!" -Lucy G., age 12

***

"I personally always listened to a little Taylor here and there, but how I became a Swiftie is actually a really funny story. Someone close to me was going through a phase where she would only listen to Ariana Grande. I said "That won't last a month." She told me that if I tried, I wouldn't either. I was committed to proving her wrong and started listening to all Taylor because I was never the biggest fan of Ariana. I realized she is amazing and so talented. I started wondering why she was re-recording her albums and also found how great of a business woman she is. I always thought she might have a songwriter but when I looked at the credits it always said "Taylor Swift," which made me admire her 100 times more. It all started as a bet, but soon became my life. Taylor is a role model and inspires me to follow my dreams. If that person never listened to Ariana, my life would be so different. I would've never became a Swiftie.

This is one of the most fun experiences I had involving Taylor Swift. I went to the Eras Tour and this will sound cliche, but the show was just as great as everything else, except the car ride. I was hanging oit with some friends and I saw a text pop up on my phone in a group chat. It was a Friday and someone said in the chat, "Do yall want to go to the Eras Tour?" I was so confused. I was like "Wait what?" She told me we can drive to Minneapolis (like an eight hour drive) and get tickets once we get there. If we didn't get tickets, we would've tailgated. I was like "Let's do it!" and so were the other two people. We grabbed our best outfits and headed there. We booked a hotel for that night and the next one. I obviously didn't have time to make bracelets, but I left the night with full wrists. I had obstructed view, but how she moves around the stage and how they use screens still made it AMAZING! I went to Minneapolis N2, I got Dear John and Daylight, and when I went it really felt like you knew everyone there. Like you were best friends with all of them since kindergarten. It was magical. It's safe to say I made 70,000 new friends that night." -Anni

***

"When I was about 8 years old, my best friend and I would always dance and sing to "You Belong with Me" and "Love Story." We loved her classics and her most popular songs. Just this past year I turned 13 and my friend really got me into becoming a true Swiftie. I love all her music and I love what Taylor does and what an amazing person she is. I recently went to her movie, and I loved it, now I am rying to turn all my friends into Swifties too." -Grace

***

"This is how I became a swiftie. One of my good friends was a swiftie long before I was. She would sing the lyrics to songs I didn't even know existed. She was over at my house and we were going to watch a movie. I let her choose the movie. She wanted to watch <u>Miss Americana.</u> I said that it was fine and we watched it. I only knew very few albums and songs. After watching this I decided to do some research on Taylor. I learned when her birthday was, her cat's names, and facts about her. I learnt her albums in order, listened to a lot more of her songs, and watched the Reputation stadium tour. With this information I also have turned m y sister into a swiftie as well. Although I wasn't able to go go the Eras tour, my friend, (Yes, the same one who turned me into a swiftie.) took me with her to the movie on opening night. It was the time of my life. Now, I know so much more about Taylor, and if it wasn't for my friend you wouldn't be reading this right now, because it wouldn't be here. I now have many Taylor things in my room, including two posters, a cup (From the movie), ten bracelets, and a keychain. Thank you for taking the time to read this!" -Violet

***

"Hi Taylor! I have been a swiftie since i was around 5-6 years old, and the story of how i grew to love you is kind of crazy. So, my family used to go on many many road trips and I actually listened to 1989 in the car to put me to sleep, funny enough, and now i get to jam out to 1989 TV with all my swiftie freinds. AHHHHH I hope u see this and happy birthday Taylor!!!!!!!!!!!!!!!!!" -Alma

***

"The day before Seattle night one I had my birthday party (that was very belated because my bday is in January) and my uncle flew out from NY to surprise me. I enjoyed the rest of the party but when I got back to my house the unimaginable happened. He gave me a gift that had a TS tshirt, some bracelets and a clear bag. My friend was also at my house because she was staying the night after the party. My uncle showed us a pic on his phone and it had four tix on it for n1 in Seattle. I broke down into tears because I had been begging my parents to go since the day it was announced. My uncle told my friend that she was going to and she also started to cry. Her family was at my house as well and her younger brother who didn't realize how big of swifties we were just said "why are you guys crying?" That night was one that I will never forget." -Reilly

***

"My story is actually a bit bittersweet. The woman who got me into your music is someone i no longer talk to, though I have known her for a good chunk of time. She was something of a teacher/ mentor/ best friend to me. There was actually a bit of trauma from what this woman did to me. You see, she built me up, she supported my musical asprirations when my parents wouldn't. She told me I was great, called me her "songbird" and "superstar".

I started performing open mic nights at a bar in Manchester, NH (that no longer exists) called RAXX Billards. We had talked an hour before I was supposed to go on. She said she "couldn't wait to hear me sing". She never showed up, she left me, she was gone, she blocked me, I had been ghosted and to this day I still don't even know why.

So there was some trauma for years that had to do with that whole thing. I even for years forgot what happened (i guess the trauma made me forget) but that wasnt the end of my pain. I developed PNES (psycogenic non epileptic seizures), which are seizure like episodes brought on by stress and trauma. The doctors didnt know why until I started remembering what happened with that mentor friend im talking about. I wasnt hooked up to the moniter and my heart rate skyrocketed and thats when they figured it out.

Since then, i've made many friends. I went to a peer support center called On the Road to Wellness and the people there are so awesome. I made some really good friends there. They helped me accept and get through my trauma and now i've started singing again. I want to get into it more. Also i've rekindled my love for your music. Thank you!" -Kelly F.

***

"When I was about 3 years old, 1989 came out. Shake It Off was my favorite song. I have many videos my parents took, mostly of my sister and I (she was 1 at the time) screaming at the top of our lungs. Even in 2018, we still sang it while holding our baby sister for the first time. It never got old. It was Our Song. Our mother would also play it every time we got in the car. We had a Playlist. Shake It Off, Bad Blood, Blank Space, and Style. When reputation came out, I was too young to understand what an album was, I just considered them my new favorite songs. Look What You Made Me Do, Ready for It...?, and Delicate quickly became a part of our favorites. Next came Me!, Paper Rings, Lover, You Need To Calm Down. Older hits also joined our playlist, like You Belong With Me, Love Story, Mean, 22, and We Are Never Ever Getting Back Together. Then covid hit. I was so caught up with online learning that I never really was introduced to the ERAS Tour in January. Tickets were really expensive, so I was okay with not going. But then a friend told me that she went to listen outside, And a man came up to her, asked if she wanted tickets, then led them inside, had them pay him, and they got really good tickets for $350 each. At that point I became determined. After getting rejected, I asked if we could go to several places. Soon, the second leg of US tickets came out. I didn't get tickets. It's the same with Vancouver. it just didn't work out. Now, I hope that Taylor will release new tour dates, and I can get a bunch of people to sign up, so I can finally get tickets. Even though I've been to the movie, the actual concert, I've heard, just Hits Different. Ever since I heard about the tour, I've been catching up on her music. ATW10MVTVFTV is amazing, but my favorite album is still reputation. It's Taylo r letting free and not caring about anyone else's opinion, and the songwriting is amazing. My other favorites are 1989 (TV) and folklore. But finally, to Taylor, I wish you a happy 34th birthday. You are amazing, and us swifties will support you!" - anonymous.

***

"Dear Taylor,

I love you so much and happy birthday!!!!! I became a swiftie quite a long time ago and before that my parents have been swifties for a long time and went to the 1989 tour which was the best concert that they have ever been to!! If you actually read this, I want you to know that you are such an inspiration to an amazing amount of great people!

I had school art homework to do so i drew you in your snake reputation outfit at the eras tour and i really liked it, and i am doing this 1989 embroidery at the moment and i am going to put it on my wall!! And i really want to start making music now because of you and your amazing inspiration.

I know you are probably not going to see this but thank you so much!!! For everything that you have done!!! And thank you in advance for every amazing thing that you will do. And I love you so much." -Lily

***

"Hello Taylor! My name is Baylee. I love all your music. How could you not? No other music can come close to your music. People who do not like your music must be an alien. I've never been to your concert , but I would love to. I did see the movie though. While you performed Betty, I almost cried! Now back to the reason I'm messaging you. I hope you have the best birthday in the existence of birthdays. May your birthday be as great as your song Paper Rings. Have a great day Taylor!" -Baylee L.

***

"I first became a Swiftie when I saw the you belong with me music video. For the next few weeks I just watched that video on my terrible tablet. I started to look more into her music when I was bored at my dads basketball games (he's a coach). The first album I like listened to in full was Lover, which funny enough I listened to at the championship basketball game. I was in summer camp when Speak Now TV came out and my camp counselor let me watch the ICSY music video on her phone. Taylor, if you see this, I just want you to know that your music has helped me so much in the past few years." -Hannah C., age 14

***

"Hello I saw the amazing idea of this birthday gift for Taylor and I'm such a big fan of her, even do I didn't go to the eras tour or even the film, Taylor would be always my childhood and i just really think she is one of the most inspirational persons in the world with her breakup songs and her love songs they would always be on my heart because they have help me and inspire me a lot thats why i became a Swiftie. I would be so happy if this gets in the book that the swifties want to make. So after all I said: Happy Birthday Taylor!" -Mapausli

***

"I started listening to Taylor Swift since I was 2 because my dad is a big swiftie too. So the first song I ever listened to was the you belong with me. That song used to be my life my dad has a video of me singing word by word when I was 3. Well fast forward when I'm in 2nd grade/6-7 years old I write a full biography on her and I remember 1989 was a big hit and I had written about how she was born on December 13 1989 and other fun facts about her. Fast forward agian to 6th grade and I had my first crush and he told me I was ugly and I'm telling you that was the worst feeling ever I remember coming home that day crying and went in my room and listened to t swift for the whole night. Last year when I was in 7th grade t swift made a big comeback and I was so excited that she is going on tour. I remember my parents saying that I can't go because we can't afford the tickets. I was devastated but I knew

I can just listen to the music my self and have my own eras tour. Then when she announced midnights I completely died I was so excited to listen to it. Then this year over the summer she announced about the eras tour movie and I was like so happy I was about to get tickets to go see the movie. Then I get a text from my bestie saying hey my mom rented out the whole theater for the eras tour movie you wanna come and I screamed and ofc I went. It was amazing I got to go to my eras tour. When the day came i was in my junior jewels shirt and pj pants and I danced and sang until I died it was the best experience of my life. About a month ago 1989 Taylor's version released and we had spirit day at school just for her and I was in a full outfit for it.

What I'm saying is Taylor Swifts music has been with me for 12 years and I love it I might not be the best swiftie but I consider myself a swiftie." -London S., North Carolina

***

"I have been a Swiftie since Red, and was introduced to her by my preschool teacher. She would constantly play her music for me and I immediately fell in love. Taylor has inspired me in so many ways and has just taught me to be confident in who I am. I have seen her in her reputation tour, and the Eras Tour. Both were so memorable and I will never forget them. Happy birthday Taylor! Love you!!!" -Izzy S.

***

"Taylor-

I've been a huge fan of yours since Reputation. I honestly can't believe how much you've improved and changed from your country era and I couldn't be happier that you are a part of my life. You have truly changed my life and I can't thank you enough for that. I can't think of a day that I didn't listen to your music and I know every lyric to every song. You are my biggest idol and sometimes I question if you are even real because of how perfect you are. I love you so much and you have changed me for the better. Your music has gotten me through so many things and I just can't thank you enough for everything. In my eyes, you are the most perfect human on earth. You are incredible and I love you. All I want is for you to be happy. If you're happy, I'm happy. I hope you keep creating music, keep being an absolute angel, keep going on tour, and just keep being happy and being you. I love you so much." -Ellia

**

"I became a swiftie about a year ago when Midnights was released. I am barely a teenager so I had never really listened to her music before but I had heard about how to album was breaking a bunch of records so I started listening to it! That led me to all her other albums, learning about taylor, and the amazing swiftie community! Midnights is still one of my favorite albums today, and I am proud to call myself a swiftie. I absolutely love Taylor's music so much and I admire her so much, she is an inspiration!" -anonymous, age 13

**

"Hey T Swizzle! From the day that I first listened to you until now I have been astonished with your work. Although I may be young I am obsessed with your songs, albums and everything. I have watched you grow over the past few years, and I can't wait to see your next piece of art! I vote for you for president Miss Swift! By the way, Happy Birthday Tay Tay!" -Emilia (a swiftie who writes a 13 on her hand every day!)

"I remember my first time hearing Taylor, everyone else was such a hater. I grew up in a town that absolutely hated her and so did it. I mean I didn't know any better. As I grew up my cousin started listening to her more and more and tried to get me to as well. I thought it was stupid. "Taylor Swift is so overrated," I would say. I didn't know at the time but I was SO wrong. My cousin finally got me to listen to all the albums in order and over time, they grew on me. I remember relating to the lyrics and feeling emotions I hadn't felt before. A few years back I lost a friend. My best friend. She was one of the happiest people in the world and I never saw her cry. When she died I was ruined. I remember going back to school and people would ask me what I did over Christmas break. I had to look them in the eye and tell them I went to my best friend's memorial. When I listened to Marjorie for the first time I felt comfort. Taylor Swift. A pop star that I refused to listen to, was comforting me through music. That's something not a lot of people can truly do and I think about that everyday. I was falling apart and after years I finally found comfort. Thank you Taylor. For all that you do." -Wesley

***

"I started listening to her more popular music a few months ago, and then I got really into it. I like all of her music, lyrics, and the way she handles things as a business woman. She paves the way for young girls everywhere, and is an awesome role model!" -anonymous

***

"I have been a swiftie for as long as I can

remember. I love Taylor and her songs. She is like a mother to me. Her songs are the reason us as swifties love her but its not just that. I love her becuase she is kind and smart. Taylor's songs are just like therapy. You can listen to them and it just heals you.

I was not able to go to the Era's tour because she did not come anywhere near I live but I got to go see the film of the tour and seeing her become a queen she is, its outstanding. Taylor deserves more than anyone in the world. She has had hate thrown at her and she did not get mad. She stood up for herself and did what was right. Things like this are what make her Taylor. I love all her songs and know most of the words to every song she has! I have never met her but she has helped me come a long way and one day I hope to become as talented, smart, generous, and popular as she is today. She is the one who inspired me to start writing music and it has changed my life. Her songs are like messages and her being a very secret person the only way to get to know her is by her songs.

She is the kindest person on Earth. If you havent heard, she has donated to every place she has gone to so far to preform. Taylor is in everyones hearts and she can change someones life. Seeing how far she has come from being a little sixteen girl on a Christmas tree farm from writing her country album "Taylor Swift" to being thirty-three and becoming a billionaire and owning 10 albums that are still in the process of being re-recorded. I would do anything to see her, like any other swiftie would. She would go far for her fans if they were injured or in a emergency. I believe Taylor is not just about her music and all the guys she dates. It is something more.

I love Taylor and all her swifties who have been by

her side since then. She is a great leader and has become one of the best female artists of all time. My parents were divorced when I was three and her music has helped me through that. I would do anything for Taylor. Thank you Taylor for helping me with everything that has happened in my life. I am very thankful for all the swifties who have been by her side in the making of becoming the popstar she is. Happy birthday Taylor. Merry Christmas to everyone!" -Juliet

***

"I became a Swiftie when I watched All Too Well (10 minute version for the first time). It was after the Eras Tour started, so I'm a new Swiftie. I slowly started listening to her more popular songs and albums but I eventually got to Folklore, Evermore and Debut, and I never appreciated Taylor more. But I caught up and I know things that happened years ago, and it's as if I've been one since Debut. I love her and my friends constantly get annoyed with me because I talk about her too much. She is such a big inspiration to me. Taylor makes me feel so much better about myself. She has a song for every occasion and whenever I'm feeling down she makes me feel better. My favorite albums are Folklore, Speak Now and 1989. My favorite songs are Wonderland. YOYOK. and Champagne Problems. I don't know why because I can't relate to any of them but there's just something about it that makes it amazing. I hope Taylor has an amazing birthday, and I thank her for everything she has done for her fans and for others. She is the sweetest and most wholesome celebrity out there. Thank you for everything you've done for us Taylor. We love you!!" -anonymous

***

"I became a swiftie quite a while ago. I used to listen to her songs on road trips and blast fearless, red and 1989. i never really acknowledged her that much until i became a bit older and learnt how to understand concepts. it was only the end of 2022 when i started listening to her songs non stop and now i know every song from every album and more. she has helped me through so much; parents divorce, moving countries and many more events in my life. i don't know what i would do with out her. i've started collecting her cds and i'm just waiting for rep tv and debut tv to be released then i'll have the full collection!! my life long dream is to meet taylor. i am going to the eras tour in 2024 so at least i'll see her in person!" -Scarlett R., age 13, Australia

***

"I became a Swiftie when I was actually pretty young. I wish I could say that I was a fan of hers when she released her first album but I wasn't into her music back then. Like a lot of Swifties, I was first introduced to her music when she released the original 1989 back in 2014. I remember I used to listen to Shake It Off all the time and it was my absolute favorite song ever. I used to say "hecka" good hair instead of "hella" during the Shake It Off bridge, and I find that hilarious nowadays.

I was still younger during the 1989 to reputation kind of transition, so I didn't really know the whole thing that went down between Taylor and Kanye and everyone else that was involved, I just knew that a lot of people were hating on Taylor. And before I knew it she had dropped a new album- reputation. Look What You Made Me Do was immediately my favorite song and I listened to it all the time! I wish I could say I went to the reputation stadium tour, but I didn't. That's alright though, I can watch it all I want to on Netflix.

When she dropped Lover, it was also one of my favorite albums. I remember singing to ME! and Cruel Summer and having the time of my life. I was devastated when Loverfest was canceled.

By this point, we were in the pandemic, and I wasn't really sure if she'd release new music any time soon. But then we got folklore out of the blue, and it made my world. By that point, reputation was my favorite album, but after that, folklore became my favorite. Until six months later when she released evermore, and that became my new favorite (and still is today!).

Then came the re-records. I was so happy for her that she was re-recording her music and taking back what she owns, and it was fun to go back to her previous eras and listen to those albums with new songs being added to those said albums.

Another surprise (as she loves to do), we got Midnights! I love that album so so much. Unfortunately I didn't get my hands on tickets to The Eras Tour, but I find myself watching live streams whenever she's performing somewhere. I love seeing what she'll play next for the surprise songs, and it's fun watching her bring back songs as far back as her debut album.

When she announced Speak Now (Taylor's Version), I was extremely excited for that album, and ended up loving it (right now it's my favorite of the four re-records). And when I watched on a grainy live stream that 1989 (Taylor's Version) would be released October 27th, I was near to tears. I could relive a part of my childhood that was so significant and important to me.

Her music has impacted me so much- no matter what mood I'm in, I can always, ALWAYS find one of her songs that fits perfectly to how I'm feeling. I find myself constantly listening to her and I know she's the top artist I've listened to all year. If I were to tell Taylor anything, it would be to just keep writing music. She's changed lives, and given so many people almost the tracklist to their life. Love you Taylor!!" -anonymous

***

"Hi Taylor,

I became a swiftie after watching your reputation tour film on Netflix. I worked at the Eras tour in Los Angeles for the first 3 nights. Luckily I got to usher on the third night! It was incredible. On the first day after the concert a little girl came up to me and asked me "Will you tell Taylor thank you for singing for us?" I told her If I see her I will. So thank you for singing for us! Also thank you for making the concert movies. They're so cool!" -Kvinde

***

"Are you Ready for It Tay? You are the most outstanding aspect of my life and although I have never met you or ever seen you, I feel a special bond with you. We were both born and raised in good ole Pennsylvania and we both have a strong passion for singing and songwriting. I became a swifte during her original 1989 album because when I hear shake it off and blank space I automatically fell in absolute love with Taylor! I now live in Florida and I am praying on everything that I get concert tickets to your Miami show. I unfortunately was unable to get them in Tampa so seeing you would mean the absolute world to me. I also live relatively near your dad in Apollo Beach and I'm always on the lookout for him! Anyways, thank you so much for everything you have done for me in my life. I've I hope you have the most beautiful and awesome birthday girly!" -Anna, age 13

***

"So I was raised on Taylor Swift, so I know the basic songs. But I didn't really listen to her after that. Then in 5th grade everyone was talking about her so I listened to more of her songs! Now she is my inspiration life style and she loves her fans, and we love her so very much." -Dayja

***

"dear taylor,
your music saved my life. i have some disability's and you and all the swifties were so accepting and kind to me. i never once felt left out, or like you didn't care. i knew how much you cared. you care so much and your such an amazing person. i was very depressed and you helped me find my way through it, and helped me begin to love myself. i believe i have you to thank for my life. i love you to the moon and saturn, always and forever. on every bad day for the past 6 years i've listened to your music to help me work through how i felt. you deserve the world taylor. i'll always be here for you, like you've been here for me." -Elisabeth M.

***

"When I was little, I used to always listen to "Shake It Off" and other popular songs at the time. I always listened to Taylor's popular songs, and I loved them. I didn't really know who Taylor Swift was until the Christmas of 2019. On that Christmas day, I got surprised with tickets to go to the Eras tour. I felt so lucky because I knew how hard the tickets were to get,

I was so excited. At the time I didn't know most of the songs on the Setlist, so I listened to them every day and tried my best to learn them. When the day of the concert finally arrived I was so excited. Once I was at the concert, I was so inspired by Taylor, and I wanted to do better things in my life. I tried harder in school, and started learning all of Taylor's songs. When people said I wasn't a swiftie, I tried harder to learn about Taylor. To this day I still look up to Taylor Swift and I hope I get lucky enough for her to read this paragraph. This is my journey of going to the Eras Tour and becoming a swiftie. I was so lucky to be able to see her in real life and I hope I am a swiftie for the rest of my life. Thank you for taking the time to read this and I hope you enjoyed it." - Julia S.

***

"I have always been swiftie, even if I didn't know it then. I was born in 2010, right when Taylor Swift was the big news, and when Shake It Off came out, I was 4. It was one of the little songs that 4-year-olds can listen to. I remember singing it by heart. Fast forward a couple of years, I listened to all the hits on 'reputation' and 'Lover' because I didn't have access to full albums then. Then, long story short, the world shut down, and when I did my schoolwork, I wanted to listen to music. It started with the country (thanks, Dad), but then, one day, I clicked on the 'The Story of Us' music video. I was instantly hooked. Suddenly, my playlist was Taylor Swift, and I could not get enough. However, that was during another artist's big break, so I became obsessed with them. However, her music always stuck with me. Then, in 2022, I found she was dropping midnights, and I decided that would become my entire personality.

I listened to every single song by her for three months straight. I discovered songs like 'King of My Heart' and 'I Think He Knows' that deserve to be singles.

After midnights, I was amazed and in love with her music. When Taylor Swift announced the eras tour, I did a little digging and didn't get tickets. But after listening to hours of Taylor Swift, I got tickets for 6/2 in Chicago by some miracle. I dressed in a 1989 version of the VMAs after-party look 2022. Finally, the day arrived, and I had matcha for breakfast. That was one of the worst mistakes I have ever made because little did I know matcha was an antioxidant to clear your intestine. It doesn't go well when you have a sensitive stomach like me. So, the entire day, I felt as if I was going to throw up. I still went, and I am not kidding when I say as soon as Taylor Swift came on, I have no stomach problems again. During 'The Archer' when she came, she looked at me. That was the single best moment in my life.

So, Taylor, if you are reading this. Thank you. Thank you. THANK YOU. You have taught me to be confident in my beliefs. To be strong. Most of all, to be proud of what you love. I love you so so so so much! Happy birthday!" -Jessica

***

"I first began my swiftie journey by casually listening to all her hits when I was younger like: 22, Shake it Off, Blank Space, etc. When 2019 hit I listening to Me! and fell in love, I would listen to it everyday on repeat. In the following year, 2020, I listened to Cardigan and watched the music video and remember thinking: "Wow, that was the greatest thing I've ever heard." Then, I remember I was watching the TV one day and I saw Taylor performing 'betty' and I was so amazed about the fact she was having so much fun performing and that the lyrics she was singing were creating a story.

Fast forward to 2022, Taylor released Midnights and that's when I absolutely fell in love with Taylor's lyricism, passion, and beautiful music. Her songs had so much power to them and so much depth that I seemed to grasp on and it was truly life changing. Then, I began listening to all her other music and I fell in love with the way she writes her music, how she can tell a story, and how she can make the song feel so real and pure is so beautiful.

Taylor has changed my life and there has been some days I truly don't want to go on another day but her music helps me pick myself up again. She was there for me when other people weren't and I love her so much for that and I thank God everyday that she is on the same Earth as me." -Ryleigh

***

"Hi, my name is Aliyah! I started listening to Taylor Swift when I was three years old because that was around the time 1989 came out. Blank Space was the song that got me into Taylor Swift. In fact, my first song I could ever sing, before ABC and Twinkle Twinkle, was Blank Space. I have loved music since I was very young. Then, a few years later, reputation came out, and there, my swiftieness intensified. I loved Look What You Made Me Do so much. And when Lover came out I was obsessed with You Need To Calm Down. Then I kind of forgot about her for a while. Until Midnights came out. Midnights changed everything for me. After Midnights was released I started re-listening all her other Albums. Then I realised, she is really my favourite Artist. And here I am, more Taylor Swift obsessed than I ever was and I could ever be. My Taylor Swift obsession has become so big that I am known for being a Swiftie between me, my friends, my classmates and even my family. I am also known for taking any free moment to listen to her, even at night. Taylor has also brought me and a bunch other People together. Because of her I have made quite a few new friends. I've also turned some of my friends into Swifties and we even got to go to The Eras Tour Movie together. It was so awesome. I hope one day I get to go to the actual Eras Tour. Taylor also got me through some tough moments in my life, and her music makes me feel much better. I feel like I can relate to most of her songs. Her songs are so powerful and fantastic. Us Swifties really care about you, Taylor, and we will do anything in our power to protect you. We will always support you. Taylor, if you are reading this, I LOVE YOU TAYLOR!" -Aliyah

***

"So how I became a swiftie is it started with my teacher for 5th grade always talking about you, and saying stuff about you and all of my cheer friends loved you! So I started to listen to your music and I automatically turned into a swiftie I love you so much and I listen to your music everyday and every song is an amazing piece of work! I have always wanted to go to one of your concerts and meet you but that sadly hasn't happened yet but at one of your concerts I will be out there in the crowd and nothing can stop me!" - anonymous

***

"Taylor- I've always grown up exposed to you. I

was born early 2007 so right around when I was born was you became a sensation for the first time. Growing up, I always heard songs like ybwm, love story, and wanegbt in public and I always vibed to them, but never knew who sang them. 1989 was my first time I think becoming a fan. One of my core memories is strutting and dancing around a frame shop to the entire album right around the time it came out (although I had no idea it was you, I thought it was Lady Gaga). I finally learned who you were in 5th grade when Reputation came out. My Swiftie teacher donated a Rep cd to the school news and I made sure we played it every day because that was the only cd I liked.

Years went by casually listening to your music and following along with all the cool things you did (I was really impressed when the ME! mural thing happened on my birthday). I became a true Swiftie around the release of Red tv. It was emmy freshman year and everyone kept talking about how they were so excited about Red being rereleased, and feeling left out of the loop I decided to check it out. I learned all about your re-recording journey and fell in love. I listened to every song from every album in order, added your songs to every playlist, and listened to Red the day it came out.

From then on I have not gone a day without listening to your music. Your songs have gotten me through everything - failing my first AP test, finding new friends and losing old ones, and losing out on the Ticketmaster lottery twice. I just want to say thank you. I have no idea who I would be if I never listened to Red tv, or even 1989. I'm so excited to hear what you have in store for the rest of my life and just remember that if you ever feel like no one loves you, me and all these lovely people do. Happy Birthday!" -Rachel

***

"I've been listening to songs like 'Shake it off' and 'Welcome to New York' since I was like 8 years old. I really grew up with the 1989 album. But maybe like a year ago I discovered Reputation and I fell in love. I immediately became a huge fan of all her music and I've been obsessing over her ever since. Recently I've been dealing with depression and self harm, and to be honest Taylor has been helping me 10 times more than any therapist could ever. I'm crying while writing this because it brings back so many memories. Taylor has been my mom when my own mom wasn't there. Her music saved me so many times. I will forever be grateful for that. My favorite song is 'Long Live' because of the deep meaning behind it.

I listen a lot to Folklore because it matches my energy level and it feels like it keeps me from drowning. Taylor, I love you and thank you so much for everything." -Juliëtte, age 13, the Netherlands

***

"I was 9 at the time when my friends used to listen to Taylor's songs like Blank Space and Bad Blood. They listened so much that I got into her. Then I explored of who she really was and her albums and songs. The first album I got into was 1989 because like literally everybody knew about it and it was like everybody's favourite at that time. I had like the vibe listening to it. The actual time I got obsessed with Taylor was when I started listening to reputation. Reputation is still my personal favourite album and the vibe is just unexplainable! After that I found out about lover and I was freaking OBSESSED I loved all the literal songs like they were amazing and lover is still one of my fav albums.

Then I got into fearless and speak now because I think I had to calm down after listening to reputation lol! Red isn't my personal favourite album because it's just not my style. The only song I like from red are: All Too Well, 22, We are never ever getting back together, I knew you were trouble, The lucky one, Sad Beautiful Tragic and State of Grace. The of course folklore and evermore came out and they were just pure talent. I got obsessed with them immediately. I loved all the songs and I think those were my favourite albums at that time. The obviously Midnights came out and it was such an amazing album. I immediatley listened to all the songs and they were like amazing no joke. In the honour of Midnights I even got a Mac Book Air that was the colour midnights and I even put some Midnights stickers on it.

The reason why I got to know about these albums without the order that they were released in was because I didn't really have that much info about the albums so I just listened to them in the order that I found out about them. Debut hasn't really been my fav like I only know: Our song, Tim Mc Grew, Teardrops on My Guitar, Picture to burn and Stay Beautiful. I think debut has its own vibe like every album. My personal fav albums are Reputation, Lover, Fearless (T.V), Speak Now (T.V), Folklore and Midnights! All the albums are amazing at their place and I'm so thankful for having these amazing songs to listen to everyday and vibe with them! Taylor has such amazing talent for creating these amazing albums and producing them for us swifties to listen to.

Taylor I love you and I wish you the happiest birthday ever. May all your wishes come true!" -Ayat

***

"I have always been a fan of her, ever since I can remember. I just love all of her songs and she is just so beautiful. I love Taylor so so so much and it would be my dream to just know that my message would get to her! I don't have many swiftie friends but I'm hoping to go with my one swiftie friend to the eras tour in London!! I am sooo excited and I can't wait! I am really hoping for tickets because that would be my dream come true! I'm also waiting for my 1989 cardigan to arrive. I bought it straight away. 1989 and Fearless were my childhood. All of the best times of my life, Taylor was there. I love her with all of my heart." -Zara

***

"Hi ! I'm just a very normal (sometimes abnormal) teenage girl from India. I am 16 and don't really have a very happening life like my fellow friends. As far as I can remember, I became a swiftie in 2019. Late,I know. Back then, I never listened to music and even if I did, I only listened to Indian folk songs and Devotional songs. Even though I grew up in an English medium school, I never actually listened to English songs that much. I was so wrong when I thought that someone's music taste shouldn't make others hate them. I was constantly bullied and laughed at when I told my friends that I only listen to Indian folk songs. Like, how is that an issue? I don't even know. I also had a phase in my life back then when I stopped listening to music altogether. Then one fine day, my cousin felt bad for me and played me "Wonderland" by Taylor Swift. Honestly, I didn't even know who Taylor was back then.

I found that song really catchy and went on to listen to all other songs by Taylor. And slowly but surely, I started falling in love with her. Not only her, I started falling in love with the music she makes and the person she is. You won't believe how many friends I gained when I said "I listen to Taylor Swift." Well, loving her music didn't make me stop loving Indian folk songs, though. Instead, it widened my interest in music and made me want to discover all the genres like she does.

One thing I love about being a Swiftie is the warmth we receive from each other and Taylor. Like, one day I was walking up the stairs at school when I noticed a Taylor Swift keychain hanging from someone's bag. When I said to my best friend, "Oh look, it's Taylor Swift", the girl with the Taylor Swift keychain turned around at me and hugged me tight saying, "Oh my God, you're a Swiftie too?!". We are very good friends now. I also like sneaking in some Taylor Swift lyrics into my English essays.

My current favourite albums are "Lover", "Folklore" and "1989 TV". Honestly, I don't really have a favourite song cuz I love all of them and it would be an injustice done to the other songs if I had to name only a few. Well, the Debut album is also my favourite.

I really think that Taylor is very radiant. For someone like me, I could only find comfort in her songs because she has a song for literally EVERY situation. EVERYTHING. I even named my diary "Taylor" so, every time I write in it, I actually write a letter to her. Helps me to connect better. It wouldn't be wrong to say that Taylor Swift has changed my life. And sometimes, I am very grateful to my sister for introducing me to Taylor. What would I do without her?

I know it's weird but I would like to end by writing a short note for Taylor.

Dear Taylor,

Firstly, a very happy birthday. I hope you get all the happiness of the world and also continue to be the infinite source of strength and happiness for so many people. Ok, secondly, PLEASE come to India. Because I can't wait to see you in person. I can't wait to scream and dance at your concerts with the other Swifties. Thirdly, I don't even know if my writing will make it to the book or if you'll ever read this but I'm hoping for the best. You have no idea how much I love you. Thank you so much for inspiring me every single day. You helped me to stand back up during the darkest phases of my life and I'll be forever grateful to you for that. You have changed my life, Taylor and I have no words to thank you. "Thank you" is never enough. And the words "I love you" are not enough to express what I feel for you. Even if I have no chances of meeting you, just know that I am there at some corner of the world and I'll forever be your well-wisher and continue to support you till the day my existence is erased from planet Earth." –Purna, age 16, India

***

"I've been a swiftie since Taylor's documentary "Miss Americana" came out. Before "Miss Americana" was released, I listened to Taylor a little, but the documentary changed my opinion about her completely. Not only because of the music in it, but her natural personality, the way she makes other people feel like they fit in, and even her problems just made me think about her differently.

After watching the documentary, I decided to

research about Taylor and her songs. And became absolutely in love with her music!" -Noa

***

"I walked in to my very first art lessson in high school, it must have been the second week of year seven, and our teacher put us in to a seating plan. As always because of my disability I was sat at the front, right by the door, next to a girl called Bella. We started talking and I soon found out that she was a huge swiftie. As the lessons went by she told me more about taylor and her music, I remember going home that night and doing my homework but instead of listening to my usual playlist I listened to Taylor. I started to listen to more and more songs and learned about the different albums. This is how I became and now am a completely devoted swiftie! My faviroute album is Reputation because when I listen to it I stop caring about what other people think of me. Taylor, if you are reading this I would like you to know that your music makes me free of my disability and that I think you are a hero." -Sorrel, age 12, UK

***

"My sister has been a Swiftie all her life and I mean all her life. It literally started in debut! So she's really the one that made me a Swiftie. Being a Swiftie means being able to listen to Taylor when you're having a horrible day and she cheers you up. Being a Swiftie makes my life so much better and so much more fun! I LOVED your tour and it was amazing and so much fun! Happy birthday Taylor! You are the QUEEN and I love you!" -Preslie

***

"To me, Taylor Swift is the best advice giver you get ever get, willing to offer the best life lesson for someone to learn. She is a walking proof that you could always start from nothing, achieve your wildest dreams you could've ever dreamt of, reach the highest point of your lifetime and even though if you get weaken by your reputation, fake relationships or what people may think of you... it'll always be possible to rose up from the dead. I will always be grateful I had joined this fandom filled with nothing but tolerance, respect and faith throughout the roughest times of my teenage years." -anonymous, France

***

"I started off my blondie journey by listening to her singles on the radio, from red and 1989 mostly but I also heard should've said no and love story! Anyway I absolutely loved these songs and I asked my mum to go to her 1989 concert, she said no as it cost too much money, so before rep when THAT happened my mum told me I should stop being a swiftie because I would get bullied for it, and she was right, but I stuck with it and became a hard-core swiftie between rep and lover (and no i couldn't go to the rep tour either because it sold out, but I did have tickets for loverfest though!!) And I tried so hard to get eras tickets but ticketmaster was glitching so much so we couldn't! Love you Taylor!! Happy birthday!" -Amelie

***

"'I've always been a fan of Taylor since kindergarten when her song 'We are never getting back together' was featured in the movie Pitch Perfect. I loved that song and found Taylor from there. Every since then I've loved her and her music and they have made me happier and apart of who I am today. Me and my best friend recently watched the movie together because we can't afford going to the concert and it was the best day ever. It felt like we were there and it was a magical experience. Her songs remind me of the little things and I love hearing her stories and watching her movies/documentaries. Taylor seems so kind as well as stunning from the inside and out. :) I've heard many stories of her like her giving her staff a huge bonus and much more. Most other singers have been in the industry longer and haven't done those things like her. Taylor is one of a kind and her music will always be in my heart. Me and my best friend love you and will forever. You mean so much to us." -Isabella

***

"Hello, my name is Maha, I have been a Swift fan since I was 7 years old (I am currently 12). I have been a fan for 5 years, and the first song of hers I ever heard on the radio was blank space, and I never went back. Some of my favourite albums are Evermore, Folklore, and Midnights. Although I have never been able to go to her concerts, I hope I can in the future. My favourite song by her is Daylight. When I first listened to her music, I felt like I would always recognize her, and I did. For some time I didn't listen to Taylor Swift much, but I got back into it in 2020, around the time Folklore came out. I decided to contribute to the book being made, because it would be a fun way to show my appreciation for Taylor Swifts hard work and her amazing songs that she has written. I also wanted to contribute to the book, because it would be a great present, and she deserves nothing less. If I make it into this book it would be amazing because Taylor Swift would get to hear my story. If Taylor Swift reads this, I hope you enjoy all the wonderful stories that will be in this book, and I hope you have a wonderful birthday!" -Maha

***

"My name is Charlotte. I'm 10 years old. I've been listening to Taylor's music for five years. My favorite albums are Lover and Reputation. My special memory is going her tour in Seattle Washington with my amazing mom. It was so cool to see her perform and was no doubt the best night of my life." -Charlotte R.

***

"Hi Taylor! My name is Hanae, I'm a French swiftie. I started listening to your music when I was 6 or 7, during road trips with my parents. I remember vibing on We Are Never Ever Getting Back Together! Then I became a swiftie a few months ago, when I saw several videos of the Eras Tour. I listened to every album and loved them all!

I wanted to say that I grew up with you and that I love you so much and I want to thank you so much for everything, and for bringing happiness back into my life. I think you're amazing as a person, I love how nice you are to all of your fans and I hope I'll get the chance to meet you someday! I love everything you do, and I love the stories you're telling us through your music! It is a work of art, I love how you write about everything, so anyone can relate to your lyrics. I am so glad I became a swiftie, it is the best thing that has ever happened to me! There are still so many things I'd like to tell you! I hope you are happy, and I wish you the happiest birthday Taylor!! I am so proud of you!" -Hanae, France

***

"I have been a swiftie since midnights, but it has been the best times of my life! I went to the rain show in 'foxy' foxbourgh, I loved it so much! You're an inspiration to people all over the world. I don't know what kind of person I'd be without you. Your smile is like a sunray reflecting on me, making me smile as well! I am at a loss for words because of you and your bravery. You ARE the music industry." -Mallory

***

"My love for Taylor and her music started when she released her fifth album, 1989 in 2014. When I saw her blank space, style, bad blood, out of the woods, and all of her videos, I really started to listen to all of her music and absolutely loved it and do to this very day. Taylor swift's music has helped me so much. I truly have no idea what I would do without it. When i lost two of my loved ones, I just listened and listened to her music and changed my life in the best way possible. I really just want to say thank you to her for helping my life and thousands of other lives. I've loved her music for about ten years now. I always wanted to attend of of her concerts, but my family couldn't ever afford it. I saw The Eras Tour Movie that was truly a masterpiece! I loved it so much and I hope I can go to a Taylor Swift concert someday! I love you Taylor and Thank you! I'm so grateful to be able to listen to your music and your such a beautiful person!" -Erin R.

***

"Taylor has forever changed me. I remember my mom playing Love Story and You Belong With Me and little 4 year old me singing along, whether I knew the words or not. When I really started to listen and pay attention to music, 1989 had just came out, and Shake it Off and Blank Space became my top car ride hits. Now, I listen to Taylor in class with my friends, in the car with my dad, and even when I'm at my lowest. I love being a swiftie, not just because of her amazing music, but because the entire community (including Taylor!) is so genuine and kind. I love you Taylor, Happy Birthday!" - Kara

***

"I had first listened to Taylor when I was little and 1989 had come out. It would be playing on the radio so I would listen to those songs. A couple years later when reputation was released I listened to the popular songs on the radio. Once she released Lover the only song I really listened to on the album was ME! because a family friend had played it for me. I had stopped listening to her as much as I had used to, but I still enjoyed some of her popular songs. She then released Folklore and I was told by the same family friend that many people were thinking that the album was weird, so I ended up not listening to it. Fast forward to early 2023 and I would keep getting things on my feed about the Eras Tour. I thought it was just like any other concert, but when I started to get more videos about it I saw how incredibly special it really was. A couple of my friends are Swifties so I decided to ask them about Taylor and her music. They played me a couple songs and gave me the basic information and I was mesmerized. Over the summer I listened to all of her albums and watched documentaries on her and just watched videos of people telling things I should know about Taylor. My parents saw how excited I was getting about this and we were able to get tickets to one of her shows. That night was the best night of my life and now I continue to listen to her music and I can safely say that I will never stop listening to her ever again.

I am forever grateful that I was reintroduced to

Taylor. She has helped me get through a lot of tough moments in my life and also never fails to put a smile on my face even when I am hysterically crying to one of her songs. She has impacted me in so many ways and I know all other Swifties can agree when I say that I don't know what I would do without her!! I just want the best for her and I want her to be happy in everything she does. I love you Taylor and Happy Birthday!" -Stella

***

"I became a swiftie during Taylor's Reputation Era (which happens to be my favorite) and fell in love with her music. I was in kindergarten at the time but instantly clicked with her music and Wildest Dreams became my favorite. I have been following her music journey since then, and cannot believe how incredible she is. I gave my blood, sweat, and tears for a ticket to the Eras Tour, and have had the lucky chance to attend one of her shows in Indiana next year! I'm counting down the days and will be attending with one of my best swiftie friends. I know this story isn't overly interesting but Taylor has changed my life in so many positive ways and I just would like to thank her for the incredibly positive impact she has had in my life. I have cried, laughed, and even screamed to her music that has helped me get through so many difficult times. Thank you Taylor so much, you have changed mine and many other Swiftie's lives through your music and we love you so much." -anonymous

***

"Happy birthday to the woman that saved my life. Taylor Alison Swift saved me in so many more ways than one. I was stuck in a dark tunnel, and she was my light. She was the daylight that I saw after being trapped in a dark night. Suddenly, I was wide awake.

I had a miserable year. I went back to school after being homeschooled for five years and it was not easy. I felt so alone, so defeated, so burnt out. I didn't know how I would ever handle another school year if the previous one was so bad. I just couldn't. I felt trapped in a dark night. A night that I had been trapped in all year long but I couldn't seem to get out of. I was sick of being surrounded by so many mean people, until I found someone who wasn't so mean at all. I found Taylor.

On May 19th, my mom and I went to the Eras Tour at Gillette and sat outside of the stadium because we were unable to get tickets. That night was the first night that I saw a glimpse of daylight inside of the dark night that I was trapped in. I don't think I fully realized it at the time, but that night was the night that changed my life. I suddenly felt happy. I became a swiftie around a year before I went and tay-gated at the tour, but after that night I started to find real comfort in Taylor's music. I felt understood by her, I didn't feel so alone anymore. I could relate to almost everything that she said. I found comfort in her lyrics, I screamed them, I sang them but I also cried to them. I had never felt such a connection with someone like the connection that I started to feel with Taylor. I felt like we understood each other, like we had been through the same rocky path. Whenever I felt alone, I would listen to her music and then I didn't feel quite so alone anymore. I didn't feel defeated, I didn't feel burnt out, I felt like I was at peace. Summer quickly came and I finally was excited about something. I was finally happy. I looked forward to every weekend so I could watch Taylor's shows. I would cuddle up next to my mom to see what the surprise songs were. I would dance around every summer day listening to her music in my ears. Little by little the dark night that I was trapped in started to disappear. I only saw daylight. The genuineness that Taylor had anytime she spoke about anything was something that really spoke out to me. Whenever she spoke about anything, I felt how genuine and sincere she was. That was something that I'd never felt before, especially in someone as famous as she is. She was always so raw and so real, and her words seeped into me and made me feel so understood. I needed one thing that would bring me happiness, and I found Taylor. I'll forever be grateful. I don't even know if I could ever thank her enough for everything she did for me. She saved my life. Not only that but she helped me and my mom bond even more, we became swiftie besties. I had never had someone as sweet, genuine, and so much like me to look up to. I told myself that I could never let go of that because it's so rare to find. Once in a lifetime really. She's inspired me in so many ways. She's really so beautiful inside and out. Whenever I felt defeated, I would listen to Taylor. Not only her music, but her speeches, her interviews, anything really. She's helped me get back on my feet multiple times. Her words hit even deeper with me because we were so similar in many of the same ways. Even when I had to inevitably go back to school, it felt different. I didn't fully feel trapped anymore. Even when I was sad, I would listen to her music, cry to it, and then feel okay again. I got back up on my feet. That was something that I needed, and that is something that I will forever be grateful for. There honestly will never be enough words to describe how much she's changed my life. When you love someone so much, it's hard to find the words to describe it, especially the right words. I hope that by reading this you realize even more what a special person Taylor is, and what a different person I'd be without her.

One of my favorite quotes from the Titanic movie was when Rose says, "And now you know that there was a man named Jack Dawson, and that he saved me, in every way a person could be saved." Well, now you know that there is a woman named Taylor Swift, and that she saved me, in every way a girl could be saved. Here's to many more incredible years ahead Taylor! Thank you for everything you've done for me. Have an amazing 34th! I love you so much it's impossible to verbalize." - Sumi (@simplysumi)

***

"Hello!! My name is Mariah and I have been a swiftie since I was 5 or 6. For as long as I can remember I have been singing my heart out to her music. Taylor is such a inspiring person that I look up too. I want to be as brave and fearless as her and I love her so much. Her words and lyrics are so powerful and reach me down to my core. Her speeches and the way she is such a strong woman incredibly inspires me. Like her middle school speech, right now I'm going through middle school and its rough but I'm getting through it and know what she said and gone through then helps me keep my head up high. Thank you for listening and I hope she gets this message. I love you all and taylor. Have a great rest of your day!" -Mariah R.

***

"Hello Taylor! First off, I want to say thank you for everything you have done. Even though we've never met, you and your music have had such a tremendous impact on me. I became a swiftie in 2020, so I'm a relatively new swiftie. I have always heard your music, but first really began listening to it during the pandemic. I was going through some tough situations and would constantly listen to "Mean" on repeat just fixated on this one person. After that song, I started listening to you more and more, constantly streaming your music. When folklore came out, I instantly fell in love with it. But I'd say that I became a hardcore swiftie with the release of "Midnights" in 2022. After that, I listened to all of your music (and have memorized most of it), I started relentlessly bringing you up to my friends any chance I got, and even started a youtube channel where I basically made edits of you and your music. Now, as of November 2023, you are my top streamed artist, I have forced my sister to go see the Eras Tour movie with me even though she's not a swiftie, i've already decided to make my senior quote a lyric from "You're On Your Own, Kid," and I make sped up versions to your songs. But out of everything that has happened when I first became a swiftie to now, by far, my greatest achievement is helping my autistic little brother memorize all of Anti-Hero (it's his favorite song by you now) and made him a swiftie. Thank you for reading this. You have done so much for me and impacted my life so much." -Gracie

***

"I first became a Swiftie when I was 5, as my mum had downloaded 1989 in the car so I would be able to listen to it whenever I was in the car. I started to absolutely adore her and wanted to listen to all her music and my mum let me listen on her phone. From then on she was and still is my idol. The first Taylor song I ever heard was Blank Space and it is definitely one of my most favourite songs in the world, it gets me every time! I love Taylor because even when she faced hard times in life she never gave up and that makes her such an inspiration. She has broken world records so many times and she is overall the most amazing person to ever walk the earth. There was a time where I was feeling really left out from my friends and was having a really hard time and the only thing that got me up in the morning was listening to Taylor's music because her songs are so special and meaningful and they make me instantly feel better. I have so many favourite songs by Taylor but one song that really stands out to me was the first song I ever heard from her, Blank Space because it brings me so much nostalgia and the lyrics are so incredible and meaningful and Taylor is just such an inspiration and amazing singer/songwriter. The best part of being a Swiftie is most certainly supporting and truly wonderful woman and the joy I get from either just listening to Taylor's songs or meeting other Swifties that love her just as much as I do is just so beautiful and brings me so much joy. If I could tell Taylor anything then I would tell her that I love her with all of my heart and that she is such an inspiration to everyone everywhere and that she truly deserves the world. She has been through so much and so many people have doubted her but look at where she is not. I don't even have word to describe how wonderful she is. I hope she sees this and knows how loved she is by all us Swifties out there!!" -Sara M.

***

"hey I'm penleigh and I became a swiftie because mum has been obsessed with her ever since she released

RED in 2012. I was born before then but as I grew up I have become more and more obsessed and she is just like my whole world like no one will ever understand how much she means to me. For her eras tour, she is not coming to my state in Australia and we couldn't get other tickets so I have not ever been able to see her but it is my dream. My favorite song is clean because it's my mums favorite and it's like my and my mum's song so it's so significant." -Penleigh, Australia

***

"4 years ago in April 2019 I was 12 years old at the time during the lover era my mom picked me up from school like any other day. Then a Taylor swift song named ME! Played on the car radio and I immediately became a swiftie as I started to sing along to it and ME! Was the first Taylor Swift song I have heard, I believe. So it's ME! That convinced me to become a swiftie although I was an off and on swiftie until midnights era were between midnights and speak now tv era I became a swifie again and I became obsessed with her and now I'm a big fan of her. The best part of being a swiftie is we're I can play and sing along to her music all the time, we're I can also attend her concerts, make her feel happy, feel special, it's like she's the Queen or our mother to us and I always get to say mother is mothering sometimes. the reason why i love Taylor swift cause she's so sweet to her fans, she makes all of us happy, she's a very special person, she has a great, lovely singing voice, she's funny, she once had those beautiful cute blonde curls and she has blonde hair, she's very gorgeous, she's also cute and amazing and she's a great storyteller. Her music means to me is that we're I feel great, and feel special it makes me happy and it's like she's trying to tell us something and it's means everything great about us swifties and it's also it can mean that's she is maybe telling us a story about something that we don't about. Taylor's music has helped me to feel good about myself and help me with grief and make me happy.

If I could tell Taylor anything I would say that I love her so much, I'm a big fan, we swifties have her back always, and that she makes us feel proud about ourselves. Im not sure exactly what my favourite song is by Taylor swift I love all of them but I like karma though Cause its a great song and I can't decide which one that's really my favourite song. I'm 16 which that's the same age when Taylor became famous and about a few days ago I attended the Eras tours concert film with my friends and it was amazing. I love every part of it and next year when I'm 17 I'm looking forward to attending her concert in Toronto next year. I'm glad for being a Swiftie!" -Abbigail M.

***

"Hi Taylor, happy birthday! I wanted to tell you how much I love your songs and how much I love you, you seem such a genuine person and I totally and definitely would like to have a pure genuine heart like yours. I'll be seeing you on the 13th of July in Milan and it'll be my first time, I'm so excited! My boyfriend gave me as a birthday gift a t-shirt of the eras tour, and told my friends to buy the folklore vinyl... He's not into pop but he thinks you're very good and he's definitely perfect! I'm sorry but I just feel like talking to you would be like talking to a friend... Anyway, happy birthday Taylor, I hope you'll be the happiest you can for, like, every day of your life. Love you!" -Giulia, Rome

"I just wanted to say thank you so much! I'm so grateful for both you and your music. I've been a massive fan ever since I was a little girl dancing to Shake It Off in my living room. I used to run upstairs to listen to your albums on my CD player (I still do). My favourite album of yours will forever be Lover. But I love the style of folklore and evermore. There lyrics are beautiful. Can I also say that I'm in love with all the vault tracks!? They are so beautifully written and are some of the best songs on the albums. Also I love the visuals of the Eras Tour. I've been to see the film twice once with my family and once with my friend and I'm in awe. Your vocals are astonishing. The suprise songs were SO well picked. You're On Your Own, Kid is and always has been one of my favourite songs. Hearing it as an acoustic piano version gave it a whole new depth and made me love it even more. I also love the strings remix on the Target exclusive CD (HMV exclusive for me as a UK fan). You've also inspired me so much as a writer and song writer. I have always loved writing stories/songs. You're helped me and inspired me so much. I feel my lyrics have grown so much better thanks to you. You've also inspired me to learn to play guitar and piano. It's thanks to you I'm so in love with music today. In short, thank you so much for everything! I'm so grateful for all your music and everything you've done as an artist." -Daisy, UK

"Hi Taylor!! My name is Charlie, and I first of all just wanted to say how extremely proud I am of you. You have made so many incredible accomplishments in your life including basically being the music industry and I love you for that. I wanted to share a bit about my Swiftie experience and how I came to be one, so here it is!

It all started when I was about 2 years old. I was born during the Speak Now era, which has had a crazy impact on my life. My older sister would sing to me every night when I would fall asleep, and she would sing "Never Grow Up". I have a 12 year age gap between my sister and I, and it's been really difficult to see her because she was in college for the past 4 years, and now has a very important job which makes her breaks very limited. I only really see her during holidays and even then we have a very small amount of time together, so your song has helped me get through so many hard times. We have a very close bond, so when I miss her I just listen to "Never Grow Up" and I feel so much closer to her. As I got older, I would sing and dance to songs from Red, like "I Knew You We're Trouble" and "22". Around that age I looked up to you very much but of course I was still very young so I would call you "Taylor Smith". Haha!! When 1989 came out "Shake it Off" was my go to song. I knew and still know every lyric. Once I started first grade, I had this bully that was very mean to me. My sister would sometimes take me on drives around our town and I would tell her the things he would do and say to me, and she would play me your song "Mean". That song helped me get through things that I can't even explain. When my sister went off to college, I felt a huge void, but your songs felt like she was standing right next to me. My fourth grade year was the hardest of my life. There were multiple girls that stabbed me in the back and made rumors about me, talked about me behind my back, called me names, and made my best friends turn on me for fake reasons. I left the school because of that, and I had such a hard time because on top of all of that COVID 19 was happening then. I started at a new school for fifth grade which changed my life. Everything was so new and different but Folklore and Evermore were so calming to me. I started to fall asleep to those songs every night and I still do. I would listen to "Willow" especially to calm my nerves. As I got into middle school, of course I started to my fair share of crushes. "Love Story", "Enchanted" and so many others, even though they are older songs, they are perfect for having a middle school crush. One of my most memorable moments was when I talked to my crush for the first time, and they told me they loved the song "All Too Well" and we both connected over that. All Too Well is my favorite song of yours. I'm actually singing it for the school talent show this year! That all leads up to right now where your lyrics help me get through my day. And I just wanted to say thank you. I love you Taylor!! Keep doing everything your doing. Make sure to take well needed breaks, and be yourself!! Don't listen to haters, because they honestly just don't know what they're doing in their life. You are so worth it, and your feelings are so valid. You make a difference on so many people's lives. I love you and so many others do as well. Oh and please tell Benjamin, Olivia and Meredith I say hi!!" - Char

***

"I became a swiftie a year and a half ago when I was in a super hard part of my life. I felt alone and scared, and I thought that if I disappeared, nobody would miss me. I felt like I couldn't trust anyone and I had to go through this alone. but then, a song came on the radio. the song was called "anti-hero." I immediately loved this song because I felt like I could relate to it. ever since then, I started listening to Taylor's music more and more, and on my birthday, I was surprised with eras tour tickets! I was so excited to finally get to see Taylor perform live, which motivated me to listen to her even more. I discovered songs that I had never heard before, and believe it or not, Taylor Swift's music helped me get out of that dark place and made me feel like myself again. so, Taylor Swift, if you read this, thank you so much for helping me out of that place. You've taught me how to step into the daylight, and let it go." - margiebargie1308

***

"Dear Taylor, I know you may have heard this a few times but I love you so much. The first time I heard one of your songs I was going through a really tough moment and somehow you understood me so well that I thought you knew me. It was as if your melodies and beautiful lyrics embraced me. You became my topic of conversation, I talked about you so much that all my friends became Swifties, even my teacher! You also encouraged me to start writing. Thank you for being yourself and always being there for us." -C.M.A., Argentina

***

"I became a Swiftie in 2022, when I found out about the re-recordings. I am extremely happy that I was a Swiftie then, because it meant I was a Swiftie for the beginning of the Eras Tour, even though I couldn't (and can't) go. I think Taylor is such an inspiration for young girls and women, because she stands up for what she believes in, and doesn't let anything stand in her way if she wants something to happen. She's an inspiration for me because I'm a 13 year old girl who wants to be a singer/guitarist/performer when I grow up, and looking at the way Taylor was so dedicated to her career has really helped me grow as a person and as a musician. I hope she keeps her career going strong, not just for or for fellow Swifties, but because it's her passion as well as her career, and I want Tayor to be happy Forever & Always. Go Taylor!!" -Amelia P.

***

"Hi Taylor, I'm so happy I get to share with you my story! I first started to listen to your songs after listening to Red and 1989 songs on the radio, falling in love with all the songs I heard. I Knew You Were Trouble was the first song I heard, and it was so amazing, from the opening to the bridge to the very end. However, it wasn't until I started listening non-stop to 1989 that I became a Swiftie. I was instantly hooked to Out Of The Woods, my favorite song from you and my favorite song of all time. The reason for that is the message of Out Of The Woods is all about anxiety, a problem I face daily. When I heard Out Of The Woods, I felt like crying because of how much I could relate to the song, even though I had never even been in a relationship. Hearing those lyrics and understanding that I wasn't alone is a feeling I will never forget. Even to this day, whenever the anxiety is getting the better of me all I have to do is listen to Out Of The Woods and I can't help but smile.

Honestly, I don't think I could ever thank you enough for all that you and your songs have done for me. You amaze me with how you continuously push back against your haters whenever they try to break you, never letting them stop you from making music.

So thank you for writing these songs that mean the world to me and tell me lessons that I never knew I would need to hear, they truly mean the world to me." - Sarah

***

"Hello Taylor, I hope you're doing well! I'm still a fairly new fan of yours but can't thank you enough for the core memories you've created in my life. I first heard of you when 1989 was released where my friend and I would sing Wildest Dreams in the back of the bus when we were in 5th grade. Even now when I hear that song I am flashed back to those days, but also to the days of middle and high school dances where your songs Shake It Off, You Belong With Me, Love Story and so many more were the center of excitement. I've always heard your music on the radio but never realized how many songs I knew until I sat down and listened to each album one by one in early 2023. I find myself humming your songs on tough days and belting them during joyful days, feeling the emotions in your voice in my life, something other songs have never done. Your lyrics are unlike any others and your dedication and passion for music is evident. But the thing that is the most admirable about you, is that you truly care. I feel as if not many people have the care and love you have, you're keeping it real when you perform and see your fans in public. This is something the world lacks and I hope you continue to keep it real, because life is ugly (as I'm sure you know), but it is also beautiful. I hope to see you continue your career and continue to grow as a musician. Thank you!" -Joan M.

***

"I remember vividly the day I saw you and heard

you for the first time: I was sitting crosslegged in my living room, after school, and 'Our song' came on. I did not become obsessed with your music, though, until I was 24. My (narcissistic) boyfriend, after 4 years of promises to spend the rest of our lives together, broke up with me the day I moved to the country he was living in and told me I was not brilliant enough. It was a few weeks after you released 'Shake it off', and I became obsessed, it was a true distraction in between the deep pain I was in. I then started listening to Red. I could not believe it! It felt like I had written it, we went through such similar things! I got shivers and tears after hearing 'I'm a crumpled up piece of paper lying here', as I had actually told people I felt like a piece of paper he crumpled up and tossed away. This was two years after Red came out, but it truly was my time to listen to it. When you released 1989, it felt like the missing piece I needed: it was the anthem of our journey towards independence. And while I was also struggling with body image (although like you I realised that some time later), I was trying every day to be me, to build myself up again, to have fun, alone and with friends, to feel beautiful and young and free in a new, big city.

Red and (even more) 1989 were so important for me. It's so cool to see how far we're both come. I am a doctor in astrophysics working in one of the best universities out there, and you are conquering the world doing things so extraordinary no woman nor artist has ever done before. You look happy and I truly hope you are. Happy birthday girl, see you in Milan!" - Giulia G.

***

" I was collapsed at the bottom of my shower,

brows furrowed in stressful sobs as Taylor Swift's song Clean began to play. When turning on the music, I intended to mask any noise entering or leaving the bathroom, but this song had its own purpose. The lyrics that seemed utterly relatable to my situation pulled me from my dramatic spiral, and I silently began to listen. Taylor's lyrics depicting the ability of rain, or in my case the shower's ability to comfort feelings of anger, frustration, and hurt had me entranced.

This touching song about trying to move on from a relationship resonated with me. The very reason I was so distressed was because of a life-long friend ending our relationship out of the blue. My friend, a victim of abuse and a deformity resulting in her having only one arm, had a difficult time growing up and coping with all her baggage. Through our years together I had been everything from her confident to her therapist. But after eight years of being best friends, I began to feel like she was pushing me away. When I confronted her about my worries she reluctantly told me that she didn't enjoy being close to me anymore because of all the things I knew about her past. Apparently, it unnerved her that someone could know and understand so much of her. This knowledge, of course, shattered my heart. Throughout our lives, living right across the street, we had daydreamed together of being each other's of honor and conspiring to make our children best friends as well. Thus this brutal slap in the face had me devastated on the bathroom floor.

As I took in the song for all that it was I realized that Taylor was singing about completely moving on from her relationship, that as time passes you create new habits and miss your person less and less. At the time of my grief this concept seemed preposterous to me, but I did want to at least try and cope with my hurt. That night, once the song came to an end I thoughtfully played it again, and again. After what had been close to 20 minutes of Clean blasting through the confined space, I gathered myself from the floor and decisively chose that

tonight was the end of my grieving. Sadly it was not the end for hers. At school, she began to spread rumors about me, for some reason she couldn't accept that I was okay with losing her. It reminded me of the words I'd heard Taylor sing just a few days ago, "You're still all over me like a wine-stained dress I can't wear anymore" (Taylor Swift). I took comfort in the fact that my experience wasn't alone.

And now, two years later, I am finally "clean" of my friendship. Whenever Clean begins to play as I do chores around the house, study, or drive to school, I can confidently say that it does not bring up emotions of sadness or sour my mood. In fact, Clean became my favorite song from the 1989 album because instead, I fondly look back on memories with my lost friend and appreciate how well I've done without her. "Just because you're clean, don't mean you don't miss it. Ten months older, I won't give in Now that I'm clean, I'm never gonna risk it" (Taylor Swift)." -Katie P., Georgia

***

"she is my biggest inspiration. ive always known that Taylor Swift had an eating disorder (and recovered!). so when i was also diagnosed with anorexia and sent to a residential, she gave me a lot of hope. when i listened to her music then, i felt like a weight was taken off my shoulders. i didn't have my mom there so taylor became a sort of "mother figure". she comforted me on my darkest days. the song, "you're on your own kid" really hit home for me, because i was on my own. but it felt like taylor was there saying, "you've got no reason to be afraid"! the song has brought me to tears many times - thank you ts!" -Lexi

***

"Hi Taylor, my name is Abby. I am 13 years old and I have been a fan since a bit after 1989 stolen version came out. Your music has helped me get through some hard times in life. I have a brother with special needs and Epilepsy so it's been hard. His favourite song is "Shake it Off... I think) and a younger brother who also loves listening to your music. His favourite song is "I Knew You Were Trouble" and mine is "All of the Girls You Loved Before". I listen to your music every day and have almost every single CD! I recently got tickets to see you live at the Eras Tour for the very first time in Melbourne (18th of February which is exactly 1 month from my birthday!) I watched the movie and it was Amazing! My mum is going with me and my cousins so she is trying to learn all of the songs on the set list! (Idk how she's gonna do it all!) You are absolutely incredible and I hope you continue to make music!" -Abby

***

"when I became a swiftie I was little in my aunt's house watching the love story video just thinking, "she's a goddess!" ever since, I have not really listened to many other artists! I think tay is loyal and kind to everyone, she will always be in my heart! my favourite era is reputation but fearless was a close winner! happy birthday taytay slayslay!" -Scarlett, age 10

"Hey Taylor! Your music is something amazing in my life. It's timeless, and hits different than any other artist. The first of your songs I ever heard were "You need to calm down" and "me" which I heard in 2019 when one of my best friends at the time showed them to me. I on and off listened to your music, and finally after COVID, in 2022, midnights was released. This was the album that 100% turned me into a Swiftie. The music was so relatable, and every song in that album became one I would want to scream. After midnights, I found folklore and speak now. Both albums are now in my top 3 favorite albums of all time. Folklore has so many songs I can relate to. Whenever I feel like crying or breaking down, your music is there for me and helps me pick myself back up. Ever since I found your music, EVERYTHING HAS CHANGED. Honestly, my daily does of your music is the only thing that keeps me going sometimes. You are such an amazingly kind person, who cares so much about your fans. I've never seen an artist who cares more for the people who love her music. When you released 1989 (Taylor's version), I fell in love with the original songs, and especially the vault tracks. Right now, my favorite songs are "Is it Over Now?", "Delicate", "the last great american dynasty", "The 1", and "Mirrorball". (Folklore is obviously a favorite). Unfortunately, My family was unable to afford eras tour tickets. I think if I had been able to go, It would've been THE BEST DAY of my life. Your music has truly changed me, for the better, and I'm so glad to be a swifie. If I could meet you and tell you anything, I think it would be everything I said in the paragraph above. (and I'd say how I wish you would put the cardigans back on the site! For a long time!) Although I've never seen you in real life, the way you care for everyone you come in contact with is amazing, and it makes me so happy and proud of you. I also love writing books and music, and I can only aspire to one day be half as famous, kind, and perfect as you. Remember, us swifties will never leave you. There will always be an invisible string tying you, to every single one of us. " -Grace N.

***

"I didn't really know any of Taylor's songs, except her big hits (Shake it off, bad blood, etc.). I didn't know many songs in general and wanted to know more. I asked my best friend who is a Swiftie for some song recommendations. Obviously they did not disappoint. Next thing I knew Taylor was all I was listening to, and my mom was buying me tickets to the eras tour movie for my birthday. I went with my friends and we all dressed up as albums, I was Speak Now! I loved it so much! I am a full Swiftie for life! I absolutely love her music and am proud to be a Swiftie! And I am proud to say I have successfully converted my sister and Dad into Swifties. Happy birthday Taylor!!! Thank you for all your amazing songs!!" - Mae H.

***

"How I became a Swiftie was because of my sister Mae, for her birthday she got to go to the eras tour movie. When I heard about it I didn't really want to go because I knew barely anything about Taylor Swift. But then we started listening to songs, and I realized some of my favorite songs were written by her. Then I couldn't wait for the eras tour movie. It was the best movie ever. We were dressed up as her albums and I was lover! Now I sing her songs every day, and am a Swiftie!

Happy b-day." - Jane H.

***

"I had known a decent amount of hit songs from various albums. My mom had gotten tickets with her friends to go to her Eras tour in Pennsylvania and started to listen to her a lot more to get prepared for the concert. Her songs are so catchy and they got stuck in my head. After my mom went to the concert, I kept listening to her. About like a month ago, my mom got tickets to the Eras tour movie! Me and my friends decided that since there were nine people going, we were going to base our outfits off of nine of her albums. I chose 1989! I went all out of course! The whole experience was AWESOME!!!! I ended up going to the movie twice because I loved it so much. I literally started crying when I saw her come on stage even though it was the movie. Now, I am a huge Swiftie. I stayed up all night waiting for 1989 Taylor's version to come out! I love all of your songs! Happy Birthday Taylor!!!!!!" -Aubrey S.

***

"My mom listens to Taylor Swift. I heard her listening to You Belong With Me and I really liked it and memorizes the whole song. I started listening to some of her other songs, unfortunately I wasn't able to go to the Eras tour but me and my friends dressed up as the 9 albums and went to the Eras tour movie so that is how I turned into a Swiftie and listen to her music every day, Thank you for all of your amazing songs and Happy birthday Taylor." - Kenzie S.

***

"I started listening to Taylor when I was in college (her debut album). I've always felt that Taylor has had a way of putting my experiences into words. Most recently, I went through a divorce. Her songs clean, Tolerate it and Bejeweled were on repeat whenever I was alone. Going to the Eras tour with friends was incredible, but going to the movie with my children and their friends was an experience I will never forget. She has given me another way to connect with my kids which I truly appreciate." -Julia K.

***

"A little under a year ago, my friend threw a party where we each got an album and had to dress like it and do karaoke with some of the songs. I picked Speak Now and I learned all of the songs and fell in love with the album. It's still my fav to this day but I also learned all of the other albums since and I love all of them!! Me and the friend who threw the party listen to all of the albums all the time and I wouldn't trade it for anything! And I'm going to one of Taylor's concerts at the end of 2024!!" -Teagan

***

"Dear Taylor,

I've been a swiftie for 8 years and in 2018, I even went to your reputation tour. I was first introduced to your music one day in the car, when my mom was playing your album, "1989." I've always loved your music and you are such an amazing person to everyone around you. I recently went to the Eras tour with my two sisters and my mom. We had the time of our lives! I sang every song. Sometimes I think about meeting you or getting the 22 hat. But those are one in a million things. Who knows? Maybe one day I will! you inspire me so much and I'm so lucky to have found your music! I hope you continue to do what you do best!" -B

"At my 3rd birthday party, I ripped up the wrapping paper in excitement the bright pink enter my eyes,it was a cd player and a cd the cd was a mix of top 100 songs from 2010. Having all these hit songs on this playlist, I went home in excitement waiting to stream every song on the playlist.

I sat down and entered the cd music started to play after the first few songs it started to play Taylor swift I got up and spun around and around vibing to the music,when the next song went on I sat straight back wanting for more then the next song came on it was shake it off one of my favourite I jumped up and down.when I finally figured out how to go back songs I played shake it off all night,falling to sleep picturing the lyrics in my head.Then when she came out with reputation I beg my mum to try for tickets so I could jump up and down again like how I used to and I definitely did while my tears ricochet. I went home crying and to this day I still remember the first time I listen to her song spinning till I couldn't see anymore." - Pip

"What is funny about my history with Taylor's music is that I discovered her when I didn't mean to but it just felt like it was meant to happen.

It was actually during Red (Taylor's version) era. As a French, we never really heard of Taylor because she was unfortunately not that popular. I did know a few songs of her, including Shake it off which really was her only well-known song in France at the time, and the very first song I had heard from her. It all happened in a day. I was suffering from that very common thing we call period, which led me to lay in bed and cry all night long. I was looking for a distraction, so I kept thinking about my favourite singer at the time who was Olivia Rodrigo, and about how Taylor Swift influenced her career. That's how, just like that, I decided to listen to a random Taylor Swift song to see if it was similar. I skipped Red (Taylor's version) and went straight to Fearless (Taylor's version), and I chose, randomly, The Way I Loved You. I think that fate really had done its job this time, because it's nearly impossible to find a better song in Taylor's discography. I listened to it about ten times in a row, amazed by the writing and the melody. I was just...speechless : the writing felt at the same time so personal and universal, I just felt like the song was always meant for me. I then moved on to three other songs which were White Horse, The Other Side Of the Door and You're Not Sorry. I think it really is impossible to describe how those songs moved me. That's when I realised that as a songwriter and composer, Taylor Swift deserved way more credit than what she actually had.

I then listened, in a day or two, to her entire discography. Even though I didn't have the contexts of those albums in mind, I paid attention to the lyrics and the melodies, and I chose my favorite album extremely quickly : it was reputation. I never really understood why, but it just felt like that album summarized me : a girl considered as weird by her peers, with a not so good reputation, but actually insanely in love deep down. I have to say it, I'm a romantic, and finding a singer as romantic as me was an amazing surprise. I'll always remember listening to Call It What You Want during an hour before meeting my boyfriend's dad because I was anxious. I'll always remember melting to Cornelia Street because it portrayed exactly my fear of losing him.

I think that Taylor has created so many good memories for each one of us. She created an imaginary space where we could all dream about a perfect life. I mean, who hasn't dreamed of being a princess while listening to Enchanted ? Who hasn't put on Welcome to New York while arriving anywhere, pretending they were landing in New York ? I definitely did. And what is strange is that, at the same time, she has this wonderful power to heal your pain by wording why you're suffering. Because we're all suffering for the same reasons. Soon You'll Get Better is a perfect example of that. Just like her, I almost lost a parent due to cancer, even thought it was my father and not my mother. But the way that she explains it in her song just hits. "Who am I supposed to talk to if there's no you ?" really is a line that highlights her unbelievable writing skills. Because it was exactly how I felt, and she knew it better than me. This is the reason why people say Taylor Swift is their psychologist. Because she knows how humans feel. She's an empath.

I believe that something people either forget or exaggerate when they talk about Taylor is her political views. Some people say it was a bold choice to express publicly her views. But that's what convinced me that she was the best role model to grow up with. The fact that she's a feminist and that she stood up for her beliefs when she wasn't supposed to is astounding to me. I think that it's so inspiring for little girls and teenagers - and even grown women - to have an international star being a feminist and fighting for her rights.

My favorite song of hers since the beginning - and probably forever since it's nearly impossible to write a better song - is Better Man. I can absolutely not believe that this song was left behind. I think it might be the song that inspired the most my songwriting because the concept may seem simple but is at the same time so true for any situation. It's at the same time a song for people who are healing and people who are still suffering and want to get better. I'll never be able to explain how much this song means to me.

I'll also never be able to explain how much every single Taylor Swift album means to me. Each song of hers gives me a particular memory. Her music is a big part of my life. My dad wakes me up every weekend with Champagne Problems. He drives me to school while listening to Love Story. We sing Wildest dreams with my mom on every car ride. My sister and I are doing our makeup to Don't Blame me. I put on Paris every day on my way home because I can see the Eiffel Tower from my school. I sing Back to December to my baby brother when he's crying. And I have so many other examples.

Thank you, Taylor, for giving us the best girlhood we could ever have. Thank you to all the swifties in this planet, because they're the most kind and generous fandom. They'll always make you feel appreciated and loved, even if they disagree with you. I have found my safe place thanks to Taylor, and I'll never forget that." - Inès B., France

***

"I became a Swiftie during the COVID Lockdown. I was very lonely and it was generally a hard time for me so I escaped with the help of music. After hours of being on YouTube I stumbled upon stay stay stay and chose to listen to more music of her. Her music helped me to overcome every hard time, like when my parents got divorced. I'm really happy that I got tickets for the eras tour and I count the days till she plays in Wien. Thank you Taylor for your fantastic music and that you're a great role model." Sophia Z., age 17, Germany

***

"I've been listening to Taylor Swift since 2018 or 2019, but I have been considering myself a swiftie since Midnights came out. I love how I can relate to her songs, whether it's a happy one like I'm Only Me When I'm With You, or a sad one Clean, or a somewhere in between one like This Is Why We Can't Have Nice Things. Even if you haven't had a relationship (like me) you can still relate to one of the songs.

My favorite memory with Taylor Swift was when I was with my aunt. She lives 7 hours away from me so seeing her is rare, but in the summer we see them. This summer, we had went up and the weather was not great, it was cold and rainy the entire time. This one day in particular, June 17, we were heading back to my aunt's house, and it was raining a little. I was in my aunts car and my mom and sister were following us. We had stopped at a place that had no cars and my aunt told me to start playing Fearless (as in the song). We got out the car and I was so confused, but we started dancing in the rain, like the lyric "And I don't know why, but with you I'd dance, in a storm in my best dress, fearless." Ever since then, it has been one of my favorite songs to dance to, because it makes me think of my aunt." -Madelyn

***

"i became a swiftie over the summer. i listened to your music ever since i was little, but never like i do now. i listen to it everyday and my days feel incomplete without ur music ! your the only artist i can always listen to without getting sick of ur music. i heard your first song when i was too young to even know what i was listening too, but i think it was you belong with me. that song brings back so many memories for me, so thank you. i know you don't really know me so this may come off a bit weird, but i really do love you and your music. your such a special person and ur really so beautiful (i know this sounds weird sorry) your music is so versatile i can listen too it no matter what mood i'm in. no other artist can do that. everyone who says ur music sounds the same is just dumb. ur music helps me get through my emotions and days im sick. it inspires me. i even tried to learn to play guitar. i kinda suck but i'm working on it. i wanna be just like you when i grow up, the biggest star in america. i already started writing some songs. i'm too scared to tell anyone right now but one day i'll have the courage, and maybe i'll be performing in stadiums just like you! my favorite song is better than revenge. it just clicked the first time i heard it and i dont care about the lyricnchange. idk why people give you so much hate for it. it has this teen angst vibe i just love it so much. the best part about being a swiftie is the community. this is the one fangroup where i feel like everyone gets eachother and no one is judgemental. the comment sections on your videos feel so welcoming. if i could tell you one thing it would be dont stop making music and that ur amazing. have a great birthday gorgeous!!" -anonymous

***

"Well, i became a swiftie when i first listened to folklore, it was 2020, i was 13 years of age and even though i knew about Taylor Swift 's music i wasn't exactly a swiftie. The folklore album came out in July 2020, and that album changed me forever, i connected to that album in ways i couldn't imagine. It was a rough period of my life, i was grieving the death of a loved one and i always found a way back to myself whenever I listened to "this is me trying", "exile", "mirrorball" and honestly, every song on that album. It described me in ways hard to even comprehend. The album saved me from my own dragons. In Taylor Swift 's music i found comfort, i spent hours listening to "soon you'll get better" cause that was my exact situation. Then, later that year, Evermore came out and the song "Marjorie", "Happiness" healed me and brought me a sense of warmth. This was the magic Taylor and her music brought in my life. She swooped in the darkest times of my life and her music sat beside me like a friend. I am forever grateful to Taylor, and her music making ability cause it brought me back to life. Her NYU commencement speech of 2022 motivates me even to this day. Her music in its own way provided me with life advices when i needed them the most. I am an Indian and i attended the Eras Tour Movie recently, it was one of the best days of my life. Even though it was the film and not the actual tour, it brought me immense joy and gave me a sense of fulfillment. Through this i just wanna say, Thank you so much Taylor, iloveyou to the moon and to saturn. I really had the time of my life fighting dragons with you, long live!" -Khyati, age 16, India

***

"Unlike Taylor, this story doesn't start when it was hot and it was summer, this story starts with a little four-year-old girl. I was four when I learned about Taylor Swift. The first song I ever loved of hers was Shake It Off. I loved that song so much. I remember seeing videos of me in a pink princess tutu, spinning around with the music video on. I faded away from Taylor until I turned 10. Sure, I still listened to her like I loved Don't Blame Me, but I wasn't a major swiftie. When I was ten, I was in a dark place, and Taylor helped me through it. I'm 11 now, and in a better place now and writing songs. I would like to say thank you Taylor, she is the one who helped me in rough times. Thank you, Taylor and Happy Birthday!" -Morganne

***

"I've liked Taylor off in on since lover, so I really liked her when lover came out and would listen to her all the time, and then all of a sudden stopped listening to her for some reason, but around when midnights came out I started loving her. And now I'm proud to call myself a swiftie. I love her so much, like I don't even have word to describe how much I love her, she's who I turn to when I'm sad, she's who I turn to when Im happy basically I turn to her when I feeling any kind of emotions. I don't know what I would do if I couldn't listen to her. And I can't go to the eras tour because it's to expensive but if I could I would, I would do anything to be able to go. I also don't know if Taylor will see this but I want her to know that none of the things that happened in Brazil were her fault, and she shouldn't blame her self. The fans who were booing her and getting mad because she postponed her show, are not real fans. And I wanted her to know how much I love her! I love her so much I literally can't live without her music and her as a person. I've been though some tough times and it's safe to say that Taylor got me out of those, as soon as I heard her voice of thought about her being happy and just being who she is I was already happier. Love you Taylor!" -Madi P.

***

"I became an official Swiftie right around the start of the Eras Tour. I wish I had long before then, but better late than never. I sort of became a Swiftie due to her name being mentioned in the media a lot during that time, so I thought "She's really popular, why not officially listen to her?" And then I played Midnights on Spotify and thought "DANG, she's good at this". So then I went to her YouTube channel and watched a bunch of her music videos, behind-the-scenes, and old vlogs, and then I just really fell in love with her character. And the rest is history.

Even though I became a Swiftie when the Eras Tour started, my family has been listening to her music for ages. One of my mom's favorite songs is Paper Rings. And whenever my dad took me and my siblings on an outing, during the car ride we would always be accompanied by either Reputation or 1989. And sometimes my younger sister and I would play a game where we would take turns humming one of Taylor's songs and the other person would guess which one it was. And a few months after it was released from the vault, Mr. Perfectly Fine was my favorite song for half a year for absolutely no reason.

I have had so much fun being a Swiftie. Our fandom is full of the nicest people and we have so much fun. The only social media apps I have are YouTube and Pinterest, so I feel really connected to the Swifttube community even though I am not an editor and am not really friends with anyone; just hanging out there and observing everyone's interactions makes me feel so connected and happy.

I could never pick a favorite Taylor song, but my favorite albums of hers are Evermore and Red TV. I love Evermore's lyricism and sadness, and I love Red's pure emotion. You get to experience all the emotions when listening to it and I really like that. And back to Evermore, there's just something ethereal about crying to heartbreakingly well-written music. I love it so much.

I have no idea what song of hers I heard first because she's been releasing music since before I was born, but I just want to share this cute memory I have: when I was in 4th grade (9-10 years old), I was walking to school one day and I felt really nervous for some reason, so to calm myself down I sang Shake It Off. I think about that a lot, and think that it is such a precious memory of mine.

I love Taylor so much. I could never even try to express how much because I wouldn't be able to truly show how much I really love her. And that's just something my family doesn't understand, so it's nice to be a part of a group of people who do. Taylor really has changed my life, even if not in big ways. She has inspired me to do more creative projects, like painting my room and writing poetry. And she is such a great role model for young women, and anyone in general. She is the kindest, most caring person I know of and deserves the world. And it's so just so nice of her to have shown us her whole life's journey to help us with our own. If I could tell Taylor one thing, it would be 'Thank you'. Thank you for bringing such a strong feeling of connectedness into my life. Thank you for being there when I was too scared to tell anyone about my problems. And thank you for giving us so much, and for loving us just as much as we love you." -Margaret Elizabeth (@kittycatmargaret13)

***

"When I was a freshman in high school, I went through a terrible eating disorder; anorexia. I felt so ugly and alone, wanting to just be thin. Coming from an Asian family, all my aunts would comment on my weight, comparing me to my cousins, which made me miserable. I stopped eating lunch and breakfast, and soon just relied on snacks to keep me alive.

It was a terrible moment in my life, but one day I heard about this singer named Taylor Swift, whom I obviously have heard of prior. Everyone hated her for the stupid stepping on the scale controversy, but I never felt more seen than when I saw that clip. It meant the world to me.

I know it's silly, but seeing this billionaire famous singer go through the same thing I was and even wrote songs and videos about it was so beautiful. I loved Anti-hero, and midnights as a whole. I continued listening to all her albums, and my swiftie friend was so happy. My favorite is Speak Now, however, You're on Your Own Kid is my favorite song for obvious reasons.

Thank you Taylor, for showing me I was never alone." -Trisha L.

***

"Hey Taylor, happy birthday!!!!!!!!!!! I love you soooo much. I have been a swiftie basically since birth as my mum had the fearless cd and used to play it in the car all the time. I absolutely love your music and I am soooooooo upset I haven't been able to get tickets for you eras tour as before you announced the tour me and my mum said it's the tour of our dreams. We did go to the eras tour film and it was magical. I love you and your music and every night dream of going to the eras tour. I have put tickets on my Christmas list but as we couldn't purchase the midnights album we can't get the tickets. But I just as that when you do perform at London even though I am more then likely not going to be please do London boy as a suprise song as I think it's very suitable. Aswell as a great singer I think you are a lovely person with a great personality. I really hope to meet you in person some day. I know many people call themselves a swiftie but trust me I am a true swiftie and will always love you. I hope you have an amazing birthday and maybe get a new cat for your birthday. I think you are out of this world. Just keep doing what your doing. I am practically crying writing this knowing you will read this. I really hope I will get tickets to your tour. Your are amazing Taylor and in case I never say anything to you again please don't take this weirdly but I love you a lot!" -Annabelle

***

"Back in 2022, I was working in a base camp for people who were going through hard times. I was sixteen at the time and although there were other people working there I spent most of my time helping people who would come in and go the next day. I started struggling with depression, loneliness, and overworking myself. The base was in an area that was not connected to the outside world. So when there was a chance to go to a place with internet I immediately took it. I was going through messages that my family had sent me and decided to look at Disney +. When I did I saw the Long Pond Studios version of Folklore was available offline so I downloaded it. I listened to that album almost non-stop for the next three months. Thank you Taylor for helping me and helping me help others with the peace of mind you gave me. Have a wonderful Birthday Taylor and may God bless your coming year." -Abby

***

"When I was about 2, every night, my mom would play me The Best Day. I loved it so much and still do to this day. It was my favorite song ever. In 2012, when Taylor released Red, my mom was in love. We had it playing almost all the time. My favorite was Begin Again. And it also was similar to the first date of my parents. When she released 1989, I was in love with the songs Blank Space, Welcome To New York, and How You Get The Girl. I had them playing all the time. When Taylor disappeared, I always asked my mom when she'd come back. My mom never knew, so I stopped listening. I didn't listen to much of Reputation or Lover, because I didn't like the songs before. I hadn't ever listened to Folklore or Evermore. I listened to a little bit of Midnights, and then started getting back into her. My mom then got me tickets to see Taylor's tour. I didn't know every single song, I wish I did though. After the tour, I started to listen to the albums I hadn't listen too. I then fell in love with her music again. As I re-listened to songs, and heard new ones, I couldn't believe I missed out on so much. I finally then understood what most swifties would talk about, but I still have some to learn.

I'm proud to say I'm a swiftie, but Taylor Swift has been my role model since I first heard The Best Day." -Shelby

***

"When they asked me: how did you become a Swiftie? Honestly I don't really remember about that because it's a very long time ago. But I'm sure that it has something to do with the Fearless album, especially the song You Belong With Me. When the music video had just been released and I found it on YouTube. That song is so ear-catching and energetic. When I like a song, I will play it continuously without getting bored. Then I started to be curious about the singer, Taylor Swift. And since that day I looked for her other songs and I fell in love her and her music. I love you, Taylor. Your music is very inspiring and will always accompany me forever!" -Nurillah

***

"Dear Taylor,

I know that you might not even get to read my message since there will be thousands of people writing to you, but to me it's really important to tell someone my experience. Not important, I was in a toxic friendship, I was being used. But one day I heard 2 or 3 girls screaming a song at school, it was just so emotional, and the song described exactly what I was feeling. That song was The Archer. Since that moment, I have been absolutely in love with every single one of your songs. Those girls are now my absolute best friends, and we bond over your lyrics every single day. Without you I would not be the person I am today. So I write this message today to say thank you, honestly, your songs saved me from going back into my self hate spiral. I have never felt like that ever again. Thank you, your songs can cheer me up any day, everything you've been through, every word you say, it inspires me. I hope you can come back to Mexico, since I wasn't able to see you last time, because I think that I would break down in tears just from being in the same city as you. Thank you, thank you, thank you for everything you do." - Natalia F., age 12, Mexico

***

"hi taylor! i'm ren, and i'm 13 years old. I was born on december 3^{rd,} ^{2010,} only 10 days from your birthday! i've been a swiftie practically since birth - my mom sang "never grow up" to me as a lullaby. i started listening to you on my own during the pandemic, and with the release of folklore, i've been a non-stop swiftie. my favorite album is reputation, and i LOVE dress, but my favorite thing about your music is how you sing about so many different things. I can find a song of yours whenever I need to listen to something, and I love it. i'm really excited for reputation (taylor's version), *wink wink*, and i hope someday, i'll be able to see you live in concert!" -Ren, age 13

***

"Taylor's music has changed my life in so many ways. I first became a swiftie right when 1989 was released. I remember listening to shake it off over a 100 times every day when I came home from school. Ever since then my love for Taylor has grown so much. Not just for her music but for her as a person. Her music inspires me in so many ways, and I am so lucky that I live in a world with Taylor Swift in it. Taylor has shown me love, compassion, and kindness in so many ways even though I have never met her or interacted with her before on social media. She's shown me to be myself and not let anyone tell me otherwise. She is the strongest and most amazing person I know." -Maylee H.

***

"When I was 4-5 years old, I heard my first Taylor song which was "Style" and I was instantly in love. It was my favorite all the way up until I was 7 years old, and between the ages 7-8, I kind of fell out of being a fan. In September 2020, I rediscovered her but didn't listen to her new music at the time. I remember watching the "You Belong With Me" music video every night before bed. I was also obsessed with "Blank Space," "We Are Never Ever Getting Back Together," and of course, "Style." During that time period, me and my parents were getting ready to move to India because the government of the United States denied my parents' VISA to live there and Taylor got me through those last weeks before moving. When I got to India, however, I no longer had a favorite artist. That was until I was 11. I spent the ages 9 and 10 in India, and then moved to Canada. In the summer of 2023, I was on a trip to Alberta and randomly decided to start blasting "Style" in my hotel room; that was the moment I realized - I wanted to become a Swiftie again, and would never go back. Now, I'm currently in the process of convincing my parents to let me go to the Eras Tour when she brings it here to Toronto. My favorite song is still "Style" and my favorite album is 1989 because of the memories it has - after all, it was my entire childhood." -Sohalia

***

"Taylor's music has helped me by giving me something to distract myself if I'm having a bad day. Since 2020 was hard on me for many reasons, her music had helped me on those bad days. Especially her Lover

315

album and her most recent albums and rerecordings that came out, I got attached to those as they would help me if life was going bad for me at the time. I will always thank Taylor's music for helping me get through everything. Thank you sooooo much!" -Charlotte

***

"Dear Taylor,

I am so excited to be able to partake in this gift. My biggest dream is to meet you in real life. But anyways, my name is Stell, and I just became a swiftie recently! My cousin introduced me to your music a couple of months ago, and I've already became obsessed. By the time this gets to you, I will already been to the movie twice. Some of my favorite songs are Lavender Haze, You belong With me, Love Story, and Don't Blame Me. I don't know alot of songs, but I basically only listen to your music. You are my favorite artist of all time, and I have the picture from the movie on my desk, in a golden frame. The first time I went to the movies, I was with my cousins, and were were running late, we snuck in candy, and we barely made it to the Cruel Summer bridge. Again, I am so honored to participate in this project. I love you so much!" -Stell

***

"i've always had such respect for taylor because no matter how much people tried to take credit for her work, she's always fought to keep it and to show others they can do the same. her music is truly magical and her fan base is insane for good reason. the family of "swifties" that she's created is so admirable!" -Lindsey, age 16

***

"Hey, I'm Mawara from Austria, and let me spin

you the tale of how I transformed into a full-fledged Swiftie. Brace yourself because my journey into Swiftie-dom is like a rollercoaster of weird, random, and unusual moments.

The story kicks off when I was 13 years old in 2019. At that time, I wasn't allowed to have social media, so I didn't know many celebrities nor anything trendy. I also wasn't allowed to listen to music on my way to school. The only melodies in my life come from the radio in our car, accompanied by a trusty CD featuring some radio hits. Now, in the midst of all this, my mom, my two younger sisters, and I were hooked on a German show called The Biggest Loser. Yes, the one where folks battle the bulge in a competition-style setting. Then, out of nowhere, they drop a scene with the words "cuz I got a Blank Space, baby, and I will write your name". Cue my teenage excitement: Oh my gosh, I've heard that song on the radio! Rushing to YouTube, I type in the search bar. Lo and behold, the first result is Blank Space by none other than Taylor Swift.

Clicking on the lyrics video, I confirm that this is the elusive song I'd been searching for. The excitement was real! I couldn't help but gush to my parents about how amazing this song was, singing and dancing to it all day. I even sneaked into my parents' room so I could get my dad's free airplane earphones he never used, so I can listen to the song on my way to school, hiding them like a secret agent to avoid getting into trouble. For the next few months, Blank Space was my anthem, and I used up mobile data streaming it on YouTube. I even played innocent when my parents questioned the rising mobile data charges, though I knew my streaming habits were the culprit.

Then came the day when I opened YouTube on my laptop, poised to dive into Blank Space once more. But before I hit play, a curious thought struck me—what other gems did Taylor

Swift have? A quick visit to her YouTube Channel revealed a brand-new song, ME, released just hours ago. Intrigued, I clicked and gave it a listen. It was good, but not as good as Blank Space.

Fast forward a couple of months, and my mom and I found ourselves glued to the final

episode of Germany's Next Topmodel. Coincidently, Taylor Swift took the stage to perform

none other than ME! live. Something magical happened during that performance—my mom and I exchanged glances, and suddenly, we were both on board. From that moment on, my playlist expanded to include not just Blank Space but also ME!.

In the next month, I stumbled upon You Need to Calm Down, and in the words of Taylor, I thought, "Can you just not step on my gown?". I loved that song.

2019 was a truly fantastic year for me. We began building our dream house in 2018, and it was an incredible experience witnessing our dream home coming together. So, when Lover was released in the summer of 2019, I was preoccupied with moving into our house, and I didn't realize that Taylor had come up with an album.

As my fourth year in Gymnasium kicked off (the American equivalent of the last year of middle school), my parents granted me the freedom to listen to music with headphones whenever I pleased. With a new phone in hand, I expanded my musical horizons, but Taylor remained my constant. YouTube's recommendations showered me with her hits. It was then that I waved goodbye to other artists, embracing a daily rotation of Taylor's 10-15 songs that I loved. Each day brought a new Taylor Swift discovery, and around my 14th birthday, I Forgot That You Existed stole my heart. Over the next few months, I really delved into her discography, and by the end of 2019, I proudly declared myself a Swiftie.

Miss Americana on Netflix was a revelation, exposing me to themes of eating disorders, success, and failure. Enter 2020 and the lockdown. When folklore and evermore came out, I wasn't obsessed, but they eventually grew on me.

The rerecordings helped me to appreciate her country music more, and the RED TV Era made me a hardcore Swiftie. Today, in 2023, I am 18 years old, and I love all of her songs. I still exclusively listen to her songs, and it doesn't bother me at all.

I have to admit, being a Swiftie in your teenage years is like the best experience ever. We get one or two albums every year, wake up to see what surprise songs Taylor has sung at the Eras Tour, and then complain about it because we wanted that song. We hunt for Easter eggs, which often leads us to a lot of clowning. But most importantly: having her music to turn to no matter what we're going through is an experience I will forever be grateful to grow up with." -Mawara A., Austria

***

"When I was younger, I would dance about to shake it off like most little kids do, but no one had ever played any other of Tay's songs to me. I usually just listened to audiobooks on repeat since I never had an artist who I just loved and listened to constantly, who I cared about, and who made me genuinely happy whenever I saw anything to do with them. Until one day, when I was listening to a general music playlist online, and Love Story came on. I remember stopping what I was doing and simply listening. I thought that it was fun, but also very cleverly written, as it told a beautiful story. I felt that there was something magical about the song's lyricism, melody, and overall romantic fairytale tone, so I looked up the songwriter and thought, "Wow, how haven't I heard this before?! I need to listen to some more of Taylor's music."...And so I did, and I have not gone back to my audiobooks since!

I really wanted to go to the Eras Tour to support Taylor, but unfortunately, I could not get tickets, however I feel like I was there in spirit, living through other people's videos, and admiringly watching and singing at the movie! I had the best time there, wore all of my friendship bracelets, and as much glitter as I could put in my hair! Taylor is so amazing, successful and such a big inspiration, as no other artists could perform for over three hours straight, and still remain as enthusiastic and lively as she does!

On a different subject, I have been studying for my exams for the past few weeks, which has made me a stress ball for ages, but just listening to Taylor really helped. I genuinely believe that she kept me sane throughout the chaotic, stressful process, so thank you so much, Tay!

Since first listening to Love Story, my love for Taylor and her music has grown; I just think she is the sweetest, most caring, and talented woman (and cat lady) ever, and she deserves the world. We love you so much Taylor." -Lottie

***

"I live in a small town in Western Australia, I am 16 years old now. I didn't listen to Music that much when I was younger but my first proper introduction to Taylor Swift was actually at school. In english class we were studying song lyrics and my Teacher put on the Love Story music video for us to analyze. I remember just loving straight away and coming home and looking up more of Taylor's songs. It has been a wonderful journey and Love Story is still a personal favorite." - Safira, age 16, Australia

***

"Hello! My name is Delfina and I'm from Argentina. I'm a swiftie since 3 or 4 years ago, and Taylor means everything to me. Something that I want to talk about is how Tay Tay helped me during the Covid 19 pandemic. Without her, I wouldn't have survived. During those days, I felt depressed and lonely. I thought no one could help me... And suddenly, she appeared. SHE. THE MUSIC INDUSTRY. THE WOMAN WHO SAVED MY LIFE.

One morning, a friend sent me a video of a song. She wrote me "This song fits you so well". So I clicked the video and couldn't believe how happy that song made me. The lyrics, the instruments, were just perfect. The singer was a woman called "Taylor Swift". I knew immediately that she was the one who played "Shake it Off". (*Something that's important to know is that Taylor Swift was not THAT popular in my country back then. I mean, now in Argentina she is way more popular).

So, I started to watch videos about her and I just

started feeling... Happy. VERY happy. HAPPIER THAN EVER. Her personality was all I needed, and her music too. Then I started learning about her past and present. Later, I learnt the meaning of a "Swiftie", and then, I just started being part of this family. I literally cried writing this. Really means a lot. Taylor changed my life, and I'm sure she also changed others. My English improved a lot because of Taylor. And I wouldn't be myself without Taylor. She's amazing. Taylor, if someday you read this, let me tell you that I love you, you changed my life: you helped me to find PEACE and HAPPINESS, to be FEARLESS, and lots of other things. You are GORGEOUS. You are AMAZING. Te amo Taylor, I Love you. HAPPY BIRTHDAY!!!" -Delfina, Argentina

***

"In 2017, my cousin made me listen to Look What You Made Me Do. It was the first Taylor Swift song I ever heard and I absolutely fell in love with it. Western music was just getting popular in my country so I didn't know who Taylor Swift was till then. I listened to most of her singles but didn't know there were a whole other bunch of songs that were just as great if not even better that her popular songs.

Later on, during the lover era I listened to paper rings and decided to dive deep into her discography. By the time folklore released I was a full on swiftie.

Learning lyrics to songs, watching interviews and learning more about her incredible songwriting process was my favourite part of becoming a swiftie. I love her so much because her songs were the only things that made me happy whenever I was going through a hard time. Her lyrics feel like it's from a part of my own life. She's been my guiding light during the darkest days.

Another thing I love about Taylor is her personality. She's sweet, kind, understanding and hilarious. She's like that one friend you have who is a walking ray of sunshine. She has also taught me to stand up for what I believe in and to be strong no matter how hard life gets. She taught me to surround myself with people who really care about you and have always been there for you.

My favourite song would probably be Dear Reader or Daylight. When it came out, Dear Reader mostly described how I felt about my life and I was actually glad that there were a lot of other people who have felt the same way at some point in their life. Daylight is such a beautiful song about love and I love the way it makes me feel. I think that everyone deserves to experience that kind of love.

I love being excited about all the hidden clues, the crazy theories we make up and counting down the days to an album release. I also love that I've made a lot of friends who also love her. Watching the eras tour movie with my friends in a theater was one of the best moments of my life. We all had so much fun dancing and singing (screaming) the lyrics together.

Taylor, I love you so much. You are amazing and you make millions of people happy with what you do. You and your music changed my life and I'm so thankful for you. Thank you for everything you do!" -Arya

***

"For a long time I was going through a time of just hating Myself and my life and just wishing it would all just end already but after rediscovering Taylor I just felt a lot less alone. her music was kind of escape from all the hurt I was feeling. I'm not sure I would even be here if not for her poetic, almost understanding music. she's the reason I'm still here and the reason I don't feel as alone as I used to. when i felt like nobody cared I had her, and for that I'm forever grateful. " -Afton C.

***

"I assume I don't have a conventional 'how i became a swiftie' story. She was a pretty major pop person while I was growing up, household name and all, and I only really knew her Red and 1989 songs. By the time I was 11, I guess I let the haters get to me and assumed Taylor Swift was overrated, had no talent for singing-songwriting, and sounded like every other song on the radio (i only came to realise later that she basically pioneered and revitalised pop as we know it today). I guess I never said it out loud, but I felt that way for the longest time until a friend of mine said- 'Hey you should listen to *this is me trying*' . I guess I was feeling adventurous, so I went onto Spotify and played it. And oh my gosh I took back everything I ever said. *This is me trying* perfectly encapsulated how I felt (mainly my struggles with academic validation), and it became clear that Taylor wasn't 'just another singer', because the emotion she managed to convey with her words moved me. I remember walking to school on frosty mornings with that playing through my headphones- and it prompted me to go further. I listened to *folklore*, and then her new release *Midnights* and my perspective completely flipped. Before long, I had listened to every album.

When people say 'Oh god, she's so basic', I think they are so very wrong. Her music is a story, and everything down to each note and time signature is so perfectly done. Heck, she's even genre hopped, which many have tried and failed at. Everything from her music, to her performance and to marketing is top notch- so before you hate on Taylor Swift, learn something from her, because I certainly did. Her songs speak to me, and they continue to speak to many others around the world." -@tejudraws- on Instagram

**

"I have been a swiftie since i was nine! The songs that first got me into you were "we are never ever getting back together", "love story", and "you belong with me"! Right now, i am OBSESSED with folklore and midnights. I have been absolutely JAMMING to you ever since. I love you so, so much and i really hope to see you live someday! I REALLY hope that you get to read my message!" -Sofia, age 12

**

"Dear Taylor Swift,

I know I could write about You being my favourite artist when I was 8 and my favourite childhood song being "Shake it Off." I know I could write about rediscovering You with "Labyrinth" a little over a year ago during hard times, and falling in love with Your music all over again, but to write that would not be enough to tell how big of an impact You made on my life. You and Your songs mean so much to me and I can't imagine my life without, even trying to go a day without listening to them feels impossible, and I know it because I tried once and guess what? I didn't work, and now it's an instinct to hear at least one of Your tracks a day. Without any more side thoughts, I'll get to the main parts, in no particular order, just what I feel is right to say at the moment.

First, I'm a fragile person, I always was. I haven't found my place in the world yet, I'm stuck fighting through storms, I'm still lost in the woods, and I make the best I can from what the world throws at me, be it from the inside or the outside. Least to say, Your music is an incredible source of comfort for me, no matter what, where, and when things happen. When I'm stuck in myself, when I feel like I'm drowning, it's here. When I feel like I'm so far behind I fear I'll never reach what I want to reach, when I need to delve deep into my soul to understand my circumstances better, it's here. I'm so lucky to know I can put my headphones on and play "Castles Crumbling", "Labyrinth", "Dear Reader" then. When those feelings change, when I feel so overwhelmed with things and people out of my control (which I hope doesn't sound too bad), when I'm so helpless and hopeless yet full of passion and emotion I can't express, I know listening to "Mean", "Haunted", or "Look What You Made Me Do" will make me feel better. "Would've, Could've, Should've" is cathartic. I don't listen to "Soon You'll Get Better" often, but it helps when memories become too much and I miss the one person who is suddenly long gone, but who feels as if she hugged me the last time only yesterday. But I'm glad to say Your songs accompany me in the better times too! There are moments when Your songs make me believe there is something out there that awaits me, new people to me, new experiences to live through, new goals to reach, I scream all those hopes to "New Romantics," and "Fearless." It's those moments when I feel indescribable happiness that makes me trip over my words when I try my best singing to Your songs, "Cruel Summer," "Getaway Car", "Hits Different". Or it's when I'm putting on a one-person-play for my cats, because I'm too lost in the moment to even notice I'm doing so, until the song reaches the bridge (or when I hit something, because I'm gesticulating a lot more than my desk allows for); this usually happens with "Mine," and "the last great american dynasty," or "Style" and "Blank Space," and many more too. Your music is also there when nothing happens, when I end up noticing how wonderful the background music "cardigan" and "So It Goes..." make... Your music is always there for me, no matter what; whenever I need it and whenever I don't entirely realize I do. I'm grateful for its presence in my life. Thank You for writing all of those songs I love, Taylor.

Second, Your art is an endless source of inspiration. I write as a hobby; fanfiction, original fiction, poetry, songs, and anything else of that sort which allows me to express my ideas and feelings through written word. I really hope to become a writer someday. Ever since I can remember I took inspiration in music, any and every music. Yours simply hits different (pun unintended, but, Lord, does it fit). Whenever I'd listen to a song, I'd always think of a story, a story I already had, a new one to create, or a tale that would fit solely the song, one to stay in it for me only. I never felt I could think of the song in a different way than when I first heard it; maybe it's because I was not as flexible in my imagination and words as I wished to be, or, as I thought "maybe that's just how things are for some people?" Little did I know. Everything changed when I started listening to Your music. All of a sudden, I found myself listening to a single song and seeing myriad different characters, scenarios, plotlines, character arcs, and more, much more. There's many examples I can give of that, but I'd lie if I say it does not reach every song of Yours. To "Love Story" I wrote exactly 13 000 words of a short story (which is impossible to think of, as it was the first short story of mine this long). "I Know Places" reminds me of a novel I want to write someday, and the relationship between another two characters I wish to write a series about someday. When listening to "Look What You Made Me Do" I feel as if I blacked out and woke up in a fantasy world to see one of my characters fight against people who'd done her wrong (which must look really funny from outside of my brain). There's "cardigan" which continues to bring me even more inspiration every time I listen to it, and "Fifteen" awaiting its own story whenever I get to finally sit down and write it. I could go on and on for hours, I promise. Your music opens a million portals to new realities I want to describe, Taylor, and I cannot thank You enough for it.

Third, your music is the most romantic I've heard. I'm a romantic, for sure, I don't think I can correctly describe the amount of time I spend thinking about The One I wish I had, romanticising my own life, writing about love, and experiencing it through characters in my favourite stories. Your music describes the concept of love in such a beautiful way that I will forever adore. Sometimes it's "Gorgeous" that feels as if You took a peek into my own diary and pieced the puzzles together. But isn't this the magic of Your music? How You understand these raw feelings so well? Pardon me if I'm being too straightforward, but it never fails to astound me. I cried to "Dancing With Our Hands Tied" way too many times, and looked with a dreamy gaze into sweet, sweet nothing to "Lover" just as much.

"You Are In Love" is what I wish to experience in my life someday, so is "Sweet Nothing." "Paris" and "Love Story" I daydream to every given moment, and I can't speak about all the times I should've been doing math homework, but was instead grinning and dancing like crazy to "Paper Rings." Love as you write it, is a wonderful experience and I'm so glad You write about it. You make this feeling that's so out of anyone's control much less scary than it used to be for me.

Fourth, You are an incredibly inspiring person to me. I always talk and gush about you to people in my life, I hope they're not tired of it, because I'm not gonna be done anytime soon. You are a great business woman and I always talk about how smart you manage to lead your career, it's impressive and intimidating in the best sense of these words. You are ambitious and creative, a combination so powerful and so magnetic that I couldn't turn my eyes away from even if I tried; the world can't too, your success continues to prove it. You inspire me to be the same in my own fields. I think that's one of Your powers; You manage to write about Your experiences, thoughts, ideas, and feelings in a universal way, as in "allowing all people throughout time and place to relate to what you write about." I hope You realize how special that is, I wouldn't be surprised if future generations will study Your work and its cultural impact. In how your work is relatable to me, least to say, I am ambitious and you inspire me to be so even more. You organize things to a point a hope to reach someday, you're incredible at it; please never stop. Even more than that, Taylor, you help me feel more comfortable in my own skin. There is something about You that continues to inspire me to be who I truly want to be.

To dress how I want, not to be afraid if people see me in a short skirt or a bright red makeup; to do what feels right, even when people tell me not to trust my own mind and gut; to listen to whoever's music I want to listen to, because listening to "reputation" and "1989" makes me as genuinely confident and as miraculously happy as I ever was. You inspire me to become a better person than I was the day before on my own terms, in contact with myself and my own feelings. Taylor, I want to thank You so much for that.

I think what I'm trying to say here is that you affected my life in a billion little ways. It sounds impossible, but it's true. It's even more impossible when you realize you're not the only one; then it turns out to be beautiful. I hope these words manage to show how much I care about You and Your art. Never give up and remember that there are millions like me who know how special You are and who will support You through all, I promise with all strength in my heart. Forgive me for a strange choice of songs throughout this whole message; blame the feelings, but the least (or the most) obvious tracks sometimes touch my heart the most and help to see things clear as day. Sometimes it's what I found years ago as a kid; sometimes it's from a year ago, heard without realizing what I'm heading into, or sometimes it's from yesterday which I know I'll love for the rest of my life. It started with "Midnights" bought blind, because I trusted You to give us the very best possible, and continues with the friendship bracelets, diary entries about how much I love "1989 (Taylor's Version)," stories inspired by Your music, and bus rides made easier when hearing Your voice. It's always special, because it's You. Thank You for reading this

Taylor, I will feel honoured enough for my lifetime even if You skim through the text. I'm honored enough that I'm here to see you thrive and experience Your art as You create it." -Aleksandra

***

"I became a swiftie after 1989 came out. I was 7 or 8 I think but I was *obsessed* with listening to blank space and welcome to new york! I streamed the album almost every day during class! When the lover album came out, I went absolutely insane! And from then on, I insisted on only listening to you and your music. If an artist that wasn't you came on the radio I would frantically tell my parents to change the station to one that was playing your music!!! Ever since then I've been listening to your music whenever I can and buying your merch on amazon. I want you to know you have made such a large impact on my life and you are such an inspiration to me. You've been through so much with me and I just want you to know you are largely appreciated by over 1 million people. You should be insanely proud of yourself and feel accomplished. Thank you so much. I love you taylor." -anonymous

***

"I'd heard of Taylor Swift, including her hits (shake it off, blank space, 22, etc) but I didn't really become a swiftie until my best friend did. We were texting, and she told me, "I reached 700 liked songs on Spotify!"

this is (still) the bane of my existence. I responded, "okay, and??"

She proceeded to give me some song recommendations, including Lavender Haze, I Think He Knows, and Cruel Summer by Taylor Swift.

following stereotypes, I replied, "tbh you don't really seem like the person to listen to Taylor Swift" and she agreed and that was the end of the conversation.

I did some, I guess. I put ME! on my playlist because it showed up in my recommended, only to later take it off because I was constantly skipping it. (not anymore - ME! is a bop)

Then, in our orchestra email thread, one of the guys brought up the 2009 vmas show, which led to a whole argument.

I got interested again. But it wasn't until half a year later that the domino reaction really started.

My friends and I were visiting one of their grandparents' lake houses, and the trip was about 30 minutes. Their dad said he hoped somebody liked Taylor Swift and put on Lover. At this point, I knew more songs. I didn't just play shake it off and blank space, but I liked Miss Americana & The Heartbreak Prince, Better Than Revenge, and ...Ready For It?

Later, we arrived at the cottage. I was interested in tubing, so I rode on the boat with the dad. He asked me my favorite Taylor Swift album and I told him Lover, not knowing many. (i did know paper rings, cruel summer, and ma&thp.)

After a while, my swiftie friend joined me on the boat. We asked him to play reputation, since we both knew Ready For It? and both screamed the lyrics over the roar of the engine (to which the dad commented "oh, two swifties on this boat!" which was my first time being called a swiftie! i was thrilled.) Later, when I actually hopped on a tube, my swiftie friend asked me "are you ready for it?" I laughed and the whole tube ride I had Ready For It? playing in my head. now I consistently associate that song with tubes and riding around the lake.

towards the new year, I became more and more interested. I started listening to less popular songs (aotgylb, christmas tree farm, marjorie, etc) and swiftie favorites (atwtmvfmvsgavralps) and discovered some new favorites (carolina, dorothea, safe and sound, etc). And that's the story of how I became a swiftie!" -Elena

***

"It's hard to pinpoint what exactly I love about Taylor Swift, it encompasses so many instances and emotions that it's hard to narrow it done. Taylor Swift has been there for me over the years, to bring comfort and understanding and solace when I needed it most. She gave me hope during good times, and more frequently the really hard times in my life. Through my parent's divorce, moving multiple times, so many new schools, not having friends, a super storm that displaced my family, even up until now where I'm not sure what I want to do in life amid health struggles. She has been and and continues to be a safe haven and she was a friend when I didn't have one, I didn't have to feel so alone by myself. I didn't always tell people how I was her fan because of fear of being picked on again, no matter because I kept listening. Through periods of my life when I went through big changes and new chapters, even when I found listening to music hard and having hope was painful, I still came back to her and her music. Once I was no longer afraid of persecution in college, I shared my love for her with a few close friends and I ended up bringing them into this part of world to become part-time swifties. They were my partners who blindly agreed to go to the era's tour with me even without being massive fans and somehow we made it happen. At first, I was a little self conscious because I could only manage to get an outfit together that so many people were going as (I didn't feel creative with my outfit). However, I had never felt so in my element; so happy and at peace. People were so kind and generous, for once I didn't feel so self conscious. We had the best time! Taylor was also the reason I found some of my favorite YouTubers and in turn is the reason I decided to take a creative writing class in my last semester at college (which I had never done before and it was completely opposite of my major and minor). She inspired me and it ended up being my favorite class of my college career and I felt a true vibrancy. Afterwards, it led me to question if my original plan of career was what I really wanted. I have come to realize that maybe the standard and reliable plan isn't what is for me. Taylor will continue to be there, her music guiding me and comforting me on this new path to find something greater and more fulfilling. The comfort of her old music and the breath of fresh air with her new music, there is always something for how I'm feeling or how I hope to be feeling. She gives me something to look forward to as I carve out my little part of life. Catching a glimpse of the sign Taylor Ave when I pick my head up in the car or catching a thirteen somewhere gives me a sense of hope and wish of good luck, a vote of confidence and I'm so glad I get to share that experience with/ like so many others. For that I say Happy Birthday friend, keep being you!" -Victoria A.

***

"I first noticed Taylor Swift in some time around 2018-2019, and what I mean by that is, I saw how big she was when our family was just having some family time and my dad put on Taylor Swift's Reputation Stadium Tour. When the intro started screaming the lyrics *Baby, let the games begin* from ...Ready For It?, my face instantly lit up and halfway through the movie when she brings the guitar onto the stage, my dad said I had to go to bed and I giggled saying I didn't want to go to bed and that I wanted to finish the film.

Eventually, I think we got through a few more songs before I went to bed. Yet, when I went to bed, I think at that moment, somewhere in my mind, I think I knew I was going to be a swiftie someday, and when I mean someday, it's not like I was too lazy to already become a swiftie but that I was still trying to figure out who I was - what music I liked, what food I enjoyed, my hobbies, I was still finding myself because I was a child

In 2020, we moved to Australia for more opportunities in education, I took piano lessons, I went to school, made friends but the thing I've never gotten to do was become a swiftie, so time moved on.. I didn't notice she released Midnights in 2022, Fearless and Red Taylor's Version in 2021, but when she announced ERAS TOUR dates for Australia, I thought about the memory (paragraph 1) and I decided to finally listen to her songs, learn about the things that have happened in her life like why she created Taylor's Version and so on.

One of my biggest regrets about becoming a swiftie was that my time was too late, I was so wrapped up around everything else when we first came to Australia, I never went back to those memories of the kinda promise I made when I went to bed. I can't say it's a regret but more like an insecurity. Once, I went on this Tumblr page and someone commented that you are not a swiftie if you liked Taylor after her Folklore and Evermore era and for a few weeks, I believed them, I made myself look so dumb until I saw youtube channels saying as long as you like Taylor, you support what she does, you listen to her music, etc, you are officially a swiftie and that made me so happy, I completely forgot about that Tumblr comment." -Insha N.

***

"I was never a person who was into english music and being an Indian I hardly understood the lyrics of any english song i heard. But I remember that once when I was scrolling through pinterest I came across this really cool song in the background and before I could look it up I accidentally pressed the home button. i was so upset that day, because one song that I liked, ONE, and that too just vanished off the face of the earth. But then a year or so later I heard my elder sister listening to the same song and I was like what is that? What are you listening to? And she just goes like Taylor Swift? And I am just attending there completely baffled like no i don't want the artist name, what is the song? And then she goes, oh the song, that's You Belong With Me and i rush up to my room and just google it up. You won't believe I spent a whole entire week listening to just that song.

That's around the time when Spotify was introduced. When I searched up some of my songs, Taylor Swift was suggested, and then somehow out of nowhere she became the only person whose songs I used to listen to. She was the one person who could make me feel like I was not the only one who went through so much drama in my life. That lyric "I swear I don't love the drama, it loves me," I have quoted it so many times in my conversations that my friends complete the line before I can.

So basically now I am a massive swiftie and I swear if someone insults Taylor in front of me, they're done for. She is a blessing to this world and her words...I wish someone would write a song about her. Although i just really want to thank her for helping me to get through life mostly and I honestly love her and wish I could tell her to please don't ever lose your uniqueness or your splendor for anyone. Just be your own awkward dancing and cat loving self. You deserve it all." -Arisha F., India

***

"I haven't been a Swiftie for that long, and I joined sometime before the Eras tour. I love your music so so much and my fav album is speak now. You're such a nice person and your lyrics are so powerful. I'm trying to learn more songs all the time and each time I hear a new song, I am amazed. I love singing and you definitely fuel that passion of mine. You inspire me and make me feel so happy when I hear your music. I've gone to the Eras movie twice now, and the second time still gave me goosebumps. I am so excited for reputation TV and wish you the best!!!" -Lucas, 8th grade, California

***

"Hi Taylor, you are such a talented music artist and I hope I become just like you. Sadly I cannot buy tickets to your tour but if I could I would dress as the fearless era because I like it and I saw the perfect dress for it. I became a swiftie when I was five because I loved dancing to shake it off and so many other classics. Even today I listen to those classics and I also listen to the newer songs. Taylor I hope you have the best birthday ever. You deserve it so much. You are an inspiration to the world. All your eras are fab!" -Rasa H.

***

"How did I become a swiftie? I never thought as myself a swiftie until "Midnights" came out, I really only liked her popular songs, anyways "Midnights" came out and I listened to it and I really liked it so I kinda just wanted to be a swiftie because of "Midnights" so thank you "Midnights". My first ever Taylor Swift song I heard? It was "Shake It Off" I remember I was in my grandma's car and it was playing on the radio.

I love Taylor for a lot of reasons, but I love her so much because she's soooo sweet to her fans and she's an amazing singer. What does Taylor's music mean to me? It means sooo much to me, her music is very valuable to me, each song is very important to me, and I'm just so obsessed with every single bridge especially how she puts so much effort into them.

How has Taylor's music helped me? Taylor's music helped/helps me not too be sad or mad. Her music always makes me happy so whenever I'm sad or just not in a very good mood I will listen to her and it makes me very happy! What's my favorite song and why? My favorite song is definitely "my tears ricochet" I really love the lyrics and the intro it's very majestic, as well as her voice it's gorgeous, and the bridge- don't even get me started it's just so amazing.

What is the best part of being a swiftie? Honestly there's so many great things about being a swiftie but if I has to choose one I would say clowning, it's so fun to try and make predictions for when she's gonna announce (Taylor's Versions) or if she's gonna make a music video, it's very fun to clown around even if it's not actually gonna happen it's still really fun. If I could tell Taylor Something what would it be? Thank you so much Taylor you have done so much for your fans and I just wanna say you're one of the sweetest people I know, i love you!" -Miley

"My earliest Taylor swift memory was me and my friends dancing around the living room to I knew you were trouble when we were six. Her music has been the soundtrack to some of my best memories. Me and my friend chanting midnight rain after coming out of the movie theatre after watching the eras tour movie. Me blasting fifteen on my fifteenth birthday. Doing a play and dancing to a remix of shake it off. Having a swiftie karaoke day at school.

I remember this one time I was having really bad anxiety. I hid in the bathroom stall and school and blasted the archer in my AirPods. It helped me calm down and go on with my day.

I really appreciate how Taylor helps give smaller artists voices, it is really commendable how she took her music off of streaming services to protest fair pay for artists. The re recording project also helps to show that you should be very careful before signing to a record label and it has inspired some other artists to follow her lead. Thank you for everything you do Taylor, happy birthday!" -@holygroundgirlie

***

"I guess you could say that I became a swiftie overnight. One night when I was around 8 years old, I was playing some music to fall asleep, and this song came on. It started, and I immediately had a weird but enlightened feeling. I listened to the song and when the lyrics went to, "the rain came pouring" it started to rain outside my window. I was astonished, I kept playing the song over and over and over again. And right before I went to sleep, I looked up what song I had been playing. It was Clean by Taylor Swift. So that's when I started to dig deeper into Taylor, and I started to like songs like mine, mean, love story and you belong with me. But as I got older, I explored more recent albums. Once I really started to listen to Folklore and Evermore, I really started to become a hardcore swiftie and appreciate Taylor Swift and her music much more.

Christmas of 2022, I got the best gift I have ever gotten in my entire life. I got to go to the Eras Tour! I was so excited, little did I know that I would be going to one of the most special Eras Tour dates. My grandparents live in Kansas City so I got to go to night 1 in Kansas city. Which happened to be the day after Speak Now taylors version came out, and speak now just happened to be my favorite album at the time. Before the show, my cousin Isabell, showed me a post about how Taylors beautiful Speak Now koi fish guitar was removed from the country music hall of fame. We both had some speculations about it, and we were both really excited.

I had the most amazing time planning my outfit and getting all ready to go. When I finally got there, I was just so happy to be there and to hear her music. Then, the clock struck 0 and the music started to play. And then there she was. I got this shiver down my spine and through my whole body, and then I burst into tears. I had no idea that I would cry, because I don't cry over very many things. I just couldn't believe that I was looking at her with my very own eyes. I was screaming singing Miss americana but balling my eyes out at the same time.

Flash forward to the speak now era, and I was just wanting that guitar to come out so badly. I just wanted to see it in real life. Then she pulled it out and started playing long live and the same shive went through my spine that I felt when I first saw her. I started crying again. I just felt so happy in that moment.

That is how I became a swiftie, and my special moment at the Eras Tour with her." -Lauren T., age 13

***

"For as long as I can remember Taylor has always been a part of my life, growing up I heard a lot of her songs on the radio especially during the red era, it wasn't until 1989 that I started to become a swiftie, I have vivid memories of me dancing around my living room to shake it off, style and blank space and I was so obsessed with the music videos from this era they all hold a special place in my heart and are still to this day some of my favourites! Wildest dreams has always been a favourite song of mine. I love old Hollywood and when I listen to this song I just have an image in my head of the aesthetic in the music video that has always reminded me of old Hollywood and it's just such a beautiful song! Style is another of my favourite songs it was one of the songs I became obsessed with when 1989 was released even more so, I loved the music video and to this day I still do!

Lover was the first album release I experienced as a full-on Swiftie and pretty much made me love Taylor even more! I instantly fell in love with Cornelia street and daylight (one of my favourite Taylor swift love songs it's just so beautiful and means so much to me.) One thing I love about Taylor is not only is she an amazing singer, but she is also an incredible songwriter and lyricist and I've always appreciated that about her songs! She can sometimes make me feel different emotions even if I've never experienced what she is singing about and she just captures feelings so well. Taylor's music has been there for me through my darkest times and my happiest times and I hope it stays that way for many years to come, I often wonder if Taylor knows just how much her and her music mean to so many people the impact she has had on my life is mind-blowing. I was just 10 years old when I heard my first Taylor swift song as a Swiftie, I'm now 18 and my love for Taylor and her music has only gotten deeper and it has been crazy to see the wonderful things she has achieved over the years and how far she has come! Her hard-work and dedication to her career is so inspiring and I can't wait to see how many other wonderful things she will continue to achieve!" -Lillie J., age 18

***

"I first got into Taylor Swift with the release of Midnights. Up until then, all I really knew about her was that she was a really big mainstream artist, and I had heard her singles on the radio and such. In 2022, though, when midnights was about to be released, a lot of my friends were talking about it and how they might stay up for it. Most of them were also relatively new swifties at the time as well. I was intrigued, because up until then, I didn't know a lot about her, and so I decided to listen to Midnights when it came out, not necessarily because I liked Taylor Swift at the time, just because I wanted to know why my friends were so interested in her. So, I convinced my parents to get spotify to listen to it, and on October 21, 2022, I listened to Taylor Swifts Midnights for the first time while getting ready for school.

I was instantly in love. I had never experienced such amazing songwriting and vocals before. I was so surprised that I hadn't started listening to her before, considering how good her music is. The rest of that year, I started to get into her music more, and that spotify wrapped, I managed to get into the top 6% of Taylor Swift listeners, which is pretty good for only having spotify for a month before it came out. (As of 2023, i'm top 0.5%) Around this time is also when Taylor's Eras Tour was announced. I desperately wanted tickets and to see Taylor live. Despite not getting pre-sale tickets and being disappointed, my parents surprised me with tickets for my birthday to Arlington night 3. I was so happy, and I wasn't even that big of a swiftie yet.

The thing is, I went to the Eras Tour quite early in terms of tour dates. It was the third location Taylor did, and the setlist was quite new. I wasn't that big of a swiftie, and some of the songs, I didn't know that well. Now, I could sing all of those songs by heart without hesitating. Looking back, I honestly kinda wish that I had gone later in the year, I could know all the songs and have the same connections with them like I do now. Still, I am and will be forever grateful that I got to go to the Eras Tour, though. As time progressed, I became an even bigger swiftie. The spring/summer of 2023 really shaped me as a swiftie. I stayed up each weekend to watch livestreams, and changed my favorite songs like every week.

Going to the Eras Tour movie in October was

an amazing experience for me. I went once with my mom and once with my friends. Going with my friends was the best time i've ever had in my life. I got a cup, and we went down to the bottom of the movie theater and danced our hearts out. We cried together for marjorie, champagne problems, and you're on your own kid. Then we blasted midnights on the way home. I absolutely loved every minute.

I honestly really love Taylor, and she has helped me get through so many stressful and difficult times in my life. And even if people say that i'm too obsessed with Taylor Swift or that I need to calm down while talking about her (really bad joke but iykyk lol), I absolutely love Taylor Alison Swift with all my heart." - Izzy M., age 13

***

"I became a Swiftie when I was in Year 5 (I'm from the UK) so I was around 9 years old. The very first song I listened to was, of course, Shake It Off. It was the last day of the school year and our class was doing karaoke. I didn't know any of the words but I remember going away for the summer and coming back with an expanded but still limited range of songs.

Since then, I have become one of her biggest fans. I made a step-by-step plan on how to get eras tickets for me and my best friend. I was so passionate about getting the tickets that when I found out my Maths teacher got tickets, I cried, that was also because she was leaving and emotions were running high. We got two access codes but tickets went on sale on my birthday and I was travelling to India at the same time. My dad tried to buy them but we didn't get any. It might sound stupid but I manifested so hard; I listened to playlists, subliminals, saved every tiktok and pinned every taylor swift related pin to a board. And luckily, two days later during the next sale we managed to get VIP tickets to the third Wembley show.

I have a wall full of her song polaroids with fairy lights (that keep annoyingly falling down) and I am still constantly adding to the wall. I have her 1989 cd, and I was in her top 0.05% of Spotify listeners. In my Textiles GCSE Culture project, I chose Taylor Swift Eras Culture. I made my final piece based on her eras and spent five very stressful hours on it. My mock GCSE piece is going to be my own interpretation of the green folklore dress, so hopefully I'll be able to capture its beauty. My 15th Birthday cake was Speak Now TV based, and I have woken up at 5am to listen to each of her album releases.

She has helped me get through so much in my life. I am now almost 16 and she is still the first artist I listen to when I need to calm down. I have laughed, danced, sung and cried to her songs and she has been someone who has helped me get through some of the worst times." -anonymous

***

"I started listening to Taylor more when reputation came out! i was around 7 years old. i have memories of screaming "look what you made me do" in the car every morning before i was dropped off for school, her music has always made me so so happy. when i was younger i remember dancing to shake it off and watching the blank space music video over, and over, and over! i remember when i was little always feeling kinda connected to taylor because my last name is taylor, i now realize that taylor is a very common name, but i feel that being young and naive really made me stick with her throughout the years. in the past two years ive become more of a swiftie than i had ever been. i've really started listening to every single one of her albums and her non popular songs too. she such a lyrical genius and the way she can make stories with her songs AND her music videos is so amazing. i can picture everything in my mind and that's what makes it so fun. after school during softball season i run through the empty halls playing taylor on my phone and screaming the lyrics!! her music brings me so so much joy. i enjoy staying up late watching the eras tour, clowning about what album comes next, and just the whole fandom of swifties! everyones so loving. taylor is such a loving person and is so sweet and i'm so happy to be a fan of her and get to experience the fun being a swiftie!!!!!!" -anonymous

***

"Dear My Beloved Taylor,

Going to start with: Happy Birthday and I love you so much! I hope you, Mer, Benj, and Olivia are doing all too well! My name is Anaya, I am a freshman in highschool, and I am from Virginia. I have been a fan of your work for as long as I could remember; from dancing to Shake It Off with my mom sister in the kitchen when I was like 6 years old, to binging your music videos and recreating dances whenever they came out, to screaming your lyrics when they came on the radio. Even though I experienced all those things growing up I never considered myself a 'Swiftie' until recently. In my 8th grade year I met this sweet, lovable girl named Emma. One of the first questions she asked me was: "Do you listen to Taylor Swift" and I kinda laughed because you were like a childhood artist to me and then I realized she was being serious. I said no and she kept begging me to listen to her requested songs but I kept refusing, but then finally one night—one in which I remember so vividly now— she texts me the All Too Well (10 minute version) while I was studying for a Spanish test. I kinda rolled my eyes at her because I was kind of annoyed that she was still begging me but I clicked play anyways. I was like halfway through the song and I was in absolute shock. I did not know you were THAT lyrically talented. Let's fast forward to 300 takeout coffees later and here I am, an absolute die hard fan.

I know every lyric from Tim McGraw to Invisible String, to Dear Reader. I love you as a person more than anything though. You are so kind, stunning, and so incredibly smart. I never understand how people could say so casually, "I hate Taylor Swift" I really just do not understand it. All of the hatred you have gotten throughout the years makes me sick, but the love from us swifties overpowers all of that hate by infinity x13.

I truly cannot imagine my life without you. You make me so insanely happy no matter what. You do not even know of my existence yet you feel like my best friend. I connect with your lyrics so strongly that it makes me feel that way. Nobody could ever make me smile the way you make me. High School is really rough to be honest. I don't ever fit into friend groups and I am always the one left out of stuff, so the peak of my day is when I finally get to come home and listen to your songs and watch my favorite interviews and Miss Americana. I have been hurt and let down by so many people in my life, but never by you. You don't know of me, yet you are still always by my side, it feels that way.

Exciting news: Soooo I begged and begged for my parents to try and get me Eras Tour tickets but they kept refusing, so I watched Miss Americana with my mom and she cried and fell in love with you (I knew she would how could anyone not) and she promised we would try our best to get tickets.......the next tour. I had no idea if the Eras Tour was going to be your last so I got upset. When my parents saw you extended the tour out til 2024 we were scared you were gonna be done. But flash forward to when you announce the USA second leg dates + Canada. I remember this exact moment so well: I was on a 2 week vacation in Italy and we were at Lake Como walking up the steps to our hotel room and I refreshed my Pinterest (my fav app ever omg its the best) homepage and BAM! "Taylor Swift second USA leg dates announced" I literally stopped in my spot and screeched. Got weird looks from the people around me but I did not care about any of that! My parents and sister turn around and look at me like I am psycho and when I tell them they say that we will register for tickets. I DIED DEAD!!!!!! But yeah that did not work out so well we got waitlisted on like 10 accounts for Toronto and New Orleans. I lost all hope. I thought I was never ever going to get to see you. Well, so I thought. I am sitting in my room, November 11, 2023 watching the Eras Tour live stream from Argentina. You are singing the Long Live bridge and I received a text from my dad. When I clicked on the image he sent me, that was the moment my life changed forever! It was a picture of Eras Tour tickets checkout for Warsaw, Poland night 3. I screamed and sobbed for like 2 hours straight. I am so excited no words could describe it!

I love you so much, Tay! I hope you have a wonderful birthday!!" -Anaya

***

"I grew up with songs like Bad Blood, Blank Space and Shake It Off. I was 4 when 1989 was released so when it was becoming popular I would know the songs but nothing about Taylor. My favorite song was Shake It Off when I was young, all because of the Sing movie. As I was growing up and Taylor was more known I really liked her songs like Love Story and You Belong with Me but they never caught my interest to listen to more of Taylor's music. Until like in 6th grade I heard paper rings and lover. I fell in love with those songs but again did not find much interest in Taylor's music.

In 7th grade I finally started to listen to Taylor. I slowly started listening to Talyor. Once this year I started to get way more interested in Taylor like her albums and songs. By April I was a swiftie but was not confident enough to show it. Once I found out about Taylor coming to my state for her eras tour I was so happy, knowing that the show was going to be on June 2,3 and 4 when my birthday is June 16th. I asked my parents for tickets for my birthday but it was too late and the only tickets were too expensive. I was so up to going just outside of the stadium and listening to the show that we were in the area but it had completely flown my mind and we were too far from the stadium once I remembered.

This summer of 2023 I truly fell in love with Taylor's music. I listen to her non-stop. I entered 8th grade and was not so afraid of what people thought of me being a swiftie. I got my first vinyl in September. It was 1989. I was so happy for the 1989 Taylor's version.

The day I came home from school and found out Taylor was going to have the eras tour film I cried happy tears of joy. I asked my parents and then regretted asking because it was almost 100 dollars from my family to go. But my parents let me pre-order the tickets on October 6th because I never really asked for anything. I could not wait for the movie. The week for the movie was really stressful. I wanted to make so many friendship bracelets and custom make my shirt along with having to study for my high school entrance exam. I was so stressed but did it all. My shirt was the 22 shirt I hand-painted each letter and then embroidered sequins to outline each letter. We went October 14 to the movie. I sang the whole movie. I lost my voice and was smiling the whole time. I did not trade bracelets because there were not many people in my theater and I was scared to ask. But I was so happy. I got the pink bucket and the movie poster. I took glow sticks for each era. After the movie, we went out to eat, and could not speak since I lost my voice. The whole time we were eating my parents were saying how much they loved the movie, how Taylor is so talented, how it was such a well-choreographed show with the tolerate it table, the dancers, the clothes she was wearing, how the stage lifted everything. My mom said that it was surprising to see a young artist who is not with a load of makeup, with nails and appropriate clothes. She really respected that. I cried tears of joy from how much they liked the movie.

Taylor has become someone I listen to in any of my moods as an escape from life or a celebration of a good day. Being swiftie is one of the things I am so happy about. We are all so grateful for Taylor and us swifties can never say how much we are grateful for you Taylor. You are an inspiration to everyone. Thank you and Happy birthday Taylor Swift." -Melina C., age 13, Illinois.

***

"Hi Taylor! I actually became one of your fans when I was about 3 or 4 (During your red era) My aunt would play your music everythime I went in her car so when I first heard her play your music I immediately became interested. I asked my aunt who sang this and then she told me it was you! Then I begged her to show me pictures. I didn't become a real swiftie till midnights but I've always been a fan! I was hanging out with one of my friends I hadn't seen in a while and her family are swifties. After listening to more of your music I feel in love with it again and I'm so greatful for everything you do! I can't wait to be that aunt that plays your music in my car and Introduce all your music to all my future family! Thank you for everything you do. You and your music has helped me get through so much. I love you!" -Cecily

***

"I was about 6 or 7 when I first listened to Taylor. The song was "Shake It Off." I remember being so in love with it. Let's fast forward to 2021 when i decided to listen to "shake it off" again and I was like "I should listen to more of her songs!" I later became obsessed with "august" and started listening to her more. A year later, when Midnights was a few days old, i started listening to Taylor forever.. Here I am today listening to Taylor 24/7. From having dreams of going to the eras tour, meeting her (in my wildest dreams),

351

making friendship bracelets, and buying my first piece of merch. I would decide that I would be a swiftie until the day I die. I love Taylor so much because she is honestly the sweetest person ever and her music has helped me so so much. Taylor has taught me so many things and I'm incredibly grateful for her. Another thing I love is the swifties ! They are just the sweetest, cutest, loving fandom ever !! The best part about being a swiftie is getting to know and meet different people. Getting to talk about Taylor, your favorite, album, etc ... I don't have a favorite Taylor Swift song because there's too many to choose from, but I do have a favorite album! My favorite album is folklore. Folklore is just so magical and so well-written. From the aesthetic, song-writing, and even the way she performs the songs ! If I could tell Taylor anything, I would tell her that she is the most amazing person ever. Her music has helped me become who I am today. I would also thank her for everything she's given and done for us." -@daylightears on YouTube

***

"I recently became a swiftie because of one of my friends. She is honestly one of the nicest people I've ever met, and she helped me see that Taylor is also an amazing person. I don't remember the first Taylor Swift song I listened to, but I do remember jamming to songs from 1989 like Bad Blood and Shake It Off. My 4th grade teacher also played Love Story for the class, and I would always dance to that song as well. Taylor has incredible song writing skills and an amazing voice. One of my favorite songs from her has to be "exile." It's such a beautiful song with amazing lyrics, and I just love the bridge so much. Taylor has changed my life, and I will always be a Swiftie!" -Lindsey R.

***

"So, Taylor Swift's debut album came out when I was 2 years old. I didn't start listening to her until I was 6, when I first received her Fearless and Speak Now Albums for Christmas I instantly fell in love with her. Many times people ask me why I became a Swiftie, or why I love Taylor Swift. "Big deal" they say or "she's highly overrated." To that I say, "you don't understand" because I want them to understand but I know that's hard sometimes. That's why I want to share why I love her.

I love Taylor Swift because she's real. She's literally sunshine in human form and does so much for everyone. She's giving and kind, authentic, and a positive role model for young girls. I see young girls who are normally serious everywhere open up and show their fun and silly side. She is an inspiration for aspiring artists everywhere and truly the real deal.

I also love Taylor Swift because she helped me get through so much. I've gone through so much in my life but I can always count on her to bring me peace and help me through whatever. I was bullied a lot growing up so being able to know that she understands that is also wonderful because I feel less alone. So much of her life has been published and scrutinized on front covers of articles, yet she still always has a smile on her face and does everything with grace, something I admire about her so much.

She also gives so much to charity in turn to help so many. She's donated to countless organizations such as literature, Survivors of Sexual Assault, and many others. This in itself is

353

so amazing. She also gives so much to fans because she knows what it's like to be a fan. This
makes me love her so much.

All in all, I could honestly go on and on about how much Taylor Swift means to me, but I would probably have to write a novel or more just to fit everything in. If I were to ever meet Taylor, I would just say thank you. Thank you for being a role model to so many. Thank you for helping us through the rough and tough times. When people refer to her as a national treasure, she really lives up to that. Thank you Taylor for all that you are and everything else. Happy Birthday!" -Kiera H.

**

"My Swiftie journey kicked off in the most random way — I heard a Taylor Swift song at some random restaurant, and damn, it was good vibes all the way. So, I get home and try to Google the song, but Google was slacking with no song search feature back then. A few days later, I stumble upon this video, and they spill the tea on the song name. From that moment, I was all in as a Swiftie. Now, the guys in my class throw shade, calling me gay, but you know what? I stand loud and proud. Taylor's music speaks to me, and I'm not letting anyone dull my Swiftie sparkle." -Arya

**

"I never listened to pop music and wasn't going to, but one day 1 saw an excerpt from some interview with Taylor on YouTube. And my thoughts were like, "I think I've found someone who just can't have any haters because how can you hate this eighth wonder of the world?" I was shocked that she is so unique and popular, but at the same time caring for everyone around her so I decided to listen to a couple of songs... and a few more..... and more.......

And then I saw the whole world in them, so now I have each one in my playlist and probably never would have a favorite, because they're all incredible! So if I had a chance to tell her something, I would say: "You bring into this world an insane flow of warmth that people need so much so please don't forget that we are also ready to share it"." -Betty

***

"I don't know what my life would be like without Taylor Swift. She came into my life at a time where I was about to go through one of my lowest lows. After being somewhat known by me enough for me to be tuning into award shows for her and watching her music videos as they came out, I became a Swiftie in her Midnights era. When my mom finally played through that album as a whole instead of just the single (like other times), I realized that I was in love with each and every song in Midnights. So, I quickly did as much research about her as possible about her, finding that so many of the songs that I had loved were actually hers! and instead of staying up late because of anxiety, I was staying up late to finish listening to 1989. I've never liked country before (or anything other than Hamilton and The Beatles because of my extremely selective music taste) but I adored her's. So, during this period of darkness, I was provided with a light that would never go out like the others: Taylor Swift. Eventually— with the help from a few other lights—I was able to live in a world of brightness that I am still in now. Out of all of the other lights, Taylor's was the brightest. Not only was it bright, but it was colorful and happy.

I will forever be grateful for that. Maybe part of the reason for my interest in her is because she grew up in the same area where I live. We were born in the same hospital, and my current house is only 15 minutes away from her Wyomissing house. Along with that, there are quite a few adults who lived here when they were young and knew her at some point. There are a good amount of swifties in the area, and we are all very grateful for living where such an amazing person grew up. Another reason why I love Taylor so much is because of how much she inspires my own music creation. I always liked poetry since second grade, and Taylor lit up my interest so that it when from a small spark of enjoyment to an inferno of obsession. I am constantly writing songs, and don't know what I would do if I wasn't. If I ever had the chance to meet Taylor outside of my dreams, I would just thank her. I'd thank her for my happiness being as prominent in my life as it is. I'd thank her for inspiring me. I'd thank her for being my comfort blanket when I need it the most. I'd thank her for replacing negative things in my life. I think this whole thing makes one thing about me clear: I love Taylor Swift to the moon and to Saturn." -anonymous

***

"Dear Taylor,

My birthday wish for you is that you feel the strength and joy that all your fans see in you. Your music is an incredible gift to us all, and you are such a dedicated artist.

I see pictures of the Taylor in her teens, and in her 20s — but they cannot compare to the Taylor we have now, in 2023. You are beautiful, strong, clever, kind, and dynamic! They say that women grow into their power as they age—and I know that is true for you.

I wish you peace, contentment, joy, and love in this new year of your life! Happy 34th Birthday!!!!" - Sandra (mom to Maddie, a 10 year old swiftie)

***

"Happy birthday Taylor! I have been a fan since 1989 was released and a super fan since the Midnight album release. You have simply given our entire family so much joy this year. Your beautifully written music, fun engagement with fans, culture of understanding and empowerment have created so many bonding opportunities for my family. We made a family road trip from Los Angeles to Denver for your July 14 Eras show, and of course the music from all your albums was the main soundtrack as we drove singing together and making friendship bracelets. We now have a fabulous pink Swiftmas tree with all the eras colors ornaments and I sewed a tiny t-shirt for our christmas elf so that he can be a "Junior Jewelf". You have sparked our music creativity; my younger daughter is learning guitar and I've started playing piano again to your sheet music (hadn't since I was a teenager). From the bottom of my heart I am forever grateful to you; and I cherish the memories and emotions you have and continue to inspire. I love you to the moon and to Saturn." -Tania S.

***

"Hi Taylor! Happy Birthday! I love you so much and I'm only 13 years old but I've loved your music for so long. I've been a fan since reputation when I was like 7-8 years old. Your songs are so well thought out and I love the way that you phrase different lyrics in your songs. When I was in 3rd grade I would make my parents play the reputation album to me on my way to school. I love your new vault tracks so much! I'm so glad that you decided to release them. Your songs are just so amazing and I really want to thank you for being a big part of my life. I was in the top .5% of your Spotify fans and you will always have a big place in my heart. Happy Birthday Taylor! I love you so much!" -Ellie M.

***

"Dear, Taylor - Happy Birthday!!!!! You are my fav singer and I am so glad that you have shared your ability to write, sing, play guitar,and play piano to influence people to become great musicians such as yourself. You have led me through guitar and choir. I auditioned for your song "long live" in choir. My whole fam are Swifties, even my dad!! Like I said,happy b-day!" -Abby M.

***

"My name is Lilia, and I am a fourteen-year-old (I like to consider myself a songwriter) from Canada. My journey to becoming a swiftie was a bit rocky towards the start, but now I am a huge fan and take so much inspiration from Taylor. That journey started off when I was five, which was when *1989* was originally released. I listened to the album 24/7, but after constantly being made fun of at school for listening to Taylor, I stopped. Since then, I have become more confident and learned how to focus on what I like versus what other people think, and I now write my own songs about my personal experiences with things like being bullied. I started consistently listening to Taylor again when she released *evermore*, and she has been such a huge inspiration for me in terms of songwriting and just being a massive role model in the music industry. I feel so lucky to be able to share my love for this amazing person with so many people now, and the release of *1989 (Taylor's Version)* was such an amazing thing for me, since I got to experience the release all over again but this time without feeling judged.

Happy birthday, Taylor! You are my biggest role model, and I hope you keep inspiring young girls all around the world through your amazing music. I love you so much!" -Lilia, age 14, Canada

***

"I live in Geneva and I kept seeing Taylor's eras tour on all social media. I started to rlly wanna go and decided to at least try to listen to her music to see if I liked it!! Turns out I was in love with her music and story, I watched her rep concert and documentary on Netflix and went to watch her movie of the eras tour! I'm a rlly big fan and find her story so inspiring!" - anonymous

***

"So 2 years ago for competitive lyrical dance, our song was Never Grow Up from Speak Now era. When I listened to it, I felt like I had something special with it. I had heard it a few times before and thought nothing of it. But that time I did. I related. I felt I had just had someone help me with all my problems, they had just well gone away. So when I went home i listened to lots of her underrated songs from other eras, I related, loved, fell in love with her. She was somewhat different than any other artist, in a great amazing understanding, unique way. I started to know her personality, what kind of person she is it felt absolutely amazing to have such amazing music that really effected my life and choices.

My favorite song by her is Ronan (Taylors Version) because my aunt died from untreatable cancer when I was five years old. I loved her so much. It broke my whole world when I found out she was gone. She is in heaven now. God has taken care of her. She is in peace now. If I had anything to say to Taylor I would say, Dear Taylor, you are such an amazing, heart warming inspiring person me. You have saved my whole life, I don't think I would be here today if I didn't start listening to that one song. I hope that you find joy, and a meaning to life, God and Jesus Christ loves you. He has a plan. I want you to know you are such a heart warming person , and those exes guess what? They didn't deserve your kind, outstanding heart.

Her music brings me joy, it heals me because I have something to relate to I don't feel like I need to give up as long as she keeps me going in life I am so grateful no matter what. She taught me so much. I want to thank her for how she made me laugh , smile , and made me love myself for who I am." -Natalie K.

***

"Hi! My name is Autumn, and I am a fairly new swiftie. Last year, I discovered that I am autistic, and during that journey, I also found your (Taylor's) music. It was a pretty weird time, considering that I was realizing so many new things about myself, and I think that your music helped so much! I found songs that were written in ways that felt so much like me, like mirrorball, mastermind, or you're on your own, kid. You songs have helped me process different things in my life, like foolish one, which describes my situationship (I think that's the right term) with this one guy (it went nowhere) and I love the way that

that song just shows how all of that went through my head. You have completely changed my life in the past year (I'm listening to the red album as I wrote this) and if you don't know this, an autistic special interest is where someone fully obsesses over something and knows everything (I swear I'm not creepy) about that thing. I can list your songs like how you can list cat breeds, and even when I'm not listening to your music, it's running through my head.

I was, sadly, a little late to the game for eras tour tickets, but I went to the movie twice and had so much fun screaming everything with my friends, and will always remember how I felt singing the mastermind bridge with them. I cant remember what I did all day when I didn't get a constant feed of possible easter eggs to decode, or always have folklore playing while I'm at school. You have turned my life around, and I really hope you're here to read this." -Autumn

***

"I think even if you gave me infinite amount of time to describe what Taylor Swift means to me, it still would never be enough. I know it might sound dramatic, but there are truly no words to describe how much I love, appreciate, and admire her! The first Taylor song I ever heard was Love Story when I was in kindergarten. I remember dancing around my childhood best friend's room with her and listening to the Fearless CD on repeat, and how we loved the song "Fifteen" because it talked about best friends. Ever since then, Taylor has always been so important in my life, and I truly feel so lucky to get to have grown up with her. My dad would buy me every new album on CD when it came out and I would play them all on my Hello

Kitty CD player. He still does to this day!

Taylor's music has been such a constant in my life. Speak Now has always felt like pure magic, both when it came out originally and when it was re-released. Red is truly the soundtrack of my childhood; I remember making up a dance to All Too Well before I ever understood the significance of the lyrics. 1989 is the first time I saw Taylor on tour, and I got to go with that same childhood best friend! It's truly a core memory for me. reputation will never never not be iconic, and I am so thankful for that album every day. Lover will always hold a special place in my heart as it is the first album release that I was actually online for! It was so so fun to read all the theories and look for all the Easter eggs. folklore got me through a really difficult period of my life, as I'm sure it did for a lot of people, and is so important to me on so many levels. I won't even go into what evermore means to me, I simply adore that album! And I will always remember Midnights as the soundtrack to my freshman year of college.

I am so incredibly grateful to Taylor, and for the community that we have created! I love getting to be a swiftie and am so happy that this community grows bigger and bigger by the day. Thank you all for creating a safe, warm, and welcoming environment.

And to Taylor, if you're reading this: we are so unbelievably proud and thankful for you! Grateful is the understatement of the century. I love you to the moon and to Saturn, forever and always!" -Katie

***

"Dear Taylor,

Oh my gosh, where do I even start! My name is Maddy, I'm 14 years old and ever since I was 12, I've been writing songs. It was you who inspired me to even start writing in the first place and I honestly don't know where I'd be without your influence. I've been listening to your music my whole life, but it used to be just the more popular songs like Love Story, You Belong With Me, and Shake It Off.

Then in 2021, I started to connect with your music more and started writing my own songs. I would say I became a true Swiftie in February of 2022, and ever since then your music has helped me get through some of my most difficult times, and has healed my heart over and over again, just by knowing that I'm not alone, that there's someone who feels the same. Your kindness has been so influential on all of us Swifties and it is so amaing to watch people around the world, who don't even know each other, come together and support one another all thanks to you! Thank you so so much for caring for us and honestly changing my life! Love you muchly!!" -Maddy B., age 14

***

"It's hard to say exactly when Taylor Swift became a staple in my home. Her music is one of those things that slowly crept in when no one was paying attention and then without me even realizing it, became an integral part of the daily lives of my family. So much so, that it almost feels like she's a member of the family who has always been with us. My teenage daughter, immersed herself in all things Taylor Swift, often playing her songs in the background of everyday life in the kitchen, family room, and of course car rides. Without even realizing it, all of us learned the lyrics to every song and even adopted our own favorite song. Despite having all brothers, they rarely asked her to turn it off, and in fact I would often find them staring at the t.v. while a Taylor Swift lyric video compilation is playing. As a mom, I was delighted knowing my daughter had an amazing role model to look up to, and who sparked creative interests in her (she taught herself guitar and began a passion for words through creative writing). I was happy that she found her thing, and most of all that she was happy.

For the first 14 years of her life, my daughter only had brothers. In May of 2020 that finally changed! Ruthie was born and Ellie was enamored. As a mom I worried about their future-how would they bond and have a close relationship with 14 years between them? Being the thoughtful, selfless, compassionate person that she is, Ellie dedicated herself to creating that bond. They are true besties, and at the heart of that connection is Taylor Swift. Ruthie is growing up on Taylor's music. But it isn't just the songs themselves. Its all of the memories they've made together with Taylor playing in the background (figuratively and literally). The cakes made for new releases, the hours spent playing Name the Song or Finish the Lyrics. The excitement for the Eras Tour. Learning the choreography for the Delicate music video and performing it too many times to count (and often in a row on the same day!) Dressing up for the Eras Tour movie. But mostly, its the little moments. The quiet moments. When they are spending time together and Taylor is playing softly in the background. Ruthie is only 3 years old, but I imagine that when she looks back on her childhood, many of her core memories will come to mind when she hears certain Taylor songs. Because Taylor was always there. I have no doubt that my girls will continue to have an incredible closeness as the years go on --what could be better than having a soundtrack to one's childhood along with a best friend?

A few months ago our family welcomed another baby and it was...another girl! She's still too little to appreciate Taylor the same way her sisters do, but I'm confident that she too will learn to love our girl and my three daughters will always have an unbreakable bond thanks to Taylor Swift-- who not only created the music, but helped to shape the kind of person that my first born is. She's turning 18 soon, and I couldn't be prouder of the young woman she has become. Thank you Taylor for being an incredible person, for instilling a good heart and a strong mind in my daughters, and for bringing my family together with laughs, love, and of course some of our favorite songs, namely--Bad Blood, Hey Stephen, Delicate, Love Story, & Willow each of which will forever be engrained in my heart for the memories they hold." - a proud mama <3

Acknowledgements

Hi! You've made it to the end of the book! I really hope that you enjoyed it, and that it was able to bring comfort to you, no matter if you're Taylor Swift or a teenage girl in her bedroom. I hope this book is able to show everyone that they're not alone and that instead, it reminds them of the unifying power of music. Wherever you may be, and whatever you may be going through, you are not alone in your struggles, and there are so many people who love you and care about you.

I'd like to thank everyone who submitted their entry- there were thousands of you, and I'm once again so sorry that not everyone could be included. I'm so grateful for all of you, and I'm sure Taylor is too. I'd especially like to thank the following swifties, whose stories were featured in this book (as well as the countless anonymous entries I received):

Evelyn R., Alice, Emily, Claire, Irelynn, Julia, Grace, Peighton, Bella, Stella (YouTube @loverlore.13), Sophie, Nate, Seunga, Ariadne, Eva K., Carly, Quinn, Kendyl, Ella, Julia, Emily, Brooke, Callie, Gaia, Merryn, Kara T., Hannanah S., Maya V., Naomi S. (@naomiischandler on YouTube), Kavya S., Isabella, Ina C., Sam M., Ela, Marisa, Ilya, Adalene, Henry, Courtney, Robert, Aurélie, Bella, Nene, Maeya W. , Samantha, Divina K., Arial, Kiera C.,

Grace, Izzy, Emilio (@GorgeouSwift_13), Maeve, Lily, @midnight_rain on YouTube, Fiona, Lizbeth C., Ella, Josie, Bridie, Delilah C. (YouTube @DELILAHVEVO & tiktok @delilah.cross3), Holly, Jil, Charlotte, Lilly D., Summer, Ellen, Ava, Tanushree, Sophia, Izabella N., Rosana, Bhavi, Izzy, Noah, Aliyah, Sarah, Alexa H., Isla, Ashlynn, Lili, Yukthi, @GoldenLikeDaylight16, Ceecee, Aditi, Julia (@cardigan_24 on YouTube), Avery, Emma, Natalie K., Ceci, Peyton, Eden B., Madeline, Evyn, Aislyn, Ruby, Atley, Jasmir, AnaLucia, Kristin, @FlamingoPink1989, Rachel, Lauren A., Genevieve, Sabrina G., Zara, Annalise, Emma, Leila, Eliana, Ellie R., Caroline, Falak, Kaydence, Karleigh, Kaylin(@urfavkaylin on YouTube), Adrianna, Liv, Gavin, Laila, Ardyn, Eva, MJ, Isla, Sophia, @Harmony13TV on YouTube, Maddy, Clara, Roha (@Style.swiftie13 on YouTube), Saanvi D., Maddie, Miriam, Pep, Eliana C., Zoe, Sadie, Palmer, Kacy, Brooklyn M., Sylvie, Mya T., Vannie, Laura, Carolina, Aislin, Brynn, Mariah S., DP, Ava, Felix, Emily, Aina, Mila, Gianna, Loa, Sarah (@TaySwift13 on YouTube), Ava, Keira J., Trinity, Tamar, Millie E., Bleuenn, Ava, Zoryana, Steph, Liliana, Emerson, Elisa C., Olivia, Claire, Marco (@meliodys on YouTube), Ava, Siesie, Jasmine, S, Campbell H., Madeline, Sullivan C., Kay, Evie, Poppy V., Lahar, Emma G., A.   Embry, Isla, Raelynn, Ryann, Rebekah, Katherine, Ashwin M., Ava, Antonia A. (@nialuvsts) on pinterest, Emily S., Sinead, EllaMarie, Livia, Eden, Sragvee, Fayrouz, Selena, Blair, Trish, Sia, Jocelyn, Kavya K.,Sophia, Kirra M., Lou, Charlotte M., Sophia R., Sarrinah, Addi, Rozzie, Emily, Bella, Holly, Nina, Marissa, Elise (@HopEsmEnola13), Kaybrea, Kayla, Karalynn, Gabrielle (Brie) P., Polina P., Marrin A.,

Callie, Andie, Emma W., Devri, Anya, Emilie H., Emma, Aayushi, Iris, Alice (@aliceramosdutra on instagram), Leo, Zeynep, Lola, Lilly, Jess H., Mehar, Emma L., Hannah, Addy, Lucia B., Colleen , Andrea, Tamar, Eva S., Piper, Talya, @Taylor_Tuesday, Isabelle (Izzy) Z., Rose, Sammie Z., Jinx, Molly D. (@tsoncorneliast on twitter), A.E.E, Clara J., Tayla, Avery W., Chloe M., @localaveragehuman, Anna P., Luna, Lucy, Sophia & Becca, Ava, Natalie, Kaila Lynn, Isabel-Alice, Meta, Rhesa Marie, Nicole, Claudia, Lapis (@lapisthelovely on YouTube & tumblr), Sara, Olivia, Zadie, Reese, Azkiya, Evie, Michaela, Annabel, Natalee K., Ian, Dorothea, Eliana C., @SwiftieNation4You on YouTube, Olive, Charleigh T., Tabitha, Rachel Q., Tarryn S., Matar, Luke, @girlinred_stan5.fanacc on YouTube, Ali, @taylorswiftieeeee13 on YouTube, Livi Q., Alicia, Ophelia, C.Q.F, Cara, Ava, Jolin N., Brooke, Evy, Daisy, August, Simona, Grace F., H.S, @Sharkbytee on YouTube, Shahrzad, Nabhya, Kathryn C., Karsyn, Avery, Juliette, Sophia, Frannie S., Zoey L., Kayla, Karina, Sanelma, Naveah G., Grace, Uzay, Remy, Kiki, Lucy G., Anni, Grace, Violet, Alma, Reilly, Kelly F., Lily, Baylee L., Mapausli, London S., Izzy S., Ellia, Emilia, Wesley, Juliet, Scarlett R., Kvinde, Anna, Dayja, Elisabeth M., Julia S., Jessica, Ryleigh, Aliyah, Theresa, Rachel, Juliëtte, Ayat, Zara, Purna, Noa, Sorrel, Preslie, Amelie, Isabella, Maha, Charlotte R., Hanae, Mallory, Erin R., Kara, Stella, Sumi (@simplysumi), Mariah R., Gracie, Sara M., Penleigh, Abbigail M., Giulia, Daisy, Char, margiebargie1308, C.M.A., Amelia P., Sarah, Joan M., Giulia G., Katie P., Lexi, Abby, Scarlett, Grace N., Mae H., Jane H., Aubrey S., Kenzie S., Julia K., Teagan, B, Pip, Inès B., Sophia Z., Madelyn, Khyati, Morganne, Madi P., Margaret Elizabeth

(@kittycatmargaret13), Trisha L., Annabelle, Abby, Shelby, Nurillah, Natalia F., Ren, Maylee H., Sohalia, Charlotte, Stell, Lindsey, Mawara A., Lottie, Safira, Delfina, Arya, Afton C., @tejudraws- on Instagram, Sofia, Aleksandra, Victoria A., Insha N., Arisha F., Lucas, Rasa H., Miley, @holygroundgirlie, Lauren T., Lillie J., Izzy M., Melina C., Cecily, @daylightears on YouTube, Lindsey R., Kiera H., Arya, Betty, Sandra (and her daughter Maddie), Tania S., Ellie M., Abby M., Lilia, Natalie K., Autumn, Katie, and Maddy.

And then, of course, I'd like to thank Taylor herself. Taylor, thank you for always being there for us when we've needed you the most. Even though you're miles away on tour, somehow your music makes it feel as though you're right there with us, cheering us on. I'll never be able to repay you for what your presence alone has done for me, but I hope this book is a nice start.

Thank you for following your dreams, and for proving everyone's doubts wrong. Thank you for standing up for what you believe in, and for showing us right from wrong. Most of all, thank you for showing all the writers like me that it's okay to believe in fairy tales, because believing in them is the only way they'll ever come true. We love you!

About The Author

Ellie Anne

She loves reading, writing, and being a swiftie! Her favorite song is willow and her favorite album is evermore, which is probably quite reflective of her personality.

She wrote and published her first novel, The Fire of Londyn, at age 16, and continues to create poetry and short stories, eagerly awaiting the day when the idea for her next novel sparks.

You can find her on Instagram @ellieanneauthor, or watch her videos on YouTube, on her channel All Too Swift. She's so thankful for the opportunity to compile a collection like this, and is eternally grateful to all those who contributed.

Printed in Great Britain
by Amazon

41554543R00219